MODERN INDIA

AND

THE INDIANS

MODERN INDIA

AND

THE INDIANS

BEING A SERIES

OF IMPRESSIONS, NOTES, AND ESSAYS

BY

MONIER WILLIAMS, D.C.L.

GYAN

Published by

GYAN

Gyan Publishing House
5, Ansari Road
Daryaganj, New Delhi-110002
Phone: 011-47034999, 9811692060
E-mail: books@gyanbooks.com

Distribution Network
gyanbooks.com
India, USA, Canada, UK, Australia

ISBN: 978-93-6208-607-5 (PB)
First Published, 1878

2nd Impression 2024

Printed at: Gyan Press, Delhi.

MODERN INDIA AND THE INDIANS
Author: MONIER WILLIAMS

MODERN INDIA

AND

THE INDIANS

BEING A SERIES

OF IMPRESSIONS, NOTES, AND ESSAYS

BY

MONIER WILLIAMS, D.C.L.

HON. LL.D. OF THE UNIVERSITY OF CALCUTTA,

HON. MEMBER OF THE BOMBAY ASIATIC SOCIETY,

BODEN PROFESSOR OF SANSKRIT IN THE UNIVERSITY OF OXFORD.

Second Edition.

LONDON:

TRÜBNER AND CO., LUDGATE HILL.

1878.

OXFORD:
BY E. PICKARD HALL, M.A., AND J. H. STACY,
PRINTERS TO THE UNIVERSITY.

ADVERTISEMENT TO FIRST EDITION.

I HAVE frequently been requested to reprint my various communications to the *Times* Newspaper, *Athenæum*, *Indian Antiquary*, and other periodicals—many of which were written during my recent travels in India. The following pages are put forth in compliance with the request.

They are not a mere reproduction of what has already appeared. Much additional matter has been added, and an attempt has been made to connect the series in some sort of order corresponding to the course of my travels. They need no preface, nor introduction. They may be left to speak for themselves.

A further series of Essays embodying my principal researches into Modern Indian religious life will, I hope, be published hereafter.

OXFORD, *April*, 1878.

ADVERTISEMENT TO SECOND EDITION.

A few misprints and inaccuracies have been corrected in this edition, and a few slight improvements introduced. Otherwise no alterations have been found necessary.

M. W.

OXFORD, *June*, 1878.

CONTENTS.

MODERN INDIA AND THE INDIANS.

THE FIVE GATES OF INDIA—GIBRALTAR, MALTA, PORT SAID, PERIM, AND ADEN.

THE good ship 'Venetia,' which took me to India on the occasion of my first expedition to the East, entered the Bay of Biscay on the 15th of October, 1875. Equinoctial gales had been raging for several days previously, and the Atlantic rollers, coming broadside on, soon discriminated between the passengers, instituting a process of natural selection, which resulted in the survival of those alone who were fittest to do justice to the diurnal bill of fare provided by the Peninsular and Oriental Company with a punctuality and regularity altogether weatherproof.

To be sure our decks were crowded with a motley assemblage of men, women, and children of all sorts and conditions; for example—a Duke and Prince of the Blood Royal, an Italian Countess, a general officer or two, some A. D. C.'s, several captains, one clergyman, numerous Indian civilians of various types, stations, and degrees, from judges of the High Court to the greenest of probationers just escaped out of the clutches of the Civil Service Examiners, sundry male oddities—long-bearded, short-bearded, and beardless, wived and wifeless—divers eccentric husbandless females of uncertain ages and vague antecedents, a few solitary wives on their way to join their husbands, one or two flirting bachelors, a bevy of pretty unmarried girls, a troop of young engineers from Cooper's

Hill, a batch of serious commercial men, an unpleasant pack of obstreperous children, and a residuum of unsortable nondescripts, not to speak of a heterogeneous crew of English sailors, Laskars, Negroes, and Chinamen. None of this miscellaneous collection of human beings made their presence felt so plainly as the children. Sea-sickness is a powerful leveller and merciless humiliator, but was powerless either to repress or depress the children. Their self-assertion was only aggravated by the prostrate condition of their natural guardians. Indian nurses easily succumb, and are generally very attenuated and miserable in appearance; but the opposite extreme is occasionally exemplified. We had one Ayah on board, who was quite a curious specimen of abnormal portliness and unnatural hypertrophy. Another was a tall graceful woman attired in a long red robe, gold necklace, bracelets and bangles. Notwithstanding her ladylike mien, she was, of course, a woman of very low caste, probably a Mhār (or Dheḍ). She had some very peculiar blue cross lines tattooed on her forehead between the eyebrows, and a similar mark on one temple. Like all Indian women of her station, she had invested all her savings in ornaments, and carried them on her person.

Our fourth night at sea brought us opposite the mouth of the Tagus, and in sight of the Lisbon lights. At daybreak next day we were approaching Cape St. Vincent.

Life is made up of compensations. Our patient endurance of four miserable days was rewarded by a grand spectacle. Noble cliffs rose to a great height out of the sea, some glowing with red tints as if covered with heather, others frowning with black crags, and shelving suddenly into perpendicular precipices or scarps of dark granite, riddled with countless holes and caverns by the sheer force of the Atlantic. Here and there isolated needle-like rocks, and others of fantastic shapes, separated from the cliffs by seething channels, stood out from the mainland, or seemed to thrust themselves forward as if to court the first dash of the waves which covered their sides with sheets of foam. In the distance were lofty mountains, whose gilded summits appeared loftier through the morning mist which still clung to them. Cape St. Vincent has a lighthouse and telegraph station. We hoisted our signals, and our approach was instantly notified at Gibraltar.

At night we were in the Straits (anciently called the Straits of Hercules), with the Bay of Tangier on our right. Tangier is a sea-port of Morocco, and is now the property of the Moors under the Emperor of Morocco; the capital of the province, Fez, being about a hundred miles inland.

In four days and a half, or 108 hours from the moment of our passing the Needles, we were close to Gibraltar. The night was dark and squally, and great caution was needed. I was kept awake by the intermittent throes and gasps of our engine, which seemed to struggle for breath like a moribund monster dying hard. Very early in the morning its fitful throbbings suddenly ceased, and the silence of death followed.

The first sight of the Bay is grand beyond all expectation. It bends round in a long curve or elongated semicircle, surrounded in the distance by ranges of high hills, the towering rock of Gibraltar—said to be nearly three miles long, and 1400 feet high—overhanging the whole of one side and forming a promontory running north and south, joined to the continent of Spain by a narrow isthmus of land called the neutral ground. The latter is washed on both sides by the Mediterranean. At the furthest extremity of the promontory is Europa Point, with a lighthouse. The town of Gibraltar, resting on a long line of batteries, climbs about one-third of the western side of the rock. Rising conspicuously above the houses is a fine ruined keep—once a strong castle when the place was possessed by the Moors, and still scarred and scored with the marks of subsequent sieges.

Nearly opposite, on the shore of the bay, is the Spanish town of Algesiras. Further inland, on a hill near the bottom of the bay, is San Roque. At both towns bull-fights are popular amusements, and not despised by some of our own people, who resort to them from Gibraltar to relieve the monotony of their cramped and cage-like existence.

The rock of Gibraltar was first known to the Phœnicians under the name of Calpe. After them the Carthaginians, Romans, and Visigoths successfully gained a footing there. It did not rank as a fortress till A.D. 711, when it was fortified by a Saracen army under Tārik (or, according to some, Tārif), a Moorish conqueror, from whom it was called Jibal Tārik, or Tārik's mountain (in Arabic *Jabalu't tārik*). In 1309 Ferdinand IV took the fortress after it had belonged to the Moors for 598 years, but it was retaken by them in 1462, and held by them altogether for 726 years. We took it from Spain in 1704, and to us it has belonged, notwithstanding three attempts on the part of the Spaniards to recover it, for about 175 years. On a hill, at the lower end of the bay, is a stone cairn called the 'Queen of Spain's chair,' because a Spanish queen is said to have seated herself there during one of the sieges, and declared she would not rise from it till she had seen the English flag hauled down. This is such a hackneyed guide-book story that one is almost ashamed to repeat it.

Opposite Europa Point, on the coast of Barbary in Africa, is Ceuta—a town close under a rocky hill (Mount Abyla) which forms a pendant to the rock of Gibraltar, and represents the second pillar of Hercules. Near it is a much higher, grander, black-looking, craggy, precipitous hill, known as the Ape's Hill, which also claims, and with more apparent justice, to represent the other pillar. From this mountain at some primeval period came the tailless apes which to this day linger on the rock of Gibraltar like wild aborigines, hopelessly struggling to hold their own against civilized settlers. Eighteen apes are still left, and every one of them is known and held inviolable. To kill or even injure any one of them would be an unpardonable offence. Ceuta belongs to Spain, and is used by the government as a penal settlement. It is a most unpleasant place of residence, convicts being allowed to roam about loose. They cannot escape by land, as, once out of the town, they would certainly be killed by the Moors, between whom and the Spaniards inveterate enmity subsists. I believe some eccentric person, or persons, once started the idea that it would be well for England to restore Gibraltar to Spain and take Ceuta in exchange.

On landing at Gibraltar we lost no time in making our way to Europa Point, passing the Alameda—a name given to a kind of public square, or esplanade, planted with trees, which is an institution in all Spanish towns, and treated as consecrated ground by the inhabitants. The drive led up a hill over the lower slope of the rock, which on the town side is much less steep than towards the Spanish frontier. The vegetation is quite tropical. Prickly pears, cactuses, and pepper trees appeared to be growing luxuriantly, and aloes were as plentiful as blackberry bushes. Europa Point commands an unequalled view of the Straits, the coast of Africa, and Gibraltar Bay. The rock itself from this point reminded us of the Bastei in the district called Saxon Switzerland, near Dresden.

Returning to the town under a royal salute which announced the landing of H. R. H. the Duke of Connaught, we found it no easy matter to thread our way through the long principal street—crowded as it was with a motley multitude of Moors from Fez, Arabs, Negroes, Jews,

Scorpions (or natives of Gibraltar familiarly so called), Spanish peasants, muleteers, English soldiers and sailors. The neutral ground on the northern side, opposite the Spanish lines, affords a striking view of the celebrated galleries which perforate the rock—here most precipitous. We could see the muzzles of monster guns protruding through innumerable port-holes. This, of course, would be the direction of an attack in case of a war with Spain. The wonderful construction of the galleries themselves, which we afterwards visited, is too well-known to need description.

As we steamed out of the Bay the eastern side of the rock, which is much wilder and more craggy in appearance than the town side, showed itself to great advantage. Here a steamer passed us, crowded with Hājjīs, or pilgrims from Mecca, bound for Tangier. They were all dressed alike in coarse grey garments, with cowls on their heads, and were packed closely together like sheep in a pen. It is alleged that they never leave the deck, lie down, or change their clothes from the moment they quit Mecca till they reach home. Next, the grand range of the Sierra Nevada, with its sharp serrated outline, came into view on our left. I believe its principal mountain is little short of 12,000 feet high. About noon on the sixth day after leaving England, we passed Cape Tenez on the coast of Africa.

At sunset the whole western sky was on fire, while the serrated line of the African mountains seemed to be cut out of the glowing heavens, as if with a sharp knife, and painted jet black. When night fell we were opposite the Bay of Algiers, and could distinguish the lights of the town. Thence to Malta little of interest marked the ship's course. We passed Zembra, a fine rocky island (occasionally resorted to for coal) on one side of the Bay of Tunis, and about twelve miles west of Cape Bon. The latter is a noble headland on the African coast, with a lighthouse more than half-way down its precipitous sides. Pantelleria, the ancient Cossyra, came in sight—a grand volcanic island eight or ten miles long and thirty in circumference, said to be remarkable for a lake of unfathomable depth at the top of its highest mountain, and two caverns, one intensely hot and the other intensely cold, and hot springs in other parts. The town consists of a long line of staring white houses, with a large church and detached villas dotted at intervals over the slopes. I believe the island now belongs to Italy, and, until recently, was used as a convict settlement.

On the eighth day after leaving England we passed Gozo, an island twelve miles long (called Gaulos by the Greeks), lying to the north-west of Malta and close to it, being only separated from the main island by a narrow channel, in the centre of which lies a much smaller island, called Comino. Soon afterwards we anchored in the quarantine harbour of Malta.

Early in the morning we took one of the boats that crowded round our vessel (in form rather like Venetian gondolas) and landed at Valetta, the principal town of Malta, built in 1566 by La Valette, the grandmaster of the Order of St. John of Jerusalem, to which Order the Emperor Charles V of Germany made over the whole island in 1530. The town is regularly built on an elevated promontory just behind the fortress of St. Elmo, which, with a lighthouse, occupies its extreme point.

On one side of the promontory is the quarantine harbour for merchant ships and steamers. On the other is the great harbour for ships of war, commanded at its entrance by the fortress of Ricasoli, and indented with numerous inlets or creeks, each forming a small separate harbour, and the whole capable of being swept by the fortress of St. Angelo, bristling with guns on a promontory in the middle. In fact, the entire line of coast on the northern side of the island is hollowed out into creeks by the force of the Mediterranean currents. It is a kind of Connemara on a small scale. One considerable inlet, forming quite a harbour, is called St. Paul's Bay, because, according to tradition, the ship which contained St. Paul and his fellow-prisoners was cast on shore here.

On landing we found it impossible to shake off a swarm of importunate natives, either vendors of the produce of the island or would-be guides, who followed us about like tiresome flies intent on settling on us. We visited the cathedral of St. John, where the knights are buried under a beautiful Mosaic floor; the Governor's palace, where there is some celebrated tapestry and a fine armoury, interesting from a well-arranged collection of the armour of the Knights of St. John; and the gardens of San Antonio, five miles in the interior.

The houses of Malta are all of white stone, with flat roofs. Their architecture has a half Italian, half Oriental character. The streets are built on each side of the rocky promontory in parallel lines, so as to join at right angles a long central main street, which forms a sort of backbone along the summit of the ridge. One or two are ascended by picturesque tiers of steps. The whole island appears to be one vast rock and stone quarry. Instead of hedges, lines of white walls intersect the interior in every direction, one rising above the other like terraces, with square look-out towers at intervals. Here and there the dull monotony of the stone terraces is relieved by tufts of dark foliage, dotted about promiscuously in every direction. These represent the tops of well-grown trees, which rear their heads above the walls, as if to bear witness to the fertility of the soil in the gardens underneath. It is difficult, indeed, to understand how any garden can be productive when nothing but rock is visible around. The explanation, I believe, is that rich soil is transported in small vessels from Sicily, and kept together by the walls. The Maltese are very industrious. Their commercial instincts are certainly developed by their brief and fitful intercourse with their Anglo-Indian visitors, and notably exhibited in the sums asked for the products of their small island. Swarms of petty traders, not content with pestering every passenger who lands for a few hours, hover about the decks of the steamers offering lace and coral ornaments at four times their value. The knowing purchaser waits till the steamer is just starting, and then bids a fourth of the first price asked. I saw a black lace shawl reduced in this way from £4 10*s.* to £1.

The population multiplies so rapidly that the island is quite inadequate to support its inhabitants. Numbers emigrate and spread themselves over the Mediterranean. No less than 10,000 Maltese are said to be settled in Tunis. Their own peculiar vernacular tongue is a corrupt form of Arabic largely intermixed with Italian words. No one who has seen the position of the noble harbours on the north coast of the island, can have any doubt that so long as we possess India and remain the greatest maritime power of the world, Malta must be held and its garrisons maintained by us in full efficiency *coûte qu'il coûte.* Protected by the guns of St. Elmo and Ricasoli, Tigne and St. Angelo, almost any number of our men-of-war and merchant vessels might find a safe anchorage. Strong north-easterly gales are the only winds that can affect them.

After leaving Malta we saw no land till we approached Port Said. The whole stretch of sea is, I believe, 900 miles long. Here would lie the danger to our commerce in case of any great naval power commanding the Black Sea and the coast of Syria. On Sunday the ship's company was mustered on deck before prayer-time. First, on the port side, appeared a line of twenty-two stewards and waiters, extending from the centre of the ship, every one in characteristic uniform. Next, on the same side, came eight or ten black, thick-lipped African negroes, commonly called Sīdīs or Sīdī boys, from the neighbourhood of Zanzibar. They were dressed in snow-white garments quite out of keeping with their occupation, which consists in shovelling the coal into the furnaces, and contrasting curiously with their glossy coal-black countenances and dark thick woolly hair. They are a happy smiling race, always in exuberant spirits, though exposed to roasting heat, drinking nothing but water and nourished by a vegetable diet. They may be seen sleeping as soundly on the iron gratings of the engine-room as on a bed of down. Then came the Āg-wālās—men employed about the engine and fires. These were described to me as Konkanī Musalmāns, from the neighbourhood of Bombay. They were also dressed in peculiar white costumes—picturesque and immaculately clean. This formed the line on the port side. At the stern were the English officers of the ship, and nearest the stern, on the starboard side, a few English quartermasters or superior English sailors. After them came the long line of Laskars (or, as they call themselves, Khalāsīs, 'free,' vulgarly Klasees), marvellously transfigured in appearance, and quite belying their own identity, in spotless dresses, embroiderod turbans, and scarves.

The word Laskar is derived from the Persian *lashkar*, an army. The name is somewhat sarcastically applied to a crew of Indian sailors who, in their ordinary work-day aspect, have nothing whatever about them suggestive of military smartness or effectiveness. To the unitiated passenger these Laskars appear a very miserable squad, and no one can look at them without conjuring up fearful pictures of disaster to the ship in the event of cyclones and other possible emergencies. Yet the captain declared that, though comparatively inefficient in a cold climate, they do better than English sailors under a hot sun; that they are more tractable and docile, and, what is more important, that they never get drunk. They are, of course, Musalmāns; for Hindūs even of the lowest caste have an unconquerable religious antipathy to voyages on the 'black water[1].' In fact, the lower the caste in India the more tenacious are its members of caste-purity, and the more pride does each man take in protecting himself from what he believes to be contamination. Nothing is more essential to the preservation of caste-purity than unpolluted water, and nowhere is it so difficult to keep water ceremonially pure as on ship-board. As to the Musalmān Laskars, the best of them come from Kathiwar (more correctly written Kāthi-āwār, the abode of the Kāthi tribes) and the neighbourhood of the Portuguese settlement of Daman. Their wages are, of course, less than those of English sailors, but if the Company save in this way, a *per contra* outlay is incurred, because more men are required to counterbalance the want of muscular power in each individual.

I asked the captain about their food, and whether they would eat meat. 'Yes,' he said, 'we sometimes, while in harbour, give them a sheep, which they kill in their own way. On the voyage they generally eat dried fish, rice, and dāl, and are not very particular about it. Though they are Muhammadans, they will even sometimes eat pork if we have nothing else to give them. They ask no inconvenient questions, but tie the forbidden animal—slaughtered, however, according to the most orthodox rules of Islām—on to the end of a line, and drag it after the ship for an hour or so; after which one of their number hauls it in, calling out with great solemnity as if he were using a formula of consecration, *Jāo sū'ar idhar āo machchī*, "go away, pig; come hither, fish."'

The regiment of Laskars was headed in the muster by the Sarang—a title corrupted from *Sarhang*, the Persian word for a general, and humorously applied to the native

[1] In Hindūstānī, *Kālā pānī*. This phrase is now commonly substituted for the more proper expression *Khārā pānī*, 'salt water.'

boatswain, who, in his turban glittering with gold embroidery, and attended by his two Tindals, or boatswain's mates, would assuredly have been mistaken for an Indian prince if he could have been transplanted into the middle of a London crowd.

Conspicuous among the Asiatics was one Chinaman—the ship's carpenter—in a broad straw hat. The whole company would have well illustrated a lecture on the ethnology of the world. At any rate, they formed a singularly picturesque and interesting line of 132 specimens of the human species, methodically arranged for inspection round the quarter-deck of the ship. The mixed crowd of passengers—some lolling lazily and apathetically in the central space, others standing up to gaze with languid curiosity or serene self-complacency on the miscellaneous assortment of their fellow-creatures, ranged round them like animals in a zoological show—offered quite as curious an exhibition of diversified humanity in their own persons, while the captain and first officer walked round with an air of calm professional assurance, casting critical glances of appreciation or depreciation at each member of the ship's company, and receiving respectful salutes in return. Then at a given signal the Sarang sounded his whistle, the whole circle of unbelievers melted away in an instant, leaving the crowd of believing Christians in the centre to settle down for Divine Service.

We reached Port Said at 6 A.M. on the 12th day after leaving England. The first sight of Egypt excites no emotions of any kind. The town of Port Said—called after the late Viceroy—is a collection of mushroom buildings which have sprung into existence since the commencement of the Suez Canal. It is now lighted with gas.

Nor is the entrance to the Canal at all imposing. The adjacent coast for miles is apparently below the sea-level, making the approach to the harbour almost impossible except by daylight; but a lofty lighthouse, which was cleverly constructed by erecting wooden moulds one above the other and filling them with concrete, stands on a pier on the right, and gives out a flashing electric light visible at an immense distance. There are also two long breakwaters, one lower than the other, constructed of huge blocks of concrete, running far into the sea on either side of the harbour, which effectually prevent the sand from drifting inside and choking the mouth of the Canal.

We entered very cautiously at dawn of day, and moored our ship to two buoys. Two British ironclads—the 'Invincible' and 'Pallas'—were already in the harbour, and another fine steamer, the 'City of Venice,' was waiting to make the passage after us, while the 'Serapis' had recently passed on ahead. In half an hour we had paid the dues, which I believe amounted in our case to about £1500, and had entered the Canal, the entrance being merely a continuation of the harbour, without lock-gates of any kind. Here, on the right, there is a narrow strip of land covered with sheds, owned by the British nation. I was informed that when the works commenced, this land was offered to our Government for £800, and was declined. It is said to have been recently purchased by us for £26,000. This story will not appear incredible to any one old enough to remember the view Lord Palmerston took of the French engineer's great project.

Although the course of the Canal for the first thirty miles is as straight as an arrow, every mile of it abounds with interesting objects. The first thing noticed is an immense lagoon stretching for miles beyond the right bank, while on the left lies a trackless desert of sand, with here and there patches of what appears to be water, but is really nothing but the mirage produced by heated vapour. Then there are the natives on the bank in their picturesque costumes, the sturdy, half-naked Arabs at work in the water, the strings of camels with their burdens, the feluccas in the lagoon with their lateen sails, the myriads of water fowl, and in the horizon long lines of flamingoes extending literally for miles, and standing motionless, like regiments of soldiers in white uniforms. But the one absorbing sight of all is the Canal itself. Such expressions as 'One of the wonders of the age,' 'a triumph of engineering skill,' give an inadequate idea of the magnitude of the work. It must be seen to be estimated at its right value.

Captain Methven, the commodore of the Peninsular and Oriental fleet, who watched the progress of the Canal from its commencement, and was one of the first of our fellow-countrymen to predict its success, favoured me with many interesting particulars which may be relied upon for accuracy. The lower platform at the base of the central channel is almost everywhere fully 70 ft. wide, and as the sides shelve off at an angle, there is generally a width of about 100 ft. at the surface of the water, the extreme depth of which is 27 ft., with a margin of 10 ft. or 12 ft. of shallow water on each side. The rule first made was that no ship drawing more than 26 ft. should be allowed to pass through. The ships in which I made the passage only drew about 22 ft. of water, and now it is found that any vessel drawing more than 25 ft. is likely to come to grief. Two large steamers (the 'Hibernia' and 'Seine'), laden with submarine cable, had just accomplished the passage. One of them, however, drawing 24 ft. 7 in., scraped her keel all through the Canal, and was obliged to steam at full speed to bring her through. The only difference in the level of the sea at the Mediterranean and Red Sea extremities is caused by the difference in the tides, the variation at the Mediterranean end being 18 in. in Spring tides, and that at the Red Sea end about 7ft. or 8 ft. The effect of this difference is to cause a current at both extremities, and of course a tolerably strong flow from the Red Sea towards the great bitter lakes, situated near the centre of the Canal.

Every six miles there is a station-house (called by the French *gare*) and siding with signal-posts, fitted with black balls, by means of which the traffic is worked on the block system. As a rule, no ship is allowed to take less than one hour in steaming from one station to the next.

Two ships advancing towards each other in opposite directions are never allowed to meet while in motion. One is compelled to draw off to a siding while the other passes. This happened to us at a station called Kantárá, where we were made to shunt, while the 'Diomed,' a Liverpool steamer, passed us. Here a road—once the great highway between Egypt and Palestine, and still a high road between Cairo and Syria—leads over the Canal by a kind of flying bridge. A large caravan from Jerusalem, with hundreds of camels and a motley crowd of way-worn travellers—men, women, and children—were waiting to pass over close to our siding. It was a strange and interesting sight, which made us think of the going down of the Children of Israel into Egypt. Thence we glided on without interruption, but with the disagreeable accompaniment of an Egyptian plague of flies, passing on the right a statue of Lieutenant Waghorn, the pioneer and first organizer of the overland route in 1835.

At considerable intervals steam dredging-machines—four or five of which are now sufficient to keep the bed clear—were seen in active work. One was of monster proportions, and appeared to be ingeniously constructed for raising the sand from the bottom and delivering it on an inclined plane over the bank. The desert is occasionally dotted with patches of a kind of scrubby bush, the only merit of which is that it serves to relieve the glare from the sand, and to furnish food for camels. Here and there high banks of sand hid everything from our view. At 4 in the afternoon (having left Port Said at 7 in the morning) we emerged into the first bitter lake, called Lake Timsah, and steamed at increased speed close to the new town of Ismailia, named after the present Khedive. Here there is an oasis of green vegetation, and a principal station of the railway between Suez and Alexandria. De Lesseps himself has a house here. There is also a palace built by the Khedive for the sole purpose of receiving the Empress Eugénie, the Emperor of Austria, and other Royal personages (but no representative from England) during the festivities at the opening of the Canal in November, 1870[1].

On we steamed through the lake, and thence through a cutting to the second or great bitter lake, where we anchored for the night soon after sunset. These two remarkable lakes had nearly dry beds before the making of the Canal. That happened to them which is now going on in the Dead Sea. The water had evaporated, and left a deposit of seven or eight feet of solid salt. The French engineers foresaw that this circumstance might be turned to account for the deepening of the central channel. When the waters of the Red Sea were allowed to flow in, the layer of salt was dissolved and nearly eight feet of depth gained. The climate in the neighbouring districts is likely to be advantageously affected by the re-creation of these lakes. We had evidence next morning of an accession of humidity which may one day turn barren ground into fruitful fields. When we attempted to move on soon after daybreak, a thick mist enveloped us, and kept us stationary for more than an hour. Meanwhile, our ship's stern stuck in the sand, but with a little wriggling worked itself off. Then we glided out of the great lake through a deep

[1] The Canal was first opened for traffic in 1869, and from 1870 to 1876 the net tonnage passing through it rose from 436,609 tons to 2,096,772 tons (the gross tonnage to 3,072,107); the receipts from £200,000 in 1870 to about £1,200,000 in 1875. Of the traffic 75 per cent. was British.

cutting, which extended for some miles. At one o'clock the same afternoon we had entered the Gulf of Suez, and were steaming rapidly towards one of its spacious open docks and quays (constructed at an immense cost and loss under exaggerated ideas of the future commercial importance of a port, converted by M. de Lesseps' great work into a mere place of call) almost before we became aware that we had emerged from the Canal. We had accomplished the whole distance of 100 miles in about fifteen hours. I was surprised to learn on good authority that the total cost from first to last of the miracle of engineering skill which had transported our huge ship from one sea to the other so easily and pleasantly, was only eighteen millions sterling. Those who are competent to pronounce an opinion on the result achieved by the outlay consider that it was cheaply done for that sum. About two millions of the amount was freely given by the late Khedive in money and labour. The compulsory system was first tried, but soon given up. Cholera broke out, and English public opinion was brought to bear on the matter.

Then it was that the genius of M. de Lesseps organized a system of paid labour, the extraordinary success of which in a country like Egypt could never have been predicted. All honour to the indomitable will and scientific ability of one man, who, fighting his way through apparently insuperable obstacles,—physical, social, and political,—carried out one of the greatest projects of this wonder-working century.

But in appreciating to the full his energy and intellect, let us not withhold an equal tribute to the amazing tact and administrative capacity which enabled one man to train a whole army of ignorant and illiterate labourers, and inspire them with something of his own ardent, energetic, and enthusiastic spirit. Every individual, to the smallest donkey-boy, employed on the Canal seemed to take a pride and pleasure in doing his allotted task well, and contributing something towards the desired end. No great work has ever before been effected in Egypt with so much goodwill, cheerfulness, and activity, and with so small a sacrifice of human life. This will appear more remarkable when it is borne in mind that nearly a hundred steam dredging-machines were in constant operation, for the effective working of which a large number of men and boys with interdependent duties was indispensable.

And yet, after all, notwithstanding one's admiration of this great monument of scientific and administrative genius, it is singular that the chief impression it leaves on one's mind is that of incompleteness. The simple truth I believe to be that before the Canal can be pronounced really finished the width of the central channel must be doubled, and the banks from one end to the other lined with stone. If, when the success of the project was assured, and before the costly plant had been sold and the trained labourers dispersed, the principal European Powers had agreed to act in concert, each contributing its quota of a few millions, a really complete result might have been achieved, the capital expended might have been blotted out, and a Canal of the right dimensions presented to the commerce of the world. Now, the whole plant will have to be reconstructed, new workmen and labourers trained, and the entire process reorganized at a vast cost. Nevertheless, English enterprise and capital can do all that is needed; and English enterprise and capital will have to do it in the end.

So surely as Russia is setting her face steadfastly towards Constantinople must England concentrate her attention on Port Said, the Suez Canal, and the coast of Syria. The day may be coming—and perhaps must come very soon—when no corner of Europe will be allowed to suffer any longer from the 'impotence' of Turkish rule. What then is to happen to Egypt? England's duty will be plain. We shall have to take the Khedive in hand ourselves, make him an independent Sovereign, and peremptorily insist on his governing his own country well, righteously, and economically. To this end we must help him, not with money, but with men.

We have a whole band of Indian civilians—men like Sir George Campbell, Mr. Seton-Karr, and Mr. Cust—who have served their time in India and yet have plenty of energy left, which they are ready to devote to the welfare of their fellow-creatures. Let them consent to aid the Khedive, and simply do in Egypt the work they have done in India as commissioners, collectors, judges, magistrates, members of council, and lieutenant-governors. The Province adjacent to the Indus, commonly called Sinde, has been significantly styled 'Young Egypt.' Old Egypt and 'Young Egypt' have certainly much community of character and many points of resemblance. Those who have made 'Young Egypt' prosperous under a strong, righteous, and energetic administration, are quite competent to raise old Egypt out of the depths of misgovernment into which she is fast sinking, and convert her from a poverty-stricken into a rich and thriving country. I submit that this would be a satisfactory solution of the Eastern Question, so far, at least, as England is concerned.

Soon after our arrival at Suez, a party of us took a Felucca, or native boat, with three men and sailed up the creek to the town of Suez, three miles distant. The behaviour of our boatmen interested me not a little. It happened to be the concluding day of the fast of Ramazān (the ninth month of the Muhammadan year), and whether on this account, or because it was the stated hour of prayer, one of the men washed his face in sea-water, and then prostrated himself with his face towards Mecca in the bow of the boat. Soon afterwards we knocked our keel against some rocks and then scraped along a sand-bank, the tide running out very rapidly. Upon this two of the boatmen—very fine-looking fellows, half-naked, with well-developed muscular limbs — started up, seized two long poles, rushed towards the bow of the little vessel, applied the end of the poles to their shoulders, and running with naked feet along the upper edge of the boat's side, while they pushed the poles towards the stern, urged each other to increased exertions in the strongest guttural Arabic, till they had driven us in this manner over rocks and shoals for more than a mile, against a strong contrary wind, to the quay opposite the Suez hotel.

Their behaviour afforded a parallel to the practice of a certain good Christian of whom it is recorded that he prayed always as if all results depended on God, but put forth all his energies as if success depended wholly on himself. It reminded one also of a story told of Muhammad. Travelling on a certain occasion through the desert, he refused to follow the example of his travelling companion, who, on arriving at the evening resting-place, turned his camel loose and then prayed fervently that God would keep the beast from straying; but, on the contrary, first took a good deal of trouble to tether his camel, and then prayed to God to prevent the animal from breaking loose.

We walked about Suez for an hour. Donkey-boys mobbed us at every corner, puffing the merits of their donkeys with much originality, if not in the most refined English. 'Dis de Claimant, Sar,' 'Try de Claimant, Sar,' 'Dis Sir Roger, Sar,' 'Dis very superior donkey, Sar,' 'Dis Kenealy, Sar,' 'Dis make loud bray, Sar.'

The town is a collection of flat-roofed ramshackle old houses, most of them in an advanced stage of decay, with crooked narrow irregular streets in which dirt, dust, and bad smells wait upon each other in close companionship.

Many of the ruined buildings looked as if they might have once sheltered the children of Israel, who are supposed to have crossed the Red Sea somewhere in the neighbourhood. Our interest in everything triumphed over our disgust, though it was difficult to say which was the strongest feeling when we entered the Bazaar, where, in addition to dirt, every hole and corner harboured vast accumulations of cobwebs, left undisturbed for years as a standing menace, I suppose, to swarms of irrepressible flies which settled in millions on the eatables exposed for sale on the open counters. The narrow lanes were thronged with a mixed multitude of turbaned men and veiled women; some respectably dressed and moderately clean, threading their way through the crowd with calm Oriental dignity; others ragged and filthy, jostling each other, and vociferating in genuine Suez vernacular.

On the morning of the fourteenth day we commenced our course down the Gulf of Suez. The line of hills overhanging Suez, called *Attāka*, looked grand, red and glowing, and stood out in striking contrast to the marvellous green and blue of the sea. Soon the rugged and majestic pile of mountains of the Sinaitic Peninsula, of which Mount Sinai forms a part, opened out upon our left. This peninsula divides the Red Sea into two narrow gulfs—one, that of Suez down which we were steaming, and the navigation of which is extremely intricate, the other, that of Akāba which is not quite so long, and is seldom navigated at all.

Towards evening we came in sight of the lofty range of Mount Aghrib, on the coast of Africa, in Egyptian territory. The highest mountain of the range is alleged to be 10,000 feet high. I certainly never before supposed that Egypt possessed anything much higher than a pyramid.

The time consumed in steaming down the Red Sea to the Straits of Bābel Mandeb was five days. The coast is insufficiently lighted, and the sea unpleasantly full of coral reefs, sunken rocks, and small volcanic islands, but the P. and O. ships thread their way through all obstructions with as much precision as a well-driven hansom passes through Fleet Street. We had a steam punka in our sleeping cabin, besides the usual punkas in the saloon, but had nevertheless, to sleep on deck when the thermometer rose to ninety.

One evening we escaped a tremendous sandstorm, which, coming from the deserts of Africa eighty miles off, gathered over our heads in a densely black, ominous cloud. Happily the wind against which we were steaming carried the storm behind us, and we saw it descend in a dark column towards the northern horizon. Had the cloud burst over our heads we should have been half-blinded as well as smothered with sand, and the whole vessel so enveloped that a dense fog would have been less dangerous. The only showers in the Red Sea are showers of sand.

On the fourth day we passed the twelve rocky volcanic islands called the Twelve Apostles. In some of them coal-black scoria and ashes, looking as if quite recently ejected from crater-like cavities, were intermixed with bright red and yellow rocks and shone brilliantly in the fiery sunlight.

At dawn on the fifth day we were opposite Mocha on the Arabian coast, and had to take soundings. Rugged dark lines of mountains, some with sugar-loaf points, some with serrated edges, one behind the other, intensely arid and sterile in appearance, lined the coast. One long line of craggy hills presented the exact appearance of an old worn-out saw lying with its edge turned upwards. The opposite coast of Abyssinia was now drawing towards us. It is fringed with dark barren mountains resembling those on the Arabian coast, and in the distance was a lofty range, with one high peak, said to be somewhere in Abyssinia.

The heat was intense, and the draught of air through the narrow channel, as the coast on each side began to close in upon us, made it penetrate more searchingly.

The small island of Perim was on our right as we steamed through the Straits of Bābel Mandeb (Arabic *bābu'l mandib*, 'gate of tears').

The land opposite Perim juts out into a long narrow promontory covered with rugged, rocky hills. Under the principal rock on its barren and burning shore the French have built a large square house. They had once a settlement here, and I believe intended converting the promontory into an island by digging a canal across. Had they accomplished their object, their next engineering operation would have been a fort to balance ours at Perim, but the excitable and bellicose Arab tribes forcibly resisted the attempt to slice off a portion of their territory, and the French have now deserted the place. The staring house still remains, apparently in good repair, glittering in the glaring sunlight. Not a human being was to be seen about, but one or two deserted Arab fishing-boats were anchored near the shore.

Every person who passes Perim is sure to be asked whether he has heard the story of the stratagem by which we took possession of the island. I believe the anecdote rests on a basis of fact. But whether it does so or not, here is an epitome of it:—A French captain was sent in a man-of-war about five-and-twenty years ago to take possession of the island, and touched at Aden. Of course the English Commandant was too polite not to ask him to dine, and too hospitable not to ply him with good wine till he had drunk enough to exemplify the old proverb *in vino veritas* and let out the secret of his expedition. Instantly the English Commandant, without leaving the dinner-table, gave private orders for despatching a gunboat with six sappers and miners, and one engineer officer, who landed on the island, planted the British flag on the heights, and next day were ready to receive the French captain and welcome him to British soil.

Certainly the island is in an important position, at the very gate of the Red Sea, but its utter sterility, without a tree or even a blade of grass or bush to temper the glare of burning suns and cloudless skies, makes it even more entitled to be called an Eden than Aden itself—of course I mean on the *lucus a non lucendo* principle. It is simply a bare rock, about four or five miles in circumference, rising to an elevation of two or three hundred feet. The channel which separates it from the opposite point of Bābel Mandeb, and through which we sailed, is only one mile wide; but a channel of nearly eleven miles in width on the other side divides it from the African coast, and on that side the island possesses a small but deep harbour. We have built a lighthouse and insignificant fort on the highest point of the rock, and huts near it for a detachment of Sepoys with one or two Europeans. Since the erection of the lighthouse ships generally take the narrow channel.

We steamed through the channel against a strong heated blast of wind which blows constantly through the straits as through a funnel. In five days after quitting Suez dock we were well out of the Red Sea, and not sorry to see Perim receding from our sight and our vessel making rapid way eastwards through the Indian Ocean in the direction of Aden, ninety miles distant. When night fell, the lightship at the entrance of Aden harbour began to be visible.

By ten o'clock at night we were safely moored to two buoys near the lights of the town. The dark outline of the great rock of Aden loomed mysteriously in the weird light; lamps of various colours gleamed on the shore; native boats with vociferant Arabs crowded round our ship; half-naked men with dusky skins swarmed over the front of the vessel. It can easily be imagined that a place where rain only falls about once in two or three years must be pleasanter by night than by day. Yet, on the occasion of my second voyage, when we reached Aden by daylight, I greatly enjoyed a visit to the wonderful tanks three or four miles distant, dug out of the solid rock to catch the precious rain-water which occasionally makes up for lost time by pouring down in a deluge. The surrounding scenery is unequalled in ruggedness and sterility by anything I have ever seen. In fact, the whole place may be compared to a congeries of gigantic cinders or heaps of colossal coke. Yet it has many most striking and almost sublime features. It is certainly the Gibraltar of the Red Sea. The principal rock is even higher and grander than that of Gibraltar. It stands on a promontory in the same way, and is joined to the mainland by a narrow isthmus.

Among the institutions of the place are the diving boys—small Somali negroes imported from the opposite coast of Africa—who gather round the ship in their toy canoes, each little curly-headed urchin paddling his own tiny coracle with wonderful dexterity. Their knowledge of English is restricted to the one sentence 'I dive, Sare, I dive,' which they all vociferate with great animation, till on the first sight of a silver coin thrown from the ship, the whole troop suddenly disappear feet uppermost in the water, leaving canoes and paddles to take care of themselves, and heedless of the presence of formidable sharks which usually follow in the wake of steamers, seeking whom or what they may devour. The smallest coin never escapes the lynx-sight of these amphibious imp-like little urchins. The fortunate finder scrambles into his own canoe, first holding up his prize in triumph, then stuffing it into the hollow of his cheek for safety, and then baling out the water with which his little cockle-shell is half-swamped, while he joins more energetically than ever in the general chorus of 'I dive, Sare, I dive,' which is kept up with spirit as long as any passenger shows himself on deck.

We left Aden on the morning of the twentieth day of our voyage. The endless serrated line of the hills on the Arabian coast continued in sight for some time. Indeed the whole interior of Arabia—so far as I was able to observe it during my voyages—seems to be shut in by a barrier of ranges of dark rugged sterile mountains, one behind the other—some rising to considerable elevations—which completely enclose it and serve as an effectual bar to the curiosity and cupidity of intruders. At Aden we had an addition of some interesting first-class passengers—a Khoja, or Bombay merchant of a particular class, who has a house of business in Zanzibar, returning to India with his wife and family. He was a stout stalwart man, with a handsome countenance. I believe some of the ancestors of the *Khojas* (a name corrupted from Khwāja, 'noble') centuries ago were pirates inhabiting the coast of Cutch. They gradually became rich, turned Muslims, and gave up disreputable practices. But, although now Muhammadans and followers of a certain Āghā Khān, they retain much of their Hindū character and often their Hindū names. Our fellow-passenger told me that the trade of Zanzibar is rapidly increasing and the place becoming very prosperous. The language spoken there is Swaheli (a kind of lingua franca of Eastern Africa), which the Khoja speaks as well as his native tongue Cutchī, and to which he adds Gujarātī, Hindūstānī, and a little English. He was accompanied by a Pathān or Afghān from Peshawar returning home from the Hajj or pilgrimage to Mecca, which every true Musalmān endeavours to perform once in his life, the other four religious duties enjoined by Muhammad being prayer five times a day, fasting for a month every year, almsgiving, and repeating the creed daily. We took in at the same time a number of Baniyahs or Hindū traders, who stationed themselves on the forecastle, and were to be seen there every evening dead-asleep, rolled up like their own bales of goods in white winding-sheets.

The run from Aden to Bombay was accomplished on calm seas and under bright skies in six days and a half. The serenity of the Indian Ocean is rarely disturbed by high winds after the termination of the monsoon.

The morning of one day was spent in visiting the mail room and post-office. The three mail agents have to work ten hours a day from the time they leave Suez, sorting about 46,000 letters and 35,000 newspapers, and distributing them in about 250 bags, ready for dispersion all over India immediately on the arrival of the ship at Bombay. The following is a specimen of the directions which occasionally tax the ingenuity of the sorters (copied literatim)—

J. Faden
Sapper
Engear
Bromeday.

This letter had been sent to three Bromleys in different parts of England before it was suspected that Engear meant India, and Bromeday, Bombay.

At daybreak on the twenty-seventh day after our departure from Southampton, the high land of the Ghāts, near Bombay, was visible about fifty miles distant. When the sun rose it disappeared in the haze. A few hours later we entered Bombay harbour, passing the 'Serapis' and several fine men-of-war lying at anchor. The advent of the Prince of Wales had preceded ours by about two days.

FIRST IMPRESSIONS.

BOMBAY, NOVEMBER 10, 1875.

WE need not quote a Western poet[1] in support of the trite truism that impressions on the mind, to be deep, must be made by scenes actually witnessed.

There is an Eastern saying that the distance between the ear and the eye is very small, but the difference between hearing and seeing is very great.

Much information can be gained about India from books and newspapers, and much by asking questions of old Indians who have spent their lives in the country, but, after all, India must be seen to be understood.

The instant I set foot on the landing-place at Bombay, I became absorbed in the interest of every object that met my sight—the magnificent harbour with its beautiful islands, secluded creeks, and grand background of hills; the picturesque native boats gliding hither and thither; the array of ships from every quarter of the globe riding at anchor—every feature in the surrounding landscape, every rock and stone under my feet, every animal and plant around me on the shore, every man, woman, and child in the motley throng passing and repassing on the quay, from the Bhīstī, or water-carrier, who laid the dust by means of a skin slung on his back, to the boy who importuned me for Bakhshīsh to exhibit a fight between

[1] 'Segnius irritant animos demissa per aurem
Quam quæ sunt oculis subjecta fidelibus.'

a snake held in his hand and a mongoose concealed in a basket.

Though I was born in India, and had lived as a child in India, and had been educated for India, and had read, thought, spoken, and dreamt about India all my life, I had entered a new world.

On the esplanade, in front of the chief public buildings of Bombay, an extraordinary spectacle presented itself. An immense concourse of people was collected, waiting for the Prince of Wales, who was expected at the Secretariat to hold his first levée—no dingy crowd of Londoners hustling each other in a foggy, smoky atmosphere, but at least a hundred thousand turbaned Asiatics, in bright coloured dresses of every hue, moving sedately about in orderly groups under a glittering sky. The whole plain seemed to glow and flash with kaleidoscopic combinations of dazzling variegated colours. Rows of well-appointed carriages belonging to rich Bombay merchants, some containing Pārsī ladies and children in gorgeous costumes with coachmen in brilliant liveries, lined the esplanade. Gem-bespangled Rājas, Mahārājas, and Nawābs dashed by in four-horsed equipages, with troops of outriders before and behind.

One part of the spacious plain was set apart for 12,000 children, from various schools—Hindū, Pārsī, Muhammadan, Roman Catholic, and Protestant—collected from Bombay and the neighbourhood. The fact that it was possible to bring together from a limited area so vast an assemblage of children, male and female, all under education in an Eastern country, was in itself full of significance and interest. They were seated in rows, one behind the other, grouped according to the communities to which they severally belonged, a passage being left in the centre for the Prince. Every child was provided with a printed hymn, or poetical address to the Prince in Gujarātī, to be sung by the whole assemblage at the moment of his appearance among them.

I was told that the children were mostly from the middle ranks of the inhabitants of Bombay. Certainly it was difficult to believe in the poverty of their parents, dressed as they were, boys and girls, in rich silks, satins, brocades, and velvets of all colours, from bright red and yellow to simple white, with gold-embroidered caps and jewels of great value on their feet and arms, necks and ears.

It is no uncommon thing for parents to deck their children on festive occasions with ornaments worth hundreds of pounds. Their appearance and bearing suggested an idea that Asiatics think more of beauty of dress than beauty of form, Europeans more of beauty of form than of beauty of dress.

That same evening I left Bombay and travelled northwards through Gujarāt by the Bombay and Baroda railway. At the very first station out of Bombay, the anthill-like density of India's teeming masses made itself apparent. At least a thousand natives were collected, waiting for the train, some bound for Bombay to see the Prince of Wales, others on their way home after having witnessed the great Tamāshā. The vast crowd vociferated and swayed to and fro in an alarming manner. The sound was like the roaring of a mighty ocean. We began to think that a second mutiny was imminent, that our carriage would be stormed, and ourselves perhaps shot down on the spot.

Our fears were allayed on learning that the lower classes of Hindūs are in the habit of talking and shouting to each other at the top of their voices, in perfect good humour, whenever they are congregated in crowds[1]. Notwithstanding their apparent excitement, noisy demonstrative-

[1] Sleeman remarks ('Rambles,' p. 77) that the stentorian voices of the natives is probably due to their meeting and discussing subjects connected with their own interests in the open air under trees.

ness, and overpowering numbers, they made no attempt (as English excursionists would have done) to force their way into the first or second class compartments, but submitted quite patiently and resignedly to be penned like sheep in third-class carriages, some of which had an upper story. It was evident that no caste prejudices interfered with their making full use of our railways.

As the morning dawned on us in our northward course, sensations of real cold made us forget we were in India, till, looking out, we were reminded of our locality by unmistakeable signs, and notably by certain ominous streaks of cloud in the horizon, which turned out to be flights of millions of locusts. When they are seen approaching, the natives assemble in crowds, fire guns, and make hideous noises to prevent their settling on their crops. After passing Surat, Broach, and Baroda, I alighted at the Mehmoodabad station, and began my Indian experiences in the Collector of Kaira's camp.

A brief description of my first day's adventures may give an idea of the kind of life led by Anglo-Indians when camping out in the country during an Indian winter.

My only room was of course a tent. It had four doors and no windows, and a fifth door leading into a kind of canvas lean-to or small annex, fitted up with a large bath. Happily no one need trouble himself with a portable bath in India, because this indispensable convenience is found everywhere. The tent had a lining of brown and yellow chintz, and for a carpet a stout blue and white cotton cloth laid on flax straw. All the doors had two coverings or rather flaps, one of the same material as the tent, the other a kind of wire screen, called a chick, to let in air, and keep out as far as possible inquisitive intruders—not men and women, but huge bees, wasps, grasshoppers, squirrels, snakes, and all manner of winged and creeping things innumerable. For furniture there were two or three chairs, a dressing-table, and a good iron bedstead with hard mattresses, woollen pillows, and musquito curtains, well tucked in all round. Let the reader, then, imagine me comfortably ensconced, after my month's voyages and travels, within my four canvas walls, and looking forward with pleasant anticipations to an undisturbed sleep in a veritable bed—my first since leaving England.

I go through every needful purificatory rite in my strange lavatory, and emerge refreshed from my tent door to peep at the scene outside and take my bearings. I find that we are in a large field or common, on one side of the Mehmoodabad station. The camp consists of about a dozen tents all under large spreading trees, with which the whole park-like country round is beautifully wooded. Most of the trees are new to me—the Mango, the Banian, the Pīpal, the Tamarind, the Nīm, and the Japanese Acacia with its lovely yellow flowers. No tent is ever pitched under a Tamarind. It is supposed, I believe, to exhale too much carbonic acid during the night-time. The Mango and Nīm are the tent-pitcher's favourite trees. Under one Mango there is a large pavilion-like erection for the Collector and his wife. Then there is another double tent, which serves as a dining-room and drawing-room, of ample dimensions, fitted up with carpets, tables, book-cases, easy chairs, sewing machine, and harmonium. Two or three others for visitors like myself; another for the baby and its Ayahs; another for the Portuguese butler, and of course a capacious tent with annexes, which together serve for the collector's Kutchery (properly written *Kacherī* or *Kachahrī*), magisterial court and other offices.

On one side under the dense foliage of a Banian is a circular canvas erection without any roof. This is the kitchen, where excellent dinners are cooked by means of two bricks and a hole in the ground. A little removed from the tents is the stable, an open space quite unprotected, except by foliage, where four Arab horses and two ponies are tethered by their heels, each attended by its man. Near them stand carriages, carts, and a curious vehicle called a Tonga (*Tāngā*), usually drawn by two ponies. It has two seats back to back, suspended on two wheels, and is covered by an awning. Not far off an all-but nude Bhīstī, dark as a negro, is seen plying his occupation. He supplies the camp with water, by means of two water-skins slung over the back of a bullock. Ranging about the field in promiscuous places are other bullocks, buffaloes, goats, sheep, geese, ducks, and fowls. The bullocks are for the carts, the buffaloes and goats for producing milk and butter. The other creatures come in usefully as raw material, out of which the excellent dinners before alluded to are supplied. A sheep in these country places only costs, I am told, about four rupees, or eight shillings. It is, however, a melancholy reflection that infliction of death is essential to the maintenance of an Englishman's life. For life is everywhere exuberant around me, and every living thing seems to enjoy itself, as if it were certain of being unmolested. Natives never willingly destroy life. They cannot enter into an Englishman's desire for venting his high spirits on a fine day by killing game of some kind. 'Live and let live' is their rule of conduct towards the inferior creation.

I walk about admiring every living creature, particularly the birds—the Hoopoo with its lovely crest hopping about near me, the doves very like those at home, the bright parrots, the jays, the woodpeckers. Then little grey and brown streaked squirrels are playing all around me. They jump about with wonderful agility, peer in at the tent doors, and try to secure little bits of cotton for their nests. The sounds are not always melodious. I hear a screeching note above my head. It comes from a kind of grey and red Toucan seated trustfully on a branch, and quite undisturbed by my presence. Then another discordant cry, and a rush—

a number of natives are driving away a troop of big, grey mischievous monkeys, some with little baby-monkeys clinging to them. They soon repel the invaders, but only by shouting in rather harsh vernacular 'the monkey-people, the monkey-people!' To shoot a monkey would be nothing short of sacrilege. I venture to follow the retreating intruders, but am arrested by hedges of prickly pear. Then I fall into ecstasies over the creepers, many of them of gigantic size, which twine themselves everywhere, covering hedges, bushes, and trees with their brilliant red, orange, and white flowers.

I must not omit to mention that dotted about the field are mounted and unmounted sepoys, with here and there a belted government servant (called a Paṭṭi-wālā, or Paṭṭa-wālā, because distinguished by a belt)—all within call—all ready to answer instantaneously to the Sahib's summons, and eager to execute his behests. As to the big Collector Sahib himself, in the eyes of the people of his district he is every inch a king. He speaks like one, acts like one, and really has the power of one. He says to one man 'come,' and he cometh, and to another 'go,' and he goeth. His title of Collector gives a very inadequate idea of his real duties and authority; unless it be taken to mean that in him all the administrative functions of the district are collected and comprehended. He not only collects the revenue, but has high judicial powers, and the whole welfare of a small territory is committed to him. He superintends police, civil engineering, road-making, rural economy, municipal government, sanitation, education, every conceivable matter.

But if every Collector is a small king, every Englishman in India is regarded as a petty prince. Obsequious natives watch his movements, and hang upon his words. I try to stroll about, but as I circle leisurely round the compound, attendant satellites hover about my path.

I am evidently expected to develope wants of some kind or other in the course of my ramble. I ransack my store of correct Hindūstānī just imported from Europe for the most polite way of requesting to be left alone; but I feel as helpless as a child, and as shy as a new boy at school. Disconcerted and humiliated, I long for a little temporary obscurity, and hastily hide my head within the walls of my tent. But my tenacious followers are not to be shaken off so easily. I am conscious of being vigilantly watched through my barrier of canvas. By way of experiment I utter the magical formula *Qui hai?* (*Ko-ī hai?*), and a dusky form seems to rise out of the ground as if by magic. There he stands in an attitude of abject reverence and attention, waiting for me to issue my commands either in the best Gujarātī or purest Hindūstānī. But I do not rise to the occasion. I am not sure whether to be exhilarated by the opportunity of bringing my knowledge of Indian languages into play, or depressed by an uncomfortable consciousness of blank inability to deliver myself of any well-turned and highly idiomatic sentence expressive of a simple desire to know the dinner hour. Just at this juncture I hear a commanding voice call out in the distance 'Khānā lāo.' This is the Collector's brief and business-like order for dinner. I repair with relief to the drawing-room and dining-room. The Collector and his wife, beaming with hospitality, make me sit down at a well-appointed dinner-table. I have a French *menu* placed before me. I eat a dinner cooked with Parisian skill, I drink wine fit for an emperor, and am waited on by a stately butler and half-a-dozen stately waiters in imposing costumes, who move about with noiseless tread behind my chair, and anticipate every eccentricity of my appetite. I am evidently on enchanted ground, and can only think of Aladdin in the Arabian Nights.

Dinner over, we sit out in the open air. The moon is

shining with a lustre unknown in northern latitudes. We recline on lounging chairs round a blazing wood-fire, not sorry to wrap ourselves up in our warm plaids. I retire early to my tent and compose myself for the luxurious slumber I had anticipated. But I am too excited to sleep immediately. With difficulty I gain the border-land between consciousness and unconsciousness. What is that sound, half snort, half snuffle, close to my head? I start, and sit up. Can it be the Brāhmanī bull I saw just before dinner roaming about at large in full enjoyment of a kind of sacred independence? Cautiously and guardedly I open my musquito curtains, intending to seize the nearest weapon of defence. Clink, clink! Clank, clank! Thank goodness! that must be the guard parading close to my tent; and sure enough there are sounds of a rush, and a chase, and a genuine bull's bellow which gradually diminish and fade away in the distance.

Again I compose myself, but as night advances begin to be painfully aware that a number of other strange sounds are intensifying outside and inside my tent—croaks, squeaks, grunts, chirps, hums, buzzes, whizzes, whistles, rustles, flutters, scuffles, scampers, and nibbles. Harmless sounds proceeding from harmless creatures! I reason with myself. A toad is attracted by the water in my bath-room, a rat has scented out my travelling biscuits, musquitoes and moths are trying to work their way through my curtains, a vampire bat is hanging from the roof of my tent, crickets and grasshoppers are making themselves at home on my floor. 'Quite usual, of course,' I say to myself, 'in these hot climates, and quite to be expected!' Ah, but that hissing sound! Do not cobras hiss? The hissing subsides, and is succeeded by a melancholy moan. Is that the hooting of an owl? No! the moan has changed to a prolonged yell, increasing in an alarming manner. Yell is taken up by yell, howl by howl. Awful sounds come from all directions. Surely a number of peasants are being murdered in the adjoining fields. I am bound to get up and rush to the rescue. No, no, I remember. I saw a few jackals slinking about the camp in the evening.

Once more I try to compose myself, disgusted with my silly sensitiveness. Shriek, shriek, and a thundering roar! The midnight luggage-train is passing with a screaming whistle fifty yards from my head. At last I drop off exhausted into a troubled slumber. I dream of bulls, snakes, tigers, and railway collisions. A sound of many voices mingles with my perturbed visions. Crowds of natives are collecting for the six o'clock train two hours before sunrise. They talk, chatter, jabber, shout, and laugh to beguile the tedium of waiting. At five minutes to six the station bell rings violently, and my servant appears with my *choṭa hāzirī*, or little breakfast. I start up, dress quickly, remembering that I am expected to drink a cup of hot tea, and go out like a veteran Anglo-Indian, to 'eat the air' (*hawā khānā*), before the sun is well up.

I conform to the spirit of the trite precept *Si Romae fueris, Romano vivito more;* but the Collector and his wife are out before me, and are seen mounting their horses and starting off to scour the country in every direction for an hour or so. I find the morning breeze bite keenly, and am glad to walk briskly up and down the camp. I amuse myself by watching the gradual gathering of natives around the Kutchery—two or three policemen with a prisoner, a cheerful-looking man in a red turban and white garments carrying a paper or petition of some kind, several emaciated half-naked villagers bowed down to the dust with the weight of their poverty and grievances, a decrepit old man attended by a decrepit old woman, underlings who come to deliver reports or receive instructions, other persons who come to be advised, encouraged, scolded or praised, and others who appear to have nothing to do, and to do it very successfully. Every one has an air of quiet resignation, and nearly all squat on the ground, awaiting the Collector Sahib's return with imperturbable patience. All these cases are disposed of by the Collector in person after our eight o'clock breakfast.

At eleven the post comes in; that is, a running messenger, nearly naked, brings in a pile of letters on his head from the neighbouring town. The Collector is immersed in a sea of papers until our next meal. Meanwhile a visitor from a neighbouring station makes his appearance riding on a camel, and is received in the drawing-room tent by the Collector's wife. Then a deputation of Brāhmans is seen approaching. They have come to greet me on my arrival; some of them are Pandits. A mat is spread for them in a vacant tent. They enter without shoes, make respectful salaams, and squat round me in a semicircle. I thoughtlessly shake hands with the chief Pandit, a dignified venerable old gentleman, forgetful that the touch of a Mleććha (English barbarian) will entail upon him laborious purificatory ceremonies on his return to his own house. We then exchange compliments in Sanskṛit, and I ask them many questions, and propound difficulties for discussion. Their fluency in talking Sanskṛit surprises me, and certainly surpasses mine. We English scholars treat Sanskṛit as a dead language, but here in India I am expected to speak it as if it were my mother-tongue. Once or twice I find myself floundering disastrously, but the polite Pandits help me out of my difficulties. Two hours pass away like lightning, the only drawback to general harmony being that all the Pandits try to speak at once. I find that no one thinks of terminating the visit. Native visitors never venture to depart till the Sāhib says plainly 'you may go.' I begin to think of the most polite Sanskṛit formula for breaking up my conclave, when I am saved from all awkwardness by a call to tiffin.

In the afternoon the sun acquires canicular power, the thermometer rises to eighty-two, and the temperature is about as trying as that of the hottest day of an English summer. Under the combined influence of tiffin, heat, exhilaration, humiliation, and general excitement, I am compelled to doze away an hour or two, till it is time to walk with the Collector to a neighbouring Bāolī, or old underground well (called in Gujarātī *Wau*), now unused and falling into ruins, but well worth a visit. It is more like a small subterranean tank than a well, and the descent to it is by a long flight of stone steps, surrounded by cool stone chambers built of solid masonry, and supported by handsome pillars. In Eastern countries, benevolent men who have become rich and wish to benefit their fellow-creatures before they die, construct wells and tanks, much as we build hospitals in Europe. I return with the Collector to his camp as the sun sets.

So much for my first day's experiences, which are so vivid that I may be pardoned for having recounted them in the present tense.

SAMĀDH, SACRIFICE, SELF-IMMOLATION, AND SELF-TORTURE.

KAIRA DISTRICTS, 1876.

A REMARKABLE attempt at achieving a kind of canonization or saintship, by the accomplishment of an apparent Samādh, occurred in the district of Kaira in Gujarāt, presided over by Mr. Frederick Sheppard, the energetic Collector in whose camp I stayed on my first arrival in India. A brief account of the circumstances attending the discovery and interruption of the attempt may be acceptable to an increasing class of readers who take an interest in the various phases and peculiarities of Indian religious life. I propose, therefore, to introduce the narrative by a few remarks about sacrifice, immolation, and self-torture, all of which were once common in India.

In what may be called the Brāhmanical period, which succeeded the Vedic period of Hindūism, human sacrifice must have prevailed among the Brāhmanical races. This is sufficiently evident from the story of Śunahśepha in the Aitareya-brāhmaṇa. It is even believed by many that the sects called Śāktas (or Tāntrikas) formerly ate portions of the flesh and drank the blood of the victims sacrificed at their secret orgies. Among the wild Hill tribes and primitive races of India, the chief idea of religion has been the necessity of appeasing the malice of malignant beings by oblations of blood, and on occasions of great emergency by the outpouring of human blood. Their gods thirsted for blood and preferred that of men, while that of children was an irresistible delicacy certain to put them in the best of humours.

Very little more than thirty years has elapsed since the suppression of human sacrifices among the Kondhs or Kandhs (often written Khonds), an aboriginal tribe of Orissa. Their terrible Earth-god was supposed to send famines and pestilences unless propitiated by blood. According to Dr. Hunter (Statistics of Bengal, xix. 235) 'the victims were of either sex, and generally of tender age. The detestable office of providing them formed a hereditary privilege of the Pāns, one of the alien low-castes attached to the Kandh villages. Procurers of this class yearly sallied forth into the plains, and bought up a herd of promising boys and girls from the poorer Hindūs. Sometimes they kidnapped their prey; and each Kandh district kept a stock of victims in reserve, "to meet sudden demands for atonement." Brāhmans and Kandhs were the only races whose purity exempted them from sacrifice, and a rule came down from remote antiquity that the victim *must be bought with a price*.

'After a village had purchased a victim, it treated him with much kindness, regarding him as a consecrated being, eagerly welcomed at every threshold. If a child, he enjoyed perfect liberty; but if an adult, the chief of the village kept him in his own house, and fed him well, but fettered him so that he could not escape [1]. When the time of atonement had come, the Kandhs spent two days in feasting and riot; on the third they offered up the victim, shouting as the first blood fell to the ground, "We bought you with a price; no sin rests with us."'

Our Government, by Act XXI of 1845, entirely suppressed these horrible sacrifices, and established a special

[1] A similar practice of feeding, fattening, and petting consecrated human victims prevailed, I believe, in Mexico.

agency for enforcing obedience to the order for their abolition. Human sacrifices were offered in the city of Saugor during the whole of the Marāṭha Government up to the year 1800, when they were put a stop to by the local native Governor, a very humane man.

'I once heard,' writes Colonel Sleeman, 'a very learned Brāhman priest say that he thought the decline of the Governor's family arose from this *innovation*. "There is," said he, "no sin in *not* offering human sacrifices to the gods where none have ever been offered; but where the gods have been accustomed to them, they are very naturally annoyed when the rite is abolished, and visit the place and people with all kinds of calamities."'

Human sacrifices, however, were probably rare among the purely Āryan races, while the sacrifice of animals became universal. The first idea of sacrifice of any kind—whether of grain, fruits, or animals—seems to have been that of supplying the deities with nourishment. Gods and men all feasted together. Then succeeded the notion of the need of vicarious suffering, or life for life, blood for blood. Some deities were believed to thirst for human blood, and the blood of animals was substituted for that of men. One of the effects of Buddhism was to cause a rapid diminution of animal sacrifice. It is now rarely seen, except at the altars of the fierce goddess of destruction (Kālī), or of forms and near relations of Kālī (such as the *Grāma-devatās*, 'village deities,' and *Mātās*, 'village mothers,') and at the altars of the tutelary deity Ayenār, and at devil-shrines in the South. I myself saw very few animals sacrificed even to the bloody goddesses, though I took pains to visit them on the proper days.

Other forms of immolation were once common in India. The Thags maintained that they sacrificed their victims to the goddess Kālī.

Now that Thaggism has been suppressed by us, a good deal of datura-poisoning is practised by the same class of people. Not long ago, an old man and his son were poisoned by a gang of these poisoners for the sake of a new blanket which the old man had purchased and imprudently hung on a tree near his hut. The gang appeared to be travellers, and effected their object by making friends with him, cooking their dinner near him, and giving him a portion previously poisoned for his own use.

The killing of female infants once prevailed extensively in the Panjāb and Rājputāna, owing to the difficulty of providing daughters with suitable husbands and the immense expenses entailed by nuptial festivities. Through our instrumentality the practice has now been discontinued, or if rare cases of female infanticide occur, they are perpetrated with great secrecy.

Again, in former days, self-immolation was common. Many fanatical pilgrims, while labouring under violent excitement amounting to religious frenzy, immolated themselves at the festivals of the god Śiva (the proper god of destruction), and even at the great car-festivals (*ratha-yātrā*) of the god Vishṇu, voluntarily throwing themselves under the enormous wheels not only of the car of Jagan-nāth (Kṛishṇa or Vishṇu, as 'lord and preserver of the world'), at Purī in Orissa, but of other similar idol-cars also.

I found such cars attached to every large Vishṇu pagoda in the South of India. They are supposed to typify the moving active world over which the god presides, and the friezes of grotesque sculptures, one under the other, with which they are covered, exhibit the world's good and bad, pure and impure characters in disgustingly incongruous juxtaposition. Some of them are so large and heavy that they require to be supported on sixteen wheels, and on a particular day, once a year, they are drawn through the streets by thousands of people. Every now and then persons are crushed under the wheels; for a rather unexpected consequence of our civilisation has been to increase religious gatherings among the natives by creating facilities of communication, and the best government cannot always prevent accidents.

Indeed, if the Orissa devotees are true to their own creed, 'accidental death' ought to be the formal verdict in every case of seeming suicide at Purī. For nothing, in fact, is more abhorrent to the principles of all Vishṇu-worship than the infliction of any kind of death on the most insignificant animal, and to die by one's own hand is a form of destruction to be shrunk from by a true Vaishṇava with the most intense religious horror.

The Jagan-nāth festival, writes Dr. W. W. Hunter in the 19th volume of his Statistical Account of Bengal (p. 59)[1], 'takes place according as the Hindū months fall, in June or July, and for weeks beforehand pilgrims come trooping into Purī by thousands every day. The whole district is in a ferment. The great car is forty-five feet in height. This vast structure is supported on sixteen wheels of seven feet diameter, and is thirty-five feet square. The brother and sister of Jagan-nāth have separate cars a few feet smaller. When the sacred images are at length brought forth and placed upon their chariots, thousands fall on their knees and bow their foreheads in the dust. The vast multitude shouts with one throat, and, surging backwards and forwards, drags the wheeled edifices down the broad street towards the country-house of the world's lord (Jagan-nāth). Music strikes up before and behind, drums beat, cymbals clash, the priests harangue from the cars, or shout a sort of fescennine medley, enlivened with broad allusions and coarse gestures, which are received

[1] In twenty volumes, just published by Messrs. Trübner and Co.

with roars of laughter from the crowd. And so the dense mass struggles forward by convulsive jerks, tugging and sweating, shouting and jumping, singing and praying. The distance from the temple to the country-house is less than a mile; but the wheels sink deep into the sand, and the journey takes several days. After hours of severe toil and wild excitement in the July tropical sun, a reaction necessarily follows. The zeal of the pilgrims flags before the garden-house is reached; and the cars, deserted by the devotees, are dragged along by the professional pullers with deep-drawn grunts and groans. These men, 4200 in number, are peasants from the neighbouring Fiscal Divisions, who generally manage to live at free quarters in Purī during the festival.

'Once arrived at the country-house, the enthusiasm subsides. The pilgrims drop exhausted upon the burning sand of the sacred street, or block up the lanes with their prostrate bodies. When they have slept off their excitement, they rise refreshed and ready for another of the strong religious stimulants of the season. The world's lord is left to get back to his temple as best he can; and in the quaint words of a writer half a century ago, but for the professional car-pullers, the god "would infallibly stick" at his country-house.

'In a closely-packed eager throng of a hundred thousand men and women, many of them unaccustomed to exposure or hard labour, and all of them tugging and straining to the utmost under the blazing tropical sun, deaths must occasionally occur. There have, doubtless, been instances of pilgrims throwing themselves under the wheels in a frenzy of religious excitement; but such instances have always been rare, and are now unknown. At one time several unhappy people were killed or injured every year, but they were almost invariably cases of accidental trampling. The few suicides that did occur were, for the most part, cases of diseased and miserable objects, who took this means to put themselves out of pain. The official returns now place this beyond doubt. Nothing, indeed, could be more opposed to the spirit of Vishṇu-worship than self-immolation. Accidental death within the temple renders the whole place unclean. The ritual suddenly stops, and the polluted offerings are hurried away from the sight of the offended god. According to Ćaitanya, the apostle of Jagan-nāth, the destruction of the least of God's creatures is a sin against the Creator. Self-immolation he would have regarded with horror.'

Self-immolation, in other ways, was once extensively prevalent. Arrian, it is well known, describes how, in the time of Alexander the Great, a man named Kalanos—one of a sect of Indian wise men who went naked—burned himself upon a pile. This description is like that of the self-cremation of the ascetic Śarabhanga in Rāmāyaṇa, iii. 9. Cicero alludes to it in a well-known passage: 'Est profecto quiddam etiam in barbaris gentibus praesentiens atque divinans: siquidem ad mortem proficiscens Calanus Indus, cum adscenderet in rogum ardentem; O praeclarum discessum, inquit, e vitâ.' (De Divin. i. 23.)

There are some sand-hills in the Sātpura range dedicated to Mahādeva—supposed, as Mahākāla, to preside over destruction—from a rock on which many youths have precipitated themselves, because their mothers, being childless, have dedicated their first-born sons to the god.

According to Col. Sleeman, 'when a woman is without children, she makes votive offerings to all the gods who can, she thinks, assist her; and promises of still greater offerings in case they should grant what she wants. Smaller promises being found of no avail, she at last promises her first-born, if a male, to the god of destruction, Mahādeva (Śiva). If she gets a son, she conceals from him her vow till he has attained the age of puberty; she then communicates it to him, and enjoins him to fulfil it. He believes it to be his paramount duty to obey his mother's call; and from that moment considers himself as devoted to the god. Without breathing to any living soul a syllable of what she has told him, he puts on the habit of a pilgrim or religious mendicant, visits all the celebrated temples dedicated to this god in different parts of India; and at the annual fair on the Mahādeva hills, throws himself from a perpendicular height of four or five hundred feet, and is dashed to pieces on the rocks below. If the youth does not feel himself quite prepared for the sacrifice on the first visit, he spends another year in pilgrimages, and returns to fulfil his mother's vow at the next fair. Some have, I believe, been known to postpone the sacrifice to a third fair; but the interval is always spent in painful pilgrimages to the celebrated temples of the god[1].'

This mode of suicide is called Bhṛigu-pāta, 'throwing one's-self from a precipice.' It was once equally common at the rock of Girnār, in Kāthiāwār, and has only recently been prohibited.

We have made great efforts to put a stop to these horrors by doing away with the fair. On one occasion our efforts were assisted by the cholera which broke out among the multitude. This visitation was considered by the people as an intimation on the part of the god, that they ought to have been more attentive to the wishes of the *white men*. It is noteworthy that Mahādeva is the only Hindū god represented of a fair colour (probably from his connexion with the Snowy Mountains).

With regard to the immolation of the faithful wife (commonly called Sutee = Sanskṛit *Satī*) who followed her husband in death, and burned herself on his funeral pile, everywhere in India I saw, scattered about in various

[1] Sleeman's 'Rambles and Recollections,' p. 133.

places, monuments erected over the ashes of Satīs, and everywhere such monuments (often enshrining the supposed footprints of the faithful wife) are still regarded with the greatest veneration by the people.

Sometimes the poor women in their horror of burning have submitted to the alternative of being buried alive with their husbands. The practice of Satī was for a long period thought to be so intimately connected with the religious belief of the Hindūs, that our Government did not venture to put a stop to it. It was known to be enjoined in certain comparatively modern Indian codes, and for some time it was not discovered that the fanatical Brāhmans, to obtain the requisite authority for insisting on the continual observance of the rite, had permitted the fraudulent substitution of the word *agneh*, 'of fire,' for *agre*, 'first,' at the end of the Ṛig-veda text (X. 18. 7), thus translatable: 'without tears, without sorrow, bedecked with jewels, let the wives go up to the altar *first*.'

Our Government prohibited the burning of any widow except under strict regulations, and except with her own full consent; but, in consequence of our half-sanction, the number of widows actually returned as burnt in Bengal rose in one year to 839, while in other years the average was 500. In Lord Amherst's time the seven European functionaries in charge of the seven newly-acquired districts, one and all declared against the abolition of widow-burning, and such great authorities as Colebrooke and H. H. Wilson were against interference. Yet under Lord William Bentinck's administration a law was passed in 1829 (Reg. XVII) which suppressed the practice with entire success, and without difficulty or disturbance of any kind, notwithstanding all the bigotry, fanaticism, and prejudice brought to bear in opposition to the measure.

We have also prevented the burying alive of lepers, and others afflicted with incurable diseases, which was once universally prevalent in the Panjāb, and common in some other parts of India.

Of course, leprosy in India, as in other Eastern countries, is a kind of living death. Lepers are excluded from society, and can find no employment. They often gave themselves up of their own accord to be buried alive, the motive simply being a desire to be released from physical suffering.

This burying one's self alive is called performing Samādh (=Sanskṛit *Samādhi*). The word properly means intense concentration of the thoughts on some holy object, or a temporary suspension of all connexion between soul and body by religious abstraction.

The tomb of a Sannyāsī, or holy Brāhman, who has given up all worldly connexions and abandoned caste-obligations, is also called a Samādh (=*Samādhi*). A holy man of this kind is never burnt, but buried; and his entombed body is supposed to lie for centuries in the Samādh trance. Such tombs are often great places of pilgrimage, resorted to by thousands from all parts of India.

Colonel Sleeman (in his 'Rambles and Recollections,' p. 345) describes how he once knew a very respectable Hindū gentleman who came to the river Narbadā, attended by a large retinue, to perform a kind of water Samādh, in consequence of an incurable disease under which he laboured. After taking leave of his family, he entered a boat, which conveyed him to the deepest part of the river. He then loaded himself with sand, and stepping into the water disappeared.

Self-immolation by drowning was once very common at Benares. Bishop Heber describes how many scores of pilgrims from all parts of India came to Benares every year expressly to end their days and secure their salvation. They purchased two large pots, between which they tied themselves. Thus equipped they paddled into the stream, the empty pots supporting their weight. Then they proceeded to fill the pots with the water which surrounded them, and in this manner sank into eternity. The British Government in the Bishop's time had not succeeded in suppressing the practice. Indeed, when a man has travelled several hundred miles to drown himself, it is never very likely that a police-officer will be able to prevent him.

I now come to the remarkable fact that two attempts at Samādh have occurred in the Collector of Kaira's district quite recently. A certain devotee announced his intention of adopting this extraordinary method of securing perfect abstraction and beatitude, and was actually buried alive in the neighbourhood of a village. His friends were detected by the villagers in pouring milk down a hollow bamboo which had been arranged to supply the buried man with air and food. The bamboo was removed, and the interred man was found dead when his friends opened the grave shortly afterwards.

The other attempt is still more recent, and I here give Mr. Sheppard's own account of it almost in his own words: 'As I was shooting near my camp one evening, a mounted orderly came up with the news that a Bhāt had performed Samādh that afternoon in a neighbouring village, and that there was much consequent excitement there. Not having a horse with me, I directed the orderly to ride off to the village (picking up my police escort as he passed through my camp), to dig up the buried man, and to take into custody any persons who might endeavour to oppose the execution of my orders.

'On returning to my camp, I ordered the apprehension of all those who had assisted in the Samādh; and soon afterwards received a report that the man had been actually buried in a vault in his own house, but had been taken out alive. He was, however, very weak, and died the following morning. It was then reported to me that the limbs, though cold, had not stiffened; and the people, ready as of old to be deceived, and always inclined to attribute the smallest departure from the ordinary course of events to supernatural agency, declared that the Bhāt was not dead, but lying in the Samādh trance. There was, however, no pulse; and as it was clear that, even if the supposition of the villagers was correct, medical treatment would be desirable, I sent the body in a cart to the nearest dispensary, distant some six or seven miles, and in due time received a certificate of death from the hospital assistant in charge of that institution, together with a report of a post-mortem examination of the body, which showed that death had resulted from heart-disease.

'Meanwhile I visited the village and ascertained the following facts:—

'The deceased was a man in fairly comfortable circumstances, and with some religious pretensions. It was well known that he aspired to a still higher reputation for sanctity, and that with this view he had for several months been contemplating Samādh. The proper date for this rite had been finally settled after many solemn ceremonies and the due observance of fasting, prayer, and charity.

'On the afternoon fixed for the Samādh he assembled the villagers, and told them that it had been imparted to him in a vision that the Deity required him to pass six weeks in religious abstraction, and that he felt compelled to obey the Divine command, and to remain in the vault prepared for him during that period. He then produced and worshipped a small earthen vessel containing the sacred Tulsī plant, and afterwards carefully planted therein twenty grains of barley, telling the villagers to watch for their growth, as it had been revealed to him that the grains represented his life. If, at the end of the six weeks, the grains had sprouted, the villagers were to understand that the Bhāt was still alive. He was then to be removed from the vault, and worshipped as a saint. If, on the other hand, germination had not taken place, they were to understand that the Bhāt was dead also, and the vault was in that case to be permanently bricked up, and the Tulsī planted over the grave.

'After giving these directions, the devotee recited some Mantras and entered the vault, bidding farewell to the world, and declaring his belief that his life would be miraculously preserved. The vault was then roofed over with boards, and plastered thickly with mud. About two hours after this event, he was removed from the vault by the police under my orders, and placed in the verandah, the house itself being locked up.

'After ascertaining the above particulars, I caused the house to be opened, and then discovered that a gross attempt at imposture had been practised. The grave was about three feet deep, being a hole dug in the floor of the inner room of the house. The wall of the room formed one side of the vault. The roof over the latter was a clumsy structure, and had been partly demolished to allow of the removal of the devotee. As usual in India, the only light admitted to the room was through the door, and the unsubstantial nature of the roof was not likely to attract the attention of the villagers. But I satisfied myself that the occupant of the vault might, with great ease, have demolished the covering which was supposed to shut him off from the world.

'The vault itself was of course dark. I entered it in order to ascertain how much space had been allotted to the occupant. I found therein the rosary of the deceased, and the chaplet of flowers which he had worn before his self-immolation. There was sufficient room for me to sit in tolerable comfort. On one side of the vault I felt a small wooden plank apparently let into the wall, and on obtaining a light I found that a trap-door about a foot square had been ingeniously contrived to communicate with the other room of the house. The trap-door was so hung as to open inwards towards the vault, at the pleasure of the inmate. On going into the outer room, into which communication had thus been opened, I found that a row of the large earthen jars, which Horace would have called *amphoræ*, and which are used in India to store grain, had been arranged against the wall. The trap-door into the vault was effectually concealed by them, and the supply of air, food, and water to the impostor within thus cleverly provided for. The arrangement was neatly contrived, and was not likely to have attracted suspicion. Had the Bhāt been a strong man, and in good health, he might, without any danger to life, and with only a minimum of discomfort, have emerged triumphantly after his six weeks' Samādh, and have earned a wide reputation. But the excitement and fasting were too much for him.'

As to the practice of self-torture this cannot be entirely prevented by our Government, but is rapidly dying out. Formerly, it was possible for devotees,—with the object of exciting admiration or extorting alms, or under the delusion that their self-torture was an act of religious merit,—to swing in the air attached to a lofty pole by means of a rope and hook passed through the muscles of the back. Such self-inflicted mutilation is now prohibited.

Yet, even in the present day, to acquire a reputation for sanctity, or to receive homage and offerings from the multitude, or under the idea of accumulating a store of merit, all sorts of bodily sufferings, penances, and austerities, even to virtual suicide, are undergone—the latter being sometimes actually perpetrated out of mere revenge, as its consequences are supposed to fall on the enemy whose action has driven the deceased to self-immolation.

Three Brāhmans in a native State, who had their

daughters forced from them by Muhammadans beyond the reach of justice, complained to the governor of the province; but finding no redress, they all swallowed poison and died at the door of his tent.

The practice of sitting in Dharnā was once common, but was made punishable by Reg. VII. 1820. It was thus performed:—A person who wished to compel payment of a debt due to him sat at the door of a debtor's house and observed a strict fast. If he died from want of food the consequences of his death were supposed to fall on the debtor, and if the person sitting was a Brāhman, the terrible guilt of Brahmanicide was believed to be incurred.

I saw a man not long since at Allahābād, who has sat in one position for fifty years on a stone pedestal exposed to sun, wind, and rain. He never moves except once a day, when his attendants lead him to the Ganges. He is an object of worship to thousands, and even high-caste Brāhmans pay him homage.

I saw two Ūṛdhva-bāhus—one at Gayā and the other at Benares—that is, devotees who hold their arms with clenched fists above their heads for years, until they become shrivelled and the finger-nails penetrate through the back of the hands.

Another man was prostrating himself and measuring every inch of the ground with his body round the hill of Govardhan when I passed. He probably intended continuing the painful process till he had completed a circuit of twenty miles one hundred and eight times.

In most of the cases I have described, the laudable humanity of our Government in endeavouring to preserve human life has given rise to fresh evils and difficulties.

In the first place, population is increasing upon us in a degree which threatens to become wholly unmanageable. Then widows never marry again; not even if their boy-husbands die, leaving them widows at the age of six.

A woman is supposed to be sacramentally united to one husband, and belongs to him for ever. Every town, every village, almost every house, is full of widows who are debarred from all amusements, and converted into household drudges. They often lead bad lives. Their life, like that of the lepers, is a kind of living death, and they would often cheerfully give themselves up to be burned alive if the law would let them. The spirit of Satī still survives.

Only the other day in Nepāl, where our supremacy is barely recognized, the widows of Sir Jung Bahādur became Satīs, and burned themselves with their husband.

Then, again, the increase in the number of girls who cannot find suitable husbands is now causing much embarrassment in some districts. Even the lepers, whose lives we preserve, involve us in peculiar difficulties. These unfortunate creatures often roam about the country, exacting food from the people by threatening to touch their children. Here and there we have built leper-villages—rows of cottages under trees devoted to their use; and we make the towns contribute from local funds to support them, while charity ekes out the miserable pittance they receive.

Yet notwithstanding all the fresh evils which our philanthropic efforts have introduced into the country, no one will, I think, dispute my assertion when I maintain that the suppression of Samādhs, human sacrifices, self-immolations, and self-tortures are among the greatest blessings which India has hitherto received from her English rulers.

THE TOWERS OF SILENCE.

The Pārsīs are descendants of the ancient Persians who were expelled from Persia by the Muhammadan conquerors, and who first settled at Sūrat about 1,100 years ago. According to the last census they do not number more than 70,000 souls, of whom about 50,000 are found in the city of Bombay, the remaining 20,000 in different parts of India, but chiefly in Gujarāt and the Bombay Presidency. Though a mere drop in the ocean of 241 million inhabitants, they form a most important and influential body of men, emulating Europeans in energy and enterprize, rivalling them in opulence, and imitating them in many of their habits. Their vernacular language is Gujarātī, but nearly every adult speaks English with fluency, and English is now taught in all their schools. Their benevolent institution for the education of at least 1,000 boys and girls is in a noble building, and is a model of good management. Their religion, as delivered in its original purity by their prophet Zoroaster, and as propounded in the Zand-Avastā, is monotheistic, or, perhaps, rather pantheistic, in spite of its philosophical dualism and in spite of the apparent worship of fire and the elements, regarded as visible representations of the Deity. Its morality is summed up in three precepts of two words each—'good thoughts,' 'good words,' 'good deeds;' of which the Pārsī is constantly reminded by the triple coil of his white cotton girdle. In its origin the Pārsī system is closely allied to that of the Hindū Āryans—as represented in the Veda—and has much in common with the more recent Brāhmanism. Neither religion can make proselytes.

A man must be born a Brāhman or Pārsī; no power can convert him into either one or the other. One notable peculiarity, however, distinguishes Pārsiism. Nothing similar to its funeral rites prevails among other nations; though the practice of exposing bodies on the tops of rocks is said to prevail among the Buddhists of Bhotan.

The Dakhmas, or Pārsī Towers of Silence, are erected in a garden, on the highest point of Malabar Hill—a beautiful rising ground on the north side of Back Bay, noted for the bungalows and compounds of the European and wealthier inhabitants of Bombay scattered in every direction over its surface.

The garden is approached by a well-constructed private road, all access to which, except to Pārsīs, is barred by strong iron gates. Thanks to the omnipotent Sir Jamsetjee, no obstacles impeded my advance. The massive gates flew open before me as if by magic. I drove rapidly through a park-like enclosure, and found the courteous Secretary of the Pārsī Panchāyat, Mr. Nusserwanjee Byramjee, awaiting my arrival at the entrance to the garden. He took me at once to the highest point in the consecrated ground, and we stood together on the terrace of the largest of the three *Sagrīs*, or Houses of Prayer, which overlook the five Towers of Silence. This principal Sagrī contains the sacred fire, which, when once kindled and consecrated by solemn ceremonial, is fed day and night with incense and fragrant sandal, and never extinguished. The view from this spot can scarcely be surpassed by any in the world. Beneath us lay the city of Bombay, partially hidden by cocoanut groves, with its beautiful bay and harbour glittering in the brilliant December light. Beyond stretched the magnificent ranges of the ghauts, while immediately around us extended a garden, such as can only be seen in tropical countries. No English nobleman's garden could be better kept, and no pen could do justice to the glories of its flowering shrubs, cypresses, and palms. It seemed the very ideal, not only of a place of sacred silence, but of peaceful rest.

But what are those five circular structures which appear at intervals rising mysteriously out of the foliage? They are masses of solid masonry, massive enough to last for centuries, built of the hardest black granite, and covered with white chunam, the purity and smoothness of which are disfigured by patches of black fungus-like incrustations. Towers they scarcely deserve to be called; for the height of each is quite out of proportion to its diameter. The largest of the five, built with such solid granite that the cost of erection was three lacs of rupees, seemed 50 or 60 feet in diameter and not more than 25 feet in height. The oldest and smallest of the five was constructed 200 years ago, when the Pārsīs first settled in Bombay, and is now only used by the Modi family, whose forefathers built it, and here the bones of many kindred generations are commingled. The next oldest was erected in 1756, and the other three during the succeeding century. A sixth tower stands quite apart from the others. It is square in shape, and only used for persons who have suffered death for heinous crimes. The bones of convicted criminals are never allowed to mingle with those of the rest of the community.

But the strangest feature in these strange, unsightly structures, so incongruously intermixed with graceful cypresses and palms, exquisite shrubs, and gorgeous flowers, remains to be described. Though wholly destitute of ornament, and even of the simplest moulding, the parapet of each tower possesses an extraordinary coping, which instantly attracts and fascinates the gaze. It is a coping formed, not of dead stone, but of living vultures. These birds, on the occasion of my visit, had settled themselves side by side in perfect order and in a complete circle around the parapets of the towers, with their heads pointed inwards, and so lazily did they sit there and so motionless was their whole mien that, except for their colour, they might have been carved out of the stonework. So much for the external aspect of the celebrated Towers of Silence. After they have been once consecrated by solemn ceremonies no one, except the corpse-bearers, is allowed to enter; nor is any one, not even a Pārsī High Priest, permitted to approach within 30 feet of the immediate precincts. An exact model of the interior was, however, shown to me.

Imagine a round column or massive cylinder 12 or 14 feet high, and 60 feet in diameter, built throughout of solid stone, except in the centre, where a well 8 or 10 feet across leads down to an excavation under the masonry, containing four drains at right angles to each other, terminated by holes filled with charcoal or sand. Round the upper surface of this solid circular cylinder and completely hiding the interior from view is a stone parapet, 10 or 12 feet in height. This it is which, when viewed from the outside, appears to form one piece with the solid stonework, and being, like it, covered with chunam, gives the whole the appearance of a low tower. The upper surface of the solid stone column is divided into seventy-two compartments, or open receptacles, radiating like the spokes of a wheel from the central well, and arranged in three concentric rings, separated from each other by narrow ridges of stone, which are grooved to act as channels for conveying all moisture from the receptacles into the well and into the lower drains. It should be noted, by the by, that the number three is emblematical of Zoroaster's three precepts, and the number seventy-two of the chapters of his Yaśna—a portion of the Zand-Avastā.

Each circle of open stone coffins is divided from the next by a pathway, so that there are three circular pathways, the last encircling the central well; and these three pathways are crossed by another pathway conducting from the solitary door which admits the corpse-bearers from the exterior. In the outermost circle of the stone coffins are placed the bodies of males, in the middle those of females, and in the inner and smallest circle, nearest the well, those of children.

While I was engaged with the Secretary in examining the model, a sudden stir among the vultures made us raise our heads. At least a hundred birds, collected round one of the towers, began to show symptoms of excitement, while others swooped down from neighbouring trees. The cause of this sudden abandonment of their previous apathy soon revealed itself. A funeral was seen to be approaching. However distant the house of a deceased person, and whether he be rich or poor, high or low in rank, his body is always carried to the towers by the official corpse-bearers, called *Nasa-sālār,* who form a distinct class, the mourners walking behind. As the bearers are supposed to contract impurity in the discharge of their duty, they are forced to live quite apart from the rest of the community, and are, therefore, highly paid.

Before they remove the body from the house where the relatives are assembled funeral prayers are recited, and the corpse is exposed to the gaze of a dog, regarded by the Pārsīs as a sacred animal. This latter ceremony is called *Sagdīd.*

Then the body, swathed in a white sheet, is placed on a curved metal trough [1], open at both ends, and the corpse-bearers, dressed in pure white garments, proceed with it towards the towers. They are followed by the mourners at a distance of at least 30 feet, in pairs, also dressed in white, and each couple joined by holding a white handker-

[1] This form of bier is only used in the case of young children. See the description of the second funeral witnessed by me.

chief between them. The particular funeral I witnessed was that of a child. When the two corpse-bearers reached the path leading by a steep incline to the door of the tower, the mourners, about eight in number, turned back and entered one of the prayer houses. 'There,' said the Secretary, 'they repeat certain Gāthās, and pray that the spirit of the deceased may be safely transported on the fourth day after death to its final resting-place.'

The tower selected for the present funeral was one in which other members of the same family had before been laid. The two bearers speedily unlocked the door, reverently conveyed the body of the child into the interior, and, unseen by any one, laid it uncovered in one of the open stone receptacles nearest the central well. In two minutes they re-appeared with the empty bier and white cloth. But scarcely had they closed the door when a dozen vultures swooped down upon the body, and were rapidly followed by flights of others. In five minutes more we saw the satiated birds fly back and lazily settle down again upon the parapet. They had left nothing behind but a skeleton. Meanwhile the bearers were seen to enter a building shaped like a huge barrel. There, as the Secretary informed me, they changed their clothes and washed themselves. Shortly afterwards we saw them come out and deposit their cast-off funeral garments on a stone receptacle near at hand. Not a thread leaves the garden, lest it should carry defilement into the city. Perfectly new garments are supplied at each funeral. In a fortnight, or at most four weeks, the same bearers return, and with gloved hands and implements resembling tongs place the dry skeleton in the central well. There the bones find their last resting-place, and there the dust of whole generations of Pārsīs commingling is left undisturbed for centuries.

The revolting sight of the gorged vultures made me turn

my back on the towers with ill-concealed abhorrence. I asked the Secretary how it was possible to become reconciled to such a usage. His reply was nearly in the following words :—' Our Prophet Zoroaster, who lived 6,000 years ago, taught us to regard the elements as symbols of the Deity. Earth, fire, water, he said, ought never, under any circumstances, to be defiled by contact with putrefying flesh. Naked, he said, we came into the world, and naked we ought to leave it. But the decaying particles of our bodies should be dissipated as rapidly as possible, and in such a way that neither Mother Earth nor the beings she supports should be contaminated in the slightest degree. In fact, our Prophet was the greatest of health officers, and, following his sanitary laws, we build our towers on the tops of the hills, above all human habitations. We spare no expense in constructing them of the hardest materials, and we expose our putrescent bodies in open stone receptacles, resting on 14 feet of solid granite, not necessarily to be consumed by vultures, but to be dissipated in the speediest possible manner, and without the possibility of polluting the earth or contaminating a single living being dwelling thereon. God, indeed, sends the vultures, and, as a matter of fact, these birds do their appointed work much more expeditiously than millions of insects would do if we committed our bodies to the ground. In a sanitary point of view nothing can be more perfect than our plan. Even the rain water which washes our skeletons is conducted by channels into purifying charcoal. Here in these five towers rest the bones of all the Pārsīs that have lived in Bombay for the last 200 years. We form a united body in life, and we are united in death. Even our leader, Sir Jamsetjee, likes to feel that when he dies he will be reduced to perfect equality with the poorest and humblest of the Pārsī community.'

When the Secretary had finished his defence of the Towers

of Silence, I could not help thinking that however much such a system may shock our European feelings and ideas, yet our own method of interment, if regarded from a Pārsī point of view, may possibly be equally revolting to Pārsī sensibilities.

The exposure of the decaying body to the assaults of innumerable worms may have no terrors for us, because our survivors do not see the assailants; but let it be borne in mind that neither are the Pārsī survivors permitted to look at the swoop of the Heaven-sent birds. Why, then, should we be surprised if they prefer the more rapid to the more lingering operation? and which of the two systems, they may reasonably ask, is more defensible on sanitary grounds?

FUNERAL CEREMONIES AND OFFERINGS TO ANCESTORS AT BOMBAY, BENARES, AND GAYĀ.

When I commenced my researches in India I was prepared to expect much perplexing variety in religious and social usages, but the actual reality far outdid my anticipations.

On one occasion, soon after my visit to the Pārsī Towers of Silence, I gained admission to the Hindū burning-ground on the shore of Back Bay at Bombay, and witnessed a curious funeral ceremony there. The body of a man about forty years of age had been burnt the day before. On the morning of my visit about twenty-four men, his relations, gathered round the ashes to perform his funeral rites and soothe his departed spirit supposed to be hovering near in a state of feverish excitement after the fiery process to which the body had just been subjected. They offered no objection to my standing close to them, nor even to my asking them questions. The ceremony commenced by one of their number examining the ashes, and carefully separating any portions of the bones that had not been calcined by the flames on the previous day. These he collected in his hands and carried outside the burning-ground, with the intention, I was told, of throwing them into the sea near at hand. This being done, the whole party gathered round the ashes of the pyre in a semicircle, and one of the twenty-four men sprinkled them with water. Then some cow-dung was carefully spread in the centre of the ashes so as to form a flat circular cake of rather more than a foot in diameter, around which a stream of cow's urine was poured from a metal vessel. Next, one of the men brought a plantain-leaf, and laid it on the circle of cow-dung so as to form a kind of dish or plate. Around the edge of the leaf were placed five round balls (*piṇḍas*) probably of rice-flour, rather smaller than cricket-balls, mixed with some brown substance. Sprigs of the Tulsī plant and fresh leaves of the betel, with a few flowers, were inserted in each ball, and a coloured cotton cord loosely suspended between them. Next, one of the relations covered the five piṇḍas with the red powder called gulāl. Then five flat wheaten cakes were placed on the plantain-leaf inside the circle of the five piṇḍas, and boiled rice was piled up on the cakes, surmounted by a small piece of ghī mixed with brown sugar.

The funeral ceremony being so far completed the deceased man's nephew, or sister's son, took an empty earthenware vase, filled it with water, and held it on his right shoulder. Starting from the north side he commenced circumambulating the five piṇḍas and the five wheaten cakes, with his left shoulder towards them, while one of the relatives with a sharp stone made a hole in the jar, whence the water spouted out in a stream as he walked round. On completing the first circuit and coming back to the north, a second incision was made with the same stone, whence a second stream poured out simultaneously with the first. At the end of the fifth round, when five streams of water had been made to spout out from five holes round the five piṇḍas, the earthenware vase was dashed to the ground on the north side, and the remaining water spilt over the ashes. Next, one of the relatives took a small metal vessel containing milk, and, with a betel-leaf for a ladle, sprinkled some drops over the rice piled on the wheaten cakes. After which, taking some water from a small loṭā—or rather making another relative pour it into his hand—he first sprinkled it in a circle round the piṇḍas, and then over the cakes. Finally, bending down and raising his hands to his head, he performed a sort of pūjā to the piṇḍas, which were supposed to represent the deceased man and four other relations. This was repeated by all twenty-four men in turn. After the completion of the ceremony, the balls and cakes were left to be eaten by crows.

At Benares, honorific ceremonies and offerings in honour of departed ancestors, called Śrāddhas, are constantly performed near the Maṇi-karṇikā-kuṇḍ. This is a well, or small pool, of fetid water, not more than three feet deep, and perhaps not more than twenty feet long by ten broad, lying at a considerable depth below the surface of the ground, and declared in the Kāśī-Khaṇḍa of the Skanda-Purāṇa to have been originally created by Vishṇu from the perspiration which exuded from his body. Its highly sacred character in the eyes of the orthodox Hindū may therefore be easily understood. It is said to have been named Maṇi-karṇikā, because Mahādeva on beholding Vishṇu's well was so enraptured that his body thrilled with emotion, causing an earring to fall from his ear into the water. It is also called Mukti-kshetra, 'holy place of emancipation,' and Pūrṇa-śubhakara, 'cause of complete felicity.' This wonderful well is on the ghāṭ, called from it, Maṇi-karṇikā, and is resorted to by thousands of pilgrims, who may be seen all day long descending the flight of steps by which the shallow pool is surrounded on all four sides. Eagerly and with earnest faces they crowd into the water, immersing their whole bodies repeatedly, while Brāhmans superintend their ablutions, repeat and make them repeat Mantras, and receive handsome fees in return. In a niche upon the steps on the north side are the figures of Vishṇu and Śiva, to which the pilgrims, after bathing, do honour by bowing down and touching the stones underneath with their foreheads. The bathers, though manifestly much dirtier from contact with the foul water, go away under the full conviction that they are inwardly purified, and that all their sins, however heinous, have been washed away for time and for eternity.

There is another well of almost equal sanctity, named the Jnāna-vāpī, or 'pool of knowledge,' situated under a handsome colonnade in the interior of the city, between the mosque built by Aurangzīb on the site of the original Viśveśvaranāth temple and the present Golden Temple. It is a real well of some depth, and not a pool, but the water is so abominably offensive, from the offerings of flowers and rice continually thrown into it and left to putrefy, that I found it impossible to do more than take a hasty glance into the interior of the well, or even to remain in the neighbourhood long enough to note all the particulars of its surroundings. All the day long a Brāhman stands near this well and ladles out putrid water from a receptacle before him into the hands of pilgrims, who either lave their faces with the fetid liquid, or drink it with the greatest reverence. The supposed sanctity of this well is owing to the circumstance that the idol of Śiva was thrown into it when the original temple of Viśveśvaranāth was destroyed by the Musalmāns. Hence the pool is thought to be the habitation of Mahādeva himself, and the water to be permeated by his essence.

Close to the pool of Maṇi-karṇikā, on the day I visited the ghāṭ, a man was performing a Śrāddha for his mother, under the guidance of a nearly naked and decidedly stout Brāhman. The ceremony was the Daśama-śrāddha, performed on the tenth day after death. The officiating Brāhman began by forming a slightly elevated piece of ground with some sand lying near at hand. This was supposed to constitute a small vedi or altar. It was of an oblong form, but only about eight or ten inches long by four or five broad. Across this raised sand he laid three stalks of kuśa grass. Then taking a number of little earthenware platters or saucers, he arranged them round the vedi, putting tila or sesamum seed in one, rice in another, honey in a third, areca or betel-nut in a fourth, chandana or sandal in a fifth. Next, he took flour of barley (*yava*) and kneaded it into one large piṇḍa, rather smaller than a cricket-ball, which he carefully deposited in the centre of the sand vedi, scattering over it jasmine flowers, khaskhas grass, and wool, and placing on one side of it a betel-leaf with areca-nut and a single copper coin. Then having poured water from a loṭā into his hand, he sprinkled it over all the offerings, arranged in the manner I have just described. Other similar operations followed:—Thus, for instance, an earthenware platter, containing a lighted wick, was placed near the offerings; ten other platters were filled with water, which was all poured over the piṇḍa; another small platter with a lighted wick was added to the first, then some milk was placed in another platter and poured over the piṇḍa, and then once more the piṇḍa was sprinkled with water. Finally the Brāhman joined his hands together and did pūjā to the piṇḍa. The whole rite did not last more than ten or fifteen minutes, and while it was proceeding, the man for whose mother it was performed continued to repeat Mantras and prayers under the direction of the officiating Brāhman, quite regardless of much loud talking and vociferation going on around him.

The ceremony was concluded by another ceremony called the 'feeding of a Brāhman'—that is to say, another Brāhman was brought and made to sit down near the oblations, while the man for whose mother the Śrāddha was celebrated fed him with flat cakes, ghī, sweetmeats, vegetables, and curds placed in a plate of palāśa leaves. I observed that these eatables were devoured with the greatest avidity by the man for whom they were prepared, as if he had been nursing his appetite with the intention of doing full justice to the feast.

I come now to the celebrated Śrāddha ceremonies performed in the neighbourhood of the well-known Vishṇu-pada temple at Gayā. The city of Gayā is most picturesquely situated on the river Phalgū about sixty miles south-west of Patna, near some isolated hills, or rather short ranges of hills rising abruptly out of the plain. The town itself crowns two low ridges, whose sides, covered with the houses of its narrow tortuous streets, slope down to an intervening hollow occupied by the temple and sacred tank dedicated to the Sun. But the most sacred temple and the great centre of attraction for all Hindūs who wish to perform once in their lives a Gayā-śrāddha for their forefathers, is the Vishṇu-pada temple, situated on one of the ridges, and built of black stone, with a lofty dome and golden pinnacle. It contains the alleged footprint of Vishṇu in a large silver basin, under a silver canopy, inside an octagonal shrine. Piṇḍas and various kinds of offerings are placed by the pilgrims inside the basin round the footprint, and near it are open colonnades for the performance of the Śrāddhas. About six miles from the city is the well-known place of pilgrimage called Bodh-Gayā, celebrated for a monastery and numerous temples, but chiefly for the ancient tower-like structure said by the natives to be more than 2,200 years old, and originally a Buddhist monument. It has near it other alleged footprints of Vishṇu (probably once assigned to Buddha), under an open shrine. Behind the tower, on an elevated stone terrace reached by a long flight of steps, is the sacred Pīpal tree, under which, according to popular belief, the Buddha attained supreme knowledge. The tree must be many centuries old, but a succession of trees is secured by planting a new one inside the decaying stem of the old. In a chamber at the bottom of the tower-like Buddhist monument—now used as a temple—a substitute for the original figure of Buddha (carried off by the Burmese about a hundred years ago) has been placed, for the sake of the Buddhist pilgrims who come to repeat prayers and meditate under the tree; and in the same place a linga has been set up, to which the Hindūs do pūjā. When I visited the spot many persons were in the act of worshipping, and several members of the Burmese embassy, who had come to meet the Prince of Wales at Calcutta, were to be seen reverentially kneeling, praying, and meditating under the sacred tree.

Before describing the Śrāddhas at Gayā, I may state that I asked several Pandits in different parts of India, to give me the reasons for attaching special efficacy to the celebration of religious rites for ancestors in that locality. The only reply I received was that in the Gayā-māhātmya and Gayā-śrāddha-paddhati it is declared that a powerful demon (*asura*), named Gayā, formerly resided there and tyrannized over the inhabitants. Vishṇu took compassion on them, fought and killed the demon, and left a print of his foot (Vishṇu-pada, commonly called Bishanpad) on the spot where the fight occured, ordaining that it should be ever after called Gayā and should be consecrated to him, and that any Śrāddha performed there for fathers, forefathers, and relatives should be peculiarly efficacious in securing the immediate conveyance of their souls to his own heaven, Vaikuṇṭha.

It is also stated in the Gayā-māhātmya that the great Rāma, hero of the Rāmāyaṇa (himself an incarnation of Vishṇu), and other heroes set the example of performing Śrāddhas to their fathers at Gayā. Brahmā is also said to have performed an Aśvamedha there, and to have consecrated the whole locality by this act. The plain truth probably is that as the Indo-Āryans proceeded southwards, the Brāhmans found it necessary to invent reasons for attaching sanctity and attracting pilgrims to other spots besides those already held sacred in the North-West.

It was on this account that the Māhātmyas of various places were gradually written and inserted in the Purāṇas. Some of these additions, intended to exalt the importance of places like Gayā, are comparatively modern, and the Māhātmyas of one or two tīrthas, such as Paṇḍharpur in the Dekhan, are said to have been added during the last fifty or a hundred years. I was even told that Paṇḍharpur has become of late years a kind of rival to Gayā. Alleged footprints of Vishṇu like those of Gayā are shown, and the Viṭhobā sects perform Śrāddhas there.

Models of the Gayā Vishṇu-pada are made in brass and in black stone, and sold for worship. Several were presented to me. They are often placed, like the Śālagrām stone, in the houses of the natives, for domestic pūjā.

With regard to the Śrāddha ceremonies generally, there seems to be much confusion of thought and obscurity, besides great inconsistency, in the accounts given by Pandits of the exact object and effect of their celebration. It may be well to explain that a distinction is made between Śrāddhas and funeral ceremonies (*antyeshṭi*). The latter are *amangala*, 'inauspicious,' while the former are *mangala*, 'auspicious.' To understand the reason for this, it should be borne in mind that when a man dies his *sthūla-śarīra* or 'gross body' is burned, but his soul quits it with the *linga-śarīra* or 'subtile body,' sometimes described as *angushṭha-mātra*, 'of the size of a thumb,' and remains hovering near. The deceased man, thus reduced to the condition of a simple individual soul invested with a subtile body, is called a preta, i. e. a departed spirit or ghost. He has no real body capable of enjoying or suffering anything, and is consequently in a restless, unsatisfactory and uncomfortable plight. Moreover, while in this condition he is held to be an impure being. Furthermore, if he dies away from his kindred, who alone can perform the funeral ceremonies, and who are perhaps unaware of his death, and unable therefore to perform them, he becomes a piśācha, or foul wandering ghost, disposed to take revenge for its misery upon all living creatures by a variety of malignant acts. I heard it remarked not long ago by a Pandit that ghosts are much less common in India now than formerly, and, on my enquiring the reason, was told that communication was now so rapid that few die without their deaths becoming known and without having funeral rites performed very soon afterwards. Besides, he added, it is now so easy to reach Gayā by rail and by good carriage roads. The object, then, of the funeral rites, which are celebrated for ten days after death, is not only to soothe or give śānti by libations of consecrated water to the troubled spirit, but to furnish the preta with an intermediate body, between the *linga* or 'subtile' and the *sthūla* or 'gross' body—with a body, that is to say, which is capable of enjoying or suffering, and which is composed of gross particles though not of the same kind as those of the earthly gross body.

In this manner only can the preta obtain *gati*, or 'progress' onward through the temporary heaven or hell (regarded in the Hindū system as a kind of purgatory) to other births and ultimate emancipation. On the first day after death a piṇḍa or 'round ball' (generally of some kind of flour) is offered, on which the preta is supposed to feed, and which endows it with the rudiment or basis of the requisite body, whatever that basis may be. Next day another piṇḍa is offered, which gives it, perhaps, limbs, such as arms and legs. Then it receives hands, feet, &c. This goes on for ten days, and the offering of the piṇḍa on the tenth day gives the head. No sooner does the preta obtain a complete body than it becomes a pitṛi, when instead of heing regarded as impure, it is held to be a *deva*, or 'deity,' and practically worshipped as such in the Śrāddha ceremonies. Hence a Śrāddha is not a funeral ceremony, but a *worship of departed ancestors*; which worship, however, is something different from pūjā to a god. It is continued at stated periods with a view to accelerate the *gati*, or 'progress,' of the pitṛis either towards heaven, and so through the various stages of bliss, called Sālokya, Sāmīpya, and Sārūpya, or through future births to final union with the Supreme (*sāyujya*). The efficacy of Śrāddhas performed at Gayā is this, that wherever in this progress onwards departed relatives may have arrived, the Śrāddhas take them at once to Vaikuṇṭha or Vishṇu's heaven. The departed relatives especially entitled to benefit by the Śrāddha rites are as follow:—1. Father, grandfather, great-grandfather; 2. Mother, mother's father and grandfather; 3. Stepmother, if any; 4. Father's mother, grandmother, and great-grandmother; 5. Father's brothers; 6. Mother's brothers; 7. Father's sisters; 8. Mother's sisters; 9. Sisters and brothers; 10. Fathers-in-law.

An eleventh person is sometimes added, viz. the family spiritual teacher (*guru*).

Let no one suppose that the process of performing Śrāddhas at Gayā is either simple or rapid. To secure the complete efficacy of such rites, a whole round of them must be performed at about fifty distinct places in and around Gayā, besides at the most holy spot of all—the Vishṇupada temple—the time occupied in the process being at least eight days, and sometimes protracted to fifteen, while the money spent in fees to the officiating priests (who at Gayā are called Gaywāls = Gayā-pālas, regarded by some as an inferior order of Brāhmans) is never less than Rs. 40. But only the poorest are let off thus easily. The Mahārāja of Kaśmīr, who is a very strict Hindū, and performed Śrāddhas at Gayā the other day on his way to Calcutta, is reported to have distributed Rs. 15,000 to the Gaywāl Brāhmans.

With regard to the Śrāddhas I myself witnessed at Gayā, they were all performed in colonnades and open courts round the Vishṇu-pada temple. One example will suffice. The party celebrating the rite consisted of six men, who were of course relations, and one Gaywāl. The men sat on their heels in a line, with the officiating Gaywāl (sometimes called Paṇḍa) priest at their head. Twelve piṇḍas were formed of rice and milk, not much larger than the large marbles used by boys (called 'alleys'). They were placed with sprigs of the sacred Tulsī plant in small earthenware platters. Then on the top of the piṇḍas were scattered kuśa grass and flowers. I was told that the piṇḍas in the present case were typical of the bodies of the twelve ancestors for whom the Śrāddha was celebrated. The men had kuśa grass twisted round their fingers, in token of their hands being perfectly pure for the due performance of the rite. Next, water was poured into the palms of their hands, part of which they sprinkled on the ground, and part on the piṇḍas. One or two of the men then took threads off their clothes and laid them on the piṇḍas, which act is alleged to be emblematical of presenting the bodies of their departed ancestors with garments.

Meanwhile Mantras, or texts, were repeated, under the direction of the Gaywāl, and the hands were sometimes extended over the piṇḍas as if to invoke blessings. When all the Mantras were finished, and one or two added to pray for pardon if any minute point in the ritual had been omitted, the whole rite was concluded by the men putting their heads to the ground before the officiating Brahmān and touching his feet. Of course the number of piṇḍas varies with the number of ancestors for whom the Śrāddhas are celebrated, and the size of the balls and the materials of which they are composed differ according to the caste and the country of those who perform the rite. I saw one party in the act of forming fourteen or fifteen piṇḍas with oatmeal, which were of a much larger size than large marbles. This party was said to have come from the Dekhan. Sometimes the piṇḍas were placed on betel-leaves with pieces of money (afterwards appropriated by the priests), and sometimes the water used was taken out of little pots with stalks of kuśa grass, and with these sprinkled over the balls. At the end of all the ceremonies the earthen platters employed were carried to a particular stone in the precincts of the temple and dashed to pieces there. No platter is allowed to be used a second time.

Amid this crash of broken crockery, the tedious round of rites, ceremonies, and vain repetitions, which, if they effect nothing else, certainly serve to enrich a goodly company of Brāhmans, is perhaps not inappropriately concluded.

INDIAN ROSARIES.[1]

Rosaries seem to be common in nearly all religious systems which attach more importance to the repetition, than to the spirituality, of prayers. It might be supposed, *à priori*, that to no one would a rosary be more useless and meaningless than to a Christian, who is taught when he prays to enter into his closet, to avoid vain repetitions, to pour out his heart before his Father in secret, and to cultivate spiritual intercessions 'which cannot be uttered.' Yet we know that in some Christian countries rosaries are regarded as indispensable aids to devotion. Palladius, who lived in the fourth century, tells of a certain abbot who used to repeat the Lord's prayer 300 times every day, and who secured a correct enumeration of the repetitions by dropping small pebbles into his lap.

The Kurān enjoins prayers five times a day, and good Muslims are very particular in going through prescribed forms morning, noon, and evening. It cannot, therefore, be matter of wonder that the use of rosaries (called *tasbīh*, 'praise,' and furnished with tassels called *shamsa*) is common among Indian Muhammadans. In all probability they were common among Hindūs and Buddhists long before the Christian era. Indeed, the Indian name for a rosary well expresses its meaning and use even in Roman Catholic countries. It is called in Sanskṛit *japa-mālā*, 'muttering-chaplet' (and sometimes *smaraṇī*, 'remembrancer'), be-

[1] This article and that on Samādh appeared first in the Athenæum.

cause by means of its beads the muttering of a definite number of prayers may be counted. But the pious Hindū not only computes his daily prayers as if they were so many rupees to be added to his capital stock in the bank of heaven, he sets himself to repeat the mere names of his favourite god, and will continue doing so for hours together.

When I was at Benares, I went early one morning to inspect the temple of the goddess Annapūrṇā. A devotee was seated at the door, with a rosary in his hand, muttering 'Rām, Rām, Rām' incessantly. When I had occasion to pass by a long time afterwards, I found him seated in precisely the same position, and engaged in precisely the same occupation, except that instead of repeating the god's name he prefixed to it that of his wife Sītā. I have no doubt that the whole day was divided between Rām and Sītā-rām, and an accurate account kept of the total number of repetitions.

In this respect, Hindūism is behind the most corrupt forms of Christianity. It has been calculated that about ninety names and attributes are applied to Christ in the Bible. But no Romanist, however ignorant and superstitious, so far as I know, attaches any merit or efficacy to the repetition of the mere names of God.

Muhammadans reckon ninety-nine sacred names, or rather attributes, of the Deity. Some consider that the principal name, Allāh, must be counted separately. The tale is thus brought up to one hundred. I saw only ninety-nine names carved on Akbar's marble tomb near Agra, Akbar, 'the Great One,' being one of the ninety-nine. (See note at the end of this chapter.)

The voracious appetite of a Hindū in any matter connected with religious superstition far outdoes that of any other nation on earth. If one hundred titles of the Deity will satisfy the piety of an earnest-minded Muslim, nothing short of that number multiplied by ten will slake the devotional cravings of an ardent Hindū. The worshippers of Vishṇu adore him by 1,000 sacred names, and the votaries of Śiva by 1,008 names. The whole catalogue is given in the Mahā-bhārata and the Purāṇas.

Curiously enough among the names of Śiva occur Haya, 'a horse,' and Gardabha, 'an ass' (Mahā-bhārata XIII. 1149), which the Vedāntist has no difficulty in accepting as suitable titles of the One all-pervading universal Being with whom the god Śiva is identified.

It is not unreasonable to conjecture that the original invention of rosaries is due to India. They were as much the offspring of necessity as was the invention of the Sūtras, or brief memorial rules for the correct performance of the complicated ritual. No other country in the world stands in such need of aids to religious exercises. Vaishṇavas, Śaivas, Buddhists, Jains, and Muhammadans depend upon these contrivances for securing the accurate discharge of their daily round of interminable repetitions.

The rosary of a Vaishṇava is made of the wood of the Tulasī (vulgarly *Tulsī*), or holy basil, a shrub sacred to Vishṇu, and regarded as a metamorphosis of Rāma's pattern-wife Sītā. This rosary should consist of 108 smooth beads. That worn by Śaivas consists of thirty-two and sometimes sixty-four berries of the Rudrāksha tree (Elæocarpus). These seeds are as rough as the Tulsī beads are smooth, and are generally marked with five lines, the roughness symbolizing, I suspect, the austerities connected with the worship of Śiva, and the five lines standing for the five faces or five distinct aspects of the god.

The Musalmān *tasbīh* contains one hundred beads, which are generally made of date-stones, or of the sacred earth of Karbalā. They are used in repeating the hundred names of God or certain words of the Kurān, every decade of beads being separated by a tassel. Some Sunnīs are prohibited from employing rosaries, and count by means of the joints of their fingers.

It might be wearisome if I were to attempt a description of the diverse uses to which different kinds of rosaries are applied in India.

I was told by a Gṛihastha, or layman of the Svāmi-Nārāyan sect of Vaishṇavas, that he was able by help of his *japa-mālā* to go on muttering Svāmi-Nārāyan, Svāmi-Nārāyan, Svāmi-Nārāyan one hundred and eight times with perfect precision at his morning and evening devotions, and that he attributed great efficacy to the act.

High-caste Brāhmans, on the other hand, merely use their rosaries to assist them in counting up their daily prayers, especially the well-known Gāyatrī from the Ṛig-veda (*Tat savitur vareṇyam bhargo devasya dhīmahi dhiyo yo naḥ pracodayāt*), which is repeated five, ten, twenty-eight, or one hundred and eight times at the dawn and sunset Sandhyās. The very sound of this precious mantra (which is called Gāyatrī, from the metre in which it is composed), quite irrespectively of the sense (which may be rendered, 'Let us adore that excellent glory of the divine Vivifier: may he enlighten our understandings'), is a mine of inexhaustible spiritual wealth to those favoured beings whose second spiritual birth—conferred by investiture with the sacred thread—entitles them to repeat it. Manu (II. 77) declares that this sacred text was 'milked out' of the three Vedas and ordains that 'a Brāhman may attain beatitude by simple repetition (of the Gāyatrī), whether he perform other rites or not,' and 'that having repeated the Gāyatrī three thousand times he is delivered (from the greatest guilt).'

It is noticeable, moreover, that the proud Brāhman who claims to be the true owner of this valuable piece of religious property is careful to conceal his hand in a sort of bag called a Gomukhī while engaged in counting out his morning and evening store of accumulated Gāyatrīs.

In fact, every Hindū is persuaded that jealous demons are ever on the watch to obstruct his religious exercises, and ever eager, like cunning thieves, to abstract a portion of their merit. This is the true secret of the universal homage paid throughout India to Gaṇeśa, lord of the demon-hosts. I have myself often seen Brāhmans seated on the margin of sacred streams, with their faces turned towards the east, and apparently intently occupied in gazing on vacancy. On a closer inspection, I found that their right hands were mysteriously concealed in a red bag. Prayers were being repeated and counted up by help of the *japa-mālā*, and the repeater, even if too proud to betray any fear of thievish demons, seemed at any rate to understand that the value of his prayers would be increased by his taking heed not 'to be seen of men.' We must not forget, too, that a Hindū is taught by many of his own sacred precepts that the merit of religious exercises is destroyed by ostentation.

Nothing, however, comes up to the Buddhist's idea of the efficacy of repeated prayers. His rosary, like that of the Vaishṇavas, consists of 108 beads, which in China are often arranged in two rings. I never met with any native who could explain the proper meaning of *om maṇi padme hūm*, 'hail to the jewel in the lotus!' although every Buddhist in Tibet believes that the oftener this six-syllabled formula is repeated by help of rosaries and prayer-wheels the greater merit will accrue to the repeater. According to some, the repetition of the six syllables exercises some sort of protective or preventive influence with reference to the six Gatis, or forms of transmigration. In China the repeated prayer is 'Omito Fat' or 'Omito Fo' (for *amita Buddha*, 'the infinite Buddha'), or 'Nama Amitābha,' and in Japan, 'Namu Amida Butsu' (for *nama amita Buddhāya*, 'honour to the infinite Buddha').

It is not uncommon to meet Buddhists in the neighbourhood of Darjīling who, while they are talking to you, continue whirling their prayer-wheels, held in their right hands, and made to revolve like a child's toy. The wheel consists of a metal cylinder on which the form of prayer is engraved. It must be whirled, by means of a handle, in a particular direction (I think with the sun); if made to revolve the other way the number of its rotations will be set down to the debtor rather than the creditor side of the owner's account.

A friend of mine who had to hold a conversation with a pious Buddhist, intent on redeeming every instant of time for the repetition of prayers, came away from the interview under the impression that all Buddhists regard all Europeans as possessed with evil spirits. The Buddhist's diligent gyration of his wheel was mistaken by my friend for a form of exorcism.

It is said that the Buddhist monks of Ladakh have a still more economical arrangement, and one not unworthy of the attention of monks in other monasteries—when regarded, I mean, from the point of view of an ingenious contrivance for saving time and making the most of both worlds. An infinite number of prayers are repeated, and yet the whole time of the monastery is saved for making money by industrial occupations. Long strips of the usual Buddhist prayer are rolled round cylinders, and these cylinders are made to revolve, like the works of a clock, by means of heavy weights wound up every morning and evening. A single monk takes five minutes to set the entire spiritual machinery in motion, and then hastens to join his brothers at their mundane occupations; the whole body of monks feeling that the happiness and prosperity of the community are greatly promoted by the substitution of the precept 'laborare est orare,' for 'orare est laborare.'

It should be mentioned that in times of emergency or difficulty additional weights are attached to the cylinders, and an additional impetus thus given to the machinery, and, of course, increased force and cogency to the rotatory prayers.

My friend the Collector of Kaira, in whose camp I stayed for about a fortnight, had occasion one day to ascend a hill in his district much overgrown with trees. There to his surprise he came suddenly upon an old hermit, who had been living for a long time without his knowledge in the jungle at the summit. Mr. Sheppard found the ancient recluse in a hut near a rude temple, concealed from observation by the dense underwood. He was engaged in his evening religious exercises, and, wholly regardless of the presence of his European visitor, continued turning with both hands and with evident exertion a gigantic rosary. A huge wooden roller, suspended horizontally from the posts of the shed, supported a sort of chain composed of fifteen rough wooden balls, each as big as a child's head. As he kept turning this enormous rosary round and round, each ball passed into his hands, and whilst he held the several balls in his grasp he repeated, or rather chanted in a low tone, a short prayer to the god Rāma. All the wooden balls underwent this process of pious manipulation several times before he desisted. The muscular exertion and consequent fatigue must have been great, yet the entire operation was performed with an air of stoical impassiveness. Then the devotee went into another shed, where on another cross-beam, supported by posts, were strung some heavy logs of hard wood, each weighing about twenty pounds. Having grasped one of these with both hands, he dashed it forcibly against the side post, and then another log against the first. Probably the clashing noise thus produced was intended to give increased effectiveness to the recitation of his prayers.

Sleeman somewhere relates how he happened once to be staying in the neighbourhood of an Indian village, the inhabitants of which were divided into two religious parties—those who advocated a noisy musical worship, and those who attributed greater efficacy to a quiet religious ceremonial. The two parties lived together very amicably, agreeing to set apart certain hours of the day for an alternate use of the village temple. When the noisy faction had possession the din was terrific.

In short, almost every religious idea that the world has ever known has in India been stimulated to excessive growth, and every religious usage carried to preposterous extremes. Hence, if a Hindū temple has a choir of musicians, its excellence is estimated by the deafening discord it gives out at the morning and evening pūjā ; and if a devotee uses a rosary its effectiveness is supposed to depend on the dimensions of its beads, which may vary from small seeds to heavy balls as big as a human skull.

Note.—The ninety-nine names or attributes of the Deity are called by the Muhammadans *ism-i'azīm,* 'The glorious names.' Some of these are as follow :—The Lord (Rabb), the King (Mālik), the Merciful (Rahmān), the Compassionate (Rahīm), the Holy (Kuddūs), the Creator (Ḳhālik), the Saviour (Salām), the Excellent ('Azīz), the Omniscient ('Ālim), the Omnipotent (Jabbār), the Pardoner (Ghafūr), the Glorious (Majīd), the Beneficent (Karīm), the Wise (Hakīm), the Just ('Ādil), the Benign (Latif), the One (Wāhid), the Eternal (Bākī), the Survivor (Wāris), the Last (Āḳhir), the Guide (Hādī), the Director (Rashīd), the Patient (Sabūr).

GENERAL IMPRESSIONS OF NORTHERN INDIA.

BOMBAY, MARCH 6, 1876.

THE 'Serapis' is now lying at anchor before our eyes in Bombay Harbour, reminding us that the Prince of Wales is on his road to this port, and that England will soon be preparing to welcome his return home. The interest excited by his tour has now culminated, and special correspondents are either bound homewards or addressing themselves to an effective winding up of their communications by a telling description of the closing scene. Even after the Prince's return his doings in India are certain to continue a fashionable theme of conversation during the London season of 1876, and the Session will assuredly be marked by a constant recurrence to Indian topics. Every Parliamentary orator will drag in, relevantly or irrelevantly, allusions to the expedition and its results for the benefit of his constituents. Newspapers, reviews, and periodicals will contain trenchant articles, bristling with point, epigram, and criticism, if they do not cut the knot of our Indian difficulties.

Meanwhile, I will endeavour to record, in plain language, a few particulars relative to our Indian possessions, which have impressed themselves on me most forcibly in the course of my tour in the Prince's track.

It must be confessed that the impressions of a flying

traveller are not generally worth recording; but as circumstances have given me peculiar opportunities of observing the country, and mixing with the natives, after many years spent in studying their languages and literature, some value may possibly attach to my experiences, which I propose to recount under distinct heads.

Climate.

India, which is in all respects a complete world in itself, seems to include all the climates of all countries. Far from being 'deadly' (at least, from November till April), as I have heard it described, I believe the winter climate of India to be more salubrious than that of England. Perpetual sunshine, balmy breezes, perfect dryness of air and soil, with lovely flowers and summer foliage constantly before the eyes, cannot fail to exhilarate the spirits and benefit the health. Many invalids, who habitually resort to Italy to escape the damp and gloom of our English climate, would do well to devote a winter to India. The facilities now offered by the Suez Canal, and the beautiful weather prevalent in the Red Sea and Indian Ocean from November to April, make the passage itself not the least delightful part of the expedition; and if English tourists would oftener turn their steps towards our Eastern possessions, the present lamentable ignorance on Indian subjects, amounting in most cases to Cimmerian darkness, would be replaced by a better appreciation of the character of the country.

How is it, too, that so few scientific men wend their way towards India? I inquired in vain for professional astronomers, and only came across one amateur during the whole course of my travels. The sight he gave me of the planet Saturn through his well-appointed telescope at Allahabad, will remain indelibly impressed on my memory. How is it, then, that there are not more telescopic batteries directed against the heavens in an atmosphere unequalled for clearness, stillness, and all the conditions favourable to new conquests in the field of astronomical research?

Physical Features.

Not only the student of physical geography and geology, but the admirers of scenery, would find no place so satisfying as India. For here, enclosed by the Himālayas and the ocean, is an immense peninsula which presents us with an epitome of the world. Where can be seen more wonderful contrasts, where such amazing variety? Monotonous plains, sandy deserts, noble rivers, fertile fields, immense districts wooded like English parks, forest, grove, and jungle, gentle undulation, hill and dale, rock, crag, precipice, snowy peak—everything is here. The one exception is lake scenery. India has nothing to offer like the picturesque lakes of Europe. But the grand distinctive feature which impresses a traveller most is the sublime range which, stretching from the east towards the west, blends with other ranges northwards, and surrounds the whole upper part of India with a mighty natural rampart, shutting it out from the rest of the continent of Asia, and, indeed, from the rest of the world (as the Alps shut out Italy from Europe) except from the sea. It is true that early incursions have always taken place through the principal Himālayan passes (especially the Khaiber and Bolan) as well as along the course of the Brahma-putra; and the later Muhammadan invasions have always followed the former route through Afghānistān, but these occurred before the existence of steam navies, ironclads, railroads, and telegraphs. Some great aggressive power like Russia may, hereafter, give us trouble by stirring up disaffection among the people of Afghānistān, and the excitable tribes in the neighbourhood of the passes, but no Power that cannot beat us at sea is ever likely to dispossess us of India.

My first view of the Himālayan range on a clear evening from a point about 150 miles distant was absolutely overpowering. Imagine the Jung Frau piled on Mont Blanc, and repeated in a succession of peaks, stretching apparently nearly half round the horizon in an unbroken line, far more extended than that of the Alps as seen from Berne, and a faint idea may be formed of the sublimity of the spectacle presented by this majestic pile of mountains, some of which tower to a height of nearly 30,000 feet above the plain.

Animal and Plant Life.

Under this head I will confine myself at present, to the expression of my surprise that zoologists and botanists do not come by scores to this country and revel in the rich fare—the endless variety spread out in every direction, and asking to be enjoyed and appreciated. For my own part, I would rather see them abound than sportsmen, of whom, indeed, there is no lack at all. As to the omnipresent insects which most people execrate as the greatest pest incident to an Indian climate, it must be confessed that they are a little too demonstrative for the ordinary traveller and resident. Various appliances may temper extremes of heat and cold, but what can repress the irrepressible mosquito, or check the unpleasant exuberance of every form of insect life? 'If I could get £200 in England,' I have often heard irritated young civilians exclaim, 'I would give up my £800 a year in this country.' Certainly there are many drawbacks to a life in Eastern climates, and the insect nuisance is not the least of them. But one man's plague may be another man's prize. To an entomologist the study of Indian ants alone would be an inexhaustible subject of interest, while to the ordinary amateur what can be more attractive than the whole butterfly world of India. I well remember how, walking in a secluded lane, I was suddenly surrounded by a flight of at least a hundred gorgeous specimens of this form of insect life. How is it then that I looked in vain for entomologists and butterfly-collectors in my travels?

Character and Condition of the Inhabitants.

I have found no people in Europe more religious—none more patiently persevering in common duties, none more docile and amenable to authority, none more courteous or respectful towards age and learning, none more dutiful to parents, none more faithful in service. Superstition, immorality, untruthfulness, pride, selfishness, avarice, all these and other faults and vices, of course, abound, but not more than they do in other countries unpenetrated by the spirit of true Christianity, and not more than will be found among those merely nominal Christians who, after all, constitute the real mass of the people in Europe.

While on this subject, let me notice a few leading particulars as to races, languages, creeds and religious usages.

Races.

First, as to races. All the principal races of the world are here represented; the Caucasian—both Āryan in Brāhmans and Rājputs, and Semitic in the Arabs (though of Arab blood there is no great admixture)—the Mongolian, and even the Negro, some of the aboriginal hill tribes being manifestly either negroid or negrito. All races are more or less blended, yet Brāhmans, Rājputs, Jāts, Baniyas (in Sanskṛit *Banijas* = *Vaiśyas*), Śūdras, and hill tribes differ as much *inter se* as Greeks, Italians, Saxons, Slaves, Celts, Finns, and Laps.

Languages.

And just as all races are represented, so are all families of languages—Āryan, Semitic, and Agglutinative (commonly called Turanian). For example, Hindī, Bengālī, Marāṭhī, and Gujarātī are closely connected with Sanskṛit, which of course is Āryan; while Tamil, Telugu, Malayālam, and Kanarese (constituting what is called the Drāviḍian family) are examples of Agglutinative languages, and Arabic, which forms Hindūstānī out of Hindī, is Semitic. Hindūstānī—the *lingua Franca* of India—exactly corresponds, like our English, to the composite character of the inhabitants of the country. It has a Hindī stock, but has taken a vast number of Arabic and Persian words from the Muhammadan conquerors, and is now taking English words largely from us. I have heard it asserted that English is likely to supplant Hindūstānī as the current language of intercourse throughout India. I see no signs whatever of this. On the contrary, English has scarcely made its way at all among the masses of the people, though common at the Presidency towns, especially at Madras. It is studied and spoken fluently by educated natives at some of the large towns in the interior, but is chiefly valued, not for its own sake, but as a channel to Government situations.

Religious Creeds.

Again, as all races and families of language are represented in India, so are the four principal religious creeds in the world—namely, Brāhmanism or Hindūism, Buddhism, Islām or Muhammadanism, and Christianity.

The term Brāhmanism should be restricted to the purely pantheistic and not necessarily idolatrous system evolved by the Brāhmans out of the partly monotheistic, party polytheistic, partly pantheistic religion expressed in the sacred works collectively termed *Veda*. This system was fully developed in a still later work following on the Veda, called the Vedānta philosophy, where it is designated by the term *Advaita*—Non-Dualism. Brāhmanism, in fact, is a mere assertion of the unity of all being. Nothing really exists, it affirms, but the one Universal Spirit (named Brahman, from the root *bṛih*, 'to spread and pervade'), and whatever appears to exist independently is identical with that Spirit.

But it has also other characteristics. It may be described as in one sense the most self-annihilating system in the world, for it asserts that there can be no real *self* (*ātman*) existing separately from the one self-existent Supreme Self—called *Paramātman*, as well as *Brahman*, and when by the act of that Self the individuated spirits of men are allowed for a time an apparent separate existence, the ultimate end and aim of such spirits should be to attain complete reunion with the one Eternal Self in entire self-annihilation. A Brāhman, who holds this doctrine, thinks the religion of the Christian, who is conscious of severance from God, and yearns for reunion with Him, and yet does not wish his own self-consciousness to be merged in God, a very selfish kind of creed, compared with his own. It is evident, however, that there may be more real selfishness in the self-annihilating creed. For whatever may be said about the bliss of complete union (*sāyujya*) with the Supreme Spirit, the true aim of Brāhmanism, pure and simple, is not so much extinction of self, as extinction of personal existence for the sake of release from the troubles of life, and from the consequences of activity.

The term Hindūism, on the other hand, may be used to express Brāhmanism after it had degenerated—to wit, that complicated system of polytheistic doctrines and caste-usages, which has gradually resulted out of the mixture of Brāhmanism, first with Buddhism and then with the non-Āryan creeds of Drāviḍians and aborigines. This system rests on the whole series of Hindū sacred writings—the four Vedas with their Brāhmaṇas and Upanishads, the

Sūtras, the laws of Manu, the Rāmāyaṇa and Mahā-bhārata, the eighteen Purāṇas and sixty-four Tantras. Hence, Hindūism is something very different from Brāhmanism, though the one is derived from the other. It encourages idolatry—that is to say, worship before the images and symbols of *Vishṇu*, the Preserver, and *Rudra-Siva*, the Destroyer and Regenerator (the highest manifestations of Brahman) and other deities, as a help for weak-minded persons; and every enlightened Brāhman admits that the unthinking and ignorant, who are by far the majority, adore the idols themselves.

In fact, Hindūism is like a huge irregular structure which has had no single architect but a whole series, and has spread itself over an immense surface by continual additions and accretions. The gradual growth of its congeries of heterogeneous doctrines is exactly reflected in the enormous mass of its disjointed sacred writings which, beginning with the Ṛig-veda, about the time of the composition of the Pentateuch, extend over a period of 2500 years. It is perhaps the only religion in the world which has neither any name derived from any single founder, nor any distinct designation of any kind. We may call it Brāhmanism and Hindūism, but these are not names recognised by the natives themselves. Its present aspect is that of an ancient overgrown fabric, with no apparent unity of design—patched, pieced, restored and enlarged in all directions, inlaid with every variety of idea, and, although looking as if ready at any moment to fall into ruins, still extending itself so as to cover every hole and corner of available ground, still holding its own with great pertinacity, and still keeping its position securely, because supported by a hard foundation of Brāhmanism and caste. It is only, however, by the practice of a kind of universal toleration and receptivity—carried on through more than 2000 years—that Hindūism has maintained its ground and arrived at its present condition [1]. It has been asserted that Hindūism is unlike Buddhism in not being a missionary religion. Certainly Buddhism was once a proselyting system (though its missionary spirit is extinct), and it is very true that a Brāhman *nascitur non fit*, but it is equally true that Hindūism could not have extended itself over India if it had never exerted itself to make proselytes. In point of fact, it has first borne with and then accepted, and, so to speak, digested and assimilated something from all creeds. It has opened its doors to all comers (and is willing to do so still) on the two conditions of their admitting the spiritual supremacy of the Brāhmans, and conforming to certain caste-rules about food, intermarriage, and professional pursuits. In this manner it has adopted much of the Fetishism of the Negroid aborigines of India; it has stooped to the practices of various primitive tribes, and has not scrupled to appropriate and naturalise the adoration of the fish, the boar, the serpent, rocks, stones, and trees; it has borrowed ideas from the various cults of the Drāviḍian races; and it may even owe something to Christianity. Above all, it has assimilated nearly every doctrine of Buddhism except its atheism, its denial of the eternal existence of soul, and its levelling of caste-distinctions.

Buddhism originated in India about 500 B.C. It was a reformation of Brāhmanism introduced by a man named Gautama (afterwards called Buddha, 'the Enlightened') of the Śākya tribe, whose father was king of a district situated under the mountains of Nepāl.

It is noteworthy that the images of Buddha generally represent him with features and hair of an Egyptian or Ethiopian type, and with the curly hair of a Negro. He

[1] Moor, in his 'Pantheon' (p. 402), tells us that a learned Pandit once observed to him that the English were a new people, and had only the record of one Avatāra, but the Hindūs were an ancient people, and had accounts of a great many, and that if the Purāṇas were examined, they would probably be found to record the incarnation of Christ.

is usually described as a Kshatriya, or man of the kingly and military class. According to some, it is not impossible that the tribe to which he belonged may have been of aboriginal extraction.

Buddhism was originally no new religion, but a mere modification or reconstruction of Brāhmanism, and even now has much in common with it. But the Buddha, in opposition to the Brāhmans, refused to acknowledge the existence of a Supreme Being, and repudiated the authority of the Veda, caste-distinctions, sacrifices, and sacrificing priests. His doctrines were afterwards collected in the sacred writings called *Tri-piṭaka* or 'Triple-collection' (written in Pāli, the ancient language of the Magadha district closely allied to Sanskṛit). He maintained that the only deity was man himself, when brought to a condition of Buddha-hood or perfection, and he made *Nirvāṇa*, 'extinction of all being,' take the place of *Sāyujya*, 'identification with the one sole Being of the Universe,' as the great end and object of all human effort. His doctrines soon spread to Ceylon, Burmah, and other countries, but pure Buddhism does not exist any longer anywhere. In India it first co-existed with Brāhmanism, then met with some persecution, and finally lapsed back into Brāhmanism, about the ninth century of our era.

Jainism, the home of cold indifferentism, even more unworthy to be called a religion than Buddhism, is now the only representative of Buddhistic ideas in India proper. I believe that, according to the last census, the number of Buddhists under our rule in British Burmah amounts to about two millions and a half. The Jainas or Jains, in India proper, only number about 380,000, at least half of whom are in the Bombay Presidency. They congregate most thickly in the districts round Ahmedābād.

The Jainas maintain that their system originated earlier than Buddhism and from an independent source. Recent researches tend to show that there is ground for this assertion. They probably represent two parallel lines of philosophical inquiry. One thing is certain, that Jainism has much in common with Buddhism, however it may differ from Buddhism in various ways. Perhaps the chief point of difference is that the Jainas retain caste-distinctions, but this again may be a later innovation. They are divided into two sects—the Śvetāmbaras, 'clothed in white,' and the Dig-ambaras, 'sky-clothed.' The doctrines of both sects rest on sacred books, called Āgamas (divided into Angas, Upāngas, &c.), many of which are common to both. They agree with the Buddhists in rejecting the Veda of the Brāhmans. Formerly the Dig-ambaras, who are the least numerous, were forbidden to wear clothing, and even now they eat naked. The principal point in the creed of Jainas (as of Buddhists) is the reverence paid to holy men who by long discipline have raised themselves to a kind of divine perfection. The Jina, or 'conquering saint,' who having conquered all worldly desires reveals true knowledge, is with Jainas what the Buddha or 'perfectly enlightened saint' is with Buddhists.

Great numbers of the Baniyas or traders of the West of India, who claim to be Vaiśyas, are Jains. If a Jain wishes to acquire religious merit, he either builds a new temple to hold an image of one or all of the twenty-four Jina saints, or a hospital for the care of worn-out animals. No one thinks of repairing the work of his predecessor, though it be that of his own father. At Pālitāna, in Kāthiāwār, there are hundreds of new temples by the side of decaying old ones.

Jainism, like Brāhmanism and Buddhism, lays great stress on the doctrine of transmigration of souls. The Jainas carry their respect for animal life—even for the life of the most minute infusoria—to a preposterous extreme. Their only worship, like that of the Buddhist, is adoration of human perfection. Though they dissent from the Veda they regard themselves as Hindūs.

I will not here enter upon the religion of the Pārsīs, or as it is called Zoroastrianism, further than to say that it represents the religion of ancient Persia imported into India by a small body of Persian immigrants, when driven out of Persia eleven or twelve hundred years ago by the Muhammadan invaders; and that it rests on certain sacred writings called the Zand-Avastā—attributed to the prophet Zoroaster about 500 B.C.—which have suffered more from the inroads of time than any of the other religious books of the world. I may, however, mention that the religion of the ancient Persians had a common origin with that of the Hindūs, and that Pārsīism, like Brāhmanism, is based on a kind of Monotheistic Pantheism. It has not, however, advanced beyond the stage of regarding Fire, Sun, Earth, and Sea as the principal manifestations of the one Supreme Being, called Ormazd (the creator of the two forces of construction and destruction, Spenta-mainyus and Ahriman). It has never lapsed, like Brāhmanism, into gross and degrading idolatry.

The Pārsīs are certainly near relations of the Brāhmans, but they have kept themselves separate from the other races of India, and retained much of the natural vigour and energy of the Āryan character.

And now, with regard to Hindū religious usages. Of ancient Vedic sacrificial ceremonial and public religious ritual very little is left. Nor is congregational worship performed in temples. The priests in charge of the idols decorate them and bathe them with sacred water on holy days, and do them homage (*pūjā*) with lights and a rude kind of music at stated periods, generally both morning and evening. Moreover, offerings of flowers, grain, fruits, &c., are presented to the idols of the most popular gods (practically to the priests) by lay worshippers, and *mantras* or texts are repeated with prostrations of the body. Common prayer, in our sense, there is none.

The religion of the mass of the people (much of which is probably aboriginal and pre-Āryan) resolves itself, I fear, into a mere matter of selfish superstition. It is principally displayed in endeavouring to avert the anger of evil demons and in doing homage to local divinities, supposed to guard their worshippers from the assaults of malignant beings, and to be specially present in rude idols, trees, rocks, stones, and shapeless symbols, often consecrated with daubs of red paint. In place of public worship, however, great attention is given to private religious usages and to the performance of domestic ceremonies at births, marriages, funerals, &c., conducted by Brāhman priests, who have nothing whatever to do with temples or with worship performed in temples. Moreover, homage to ancestors and to the spirits of deceased fathers, grandfathers, and great-grandfathers, enters largely into the religious rites of the Hindūs as into those of the Chinese.

All these observances vary with caste, and caste is now so divided and subdivided that even the Brāhmans are broken up into innumerable classes and tribes, one claiming superiority over the other. Some of these are little more than groups of families bound together by peculiar usages. In other cases, caste is only another name for an association of men united by common occupation in a kind of trade union, every such combination being cemented in the same way by the practice of distinctive religious observances. In fact, caste in India is an essential part of religion. It is no longer to the same extent as it once was, a bond of union among large bodies of men. Its action tends to split up the social fabric into numerous independent communities and to prevent all national and patriotic combinations. In the present day the family-bond (*bhāī-band*) appears to be stronger than that of caste. Certainly both these ties operate far more powerfully in India than in Europe, because they are both intimately associated with religion. I fear, however, that other ties are proportionately weak, and that Indians, as a rule, have few sympathies and little disposition to co-operate with others beyond the circle of their own families, and none at all beyond the limits of their own immediate castes.

Indian Muhammadanism.

I come now to a brief description of Indian Muhammadanism:—The position of Islām, with reference to the idolatry of India, is very similar to that once occupied by Judaism relatively to the idolatry of Egypt and Canaan, and very similar to its own original position relatively to the Sabeanism of Arabia. In fact, Islām may be regarded as an illegitimate child of Judaism born in Arabia in the seventh century. It was a protest against the Sabeanism, idolatry, and fetish stone-worship prevalent in that country, and a declaration of God's Unity made by Muhammad in supposed continuation of the original revelation transmitted by Abraham through Ishmael, rather than through Isaac[1].

Indeed at one time it seemed likely that the religious reform preached by Muhammad would develope into a sect of Christianity, and had not the corrupt Christian doctrines with which Muhammad came in contact prevented his perceiving that the statement of a Trinity in Unity is also the strongest assertion of a Unity in Trinity, we might have had another Eastern Church in Arabia answering to those founded in Egypt, Syria, Armenia, and Constantinople.

The name Muhammad is simply the passive participle of

[1] The Kaaba, or small cube-shaped temple of Mecca, is supposed to have been built by Abraham (who is called by Muhammad the first Muslim) over the spot where he was about to sacrifice Ishmael. The sacredness of the small black stone imbedded in the eastern angle is probably the result of the fetish stone-worship once prevalent in Arabia. Abraham is supposed to have stood upon this stone when he built the Kaaba.

the Arabic verb *hamada*, 'to praise,' and no more admits of any variety of spelling than our word 'praised,' nor can I see why the numerous arbitrary violations of orthography to which the false prophet's name has given rise should be perpetuated any longer.

It should be noted that although Muhammad was a self-deluded enthusiast, he did not put himself forward as the founder of a new religion, and would have indignantly forbidden the use of such a term as Muhammadanism. According to his own views he was simply the latest of four prophets (the others being Moses, Elias, and Christ), who were all followers of Abraham, the true founder of the doctrine of Islām, and were all Muslims because all preached the Unity of God and submission to His will[1]. In this respect he was like the other great religious leaders—Zoroaster, Buddha, and Confucius.

In the end, however, the necessities of his position obliged him to break away from both Jews and Christians, with whom at first on his flight to Medina (A.D. 622) he contemplated an alliance. Nor did his doctrine, like that of Buddhism, win its way anywhere in the world by persuasiveness, except on its first propagation. It is true that Muhammad at the commencement of his career fought his way through the idolatry around him with no other weapons but argument and persuasion, but when he had collected sufficient adherents, the force of circumstances compelled him to adopt a more summary method of conversion. His conversions were then made at the point of the sword, Muhammad became a conqueror and a ruler, and Islām became as much a polity as a religion.

About forty-one millions of the inhabitants of India are

[1] In the Kurān, the Old Testament and the Gospel are spoken of with the greatest reverence, as the word of God. Muhammad never threw any doubts on the inspiration of either; faith in them was enjoined on penalty of hell. But the Kurān was a later revelation, and therefore a higher authority.

Muhammadans. Indeed, one of the unexpected facts brought out by the last census was the vast increase of Indian Muslims. Great numbers of them are the descendants of Hindūs converted to Islām by the Muhammadan conquerors, and are much Hindūized in their habits and ways. In some places the lower classes of Musalmāns do homage to the Hindū goddess of smallpox, and take part in the Holī festival. It is certain that numbers of low-caste Hindūs formerly became Muhammadans with the sole object of raising themselves in the social scale. For all Muslims are theoretically equal, and since there is no equality, nor even any real citizenship, in a Muhammadan State for those who are not Muslims, it has often happened that whole communities have adopted Islām merely to place themselves within the pale of State protection, patronage, jurisdiction, and authority.

Unhappily, however, the Indian Muslims do not imitate the Hindūs in their toleration of each other's sectarian divisions.

There are, as most people know, two principal sects of Muslims, called Sunnīs and Shī'as. The Shī'as reject some of the traditions (*Sunnah*), denying that the three immediate successors of the prophet—Abūbakr, Omar, and Othmān—were true Khalīfas. They declare that Alī, Muhammad's son-in-law, was his first rightful successor. The Turks and nearly all Indian Musalmāns, except those connected in any way with Persia, are Sunnīs. All Persians are Shī'as, and the animosity between the two divisions is even greater than between Roman Catholics and Protestants. I have heard it humorously said that, besides the Shī'as, there are seventy-two subordinate sects, each of which considers that the other seventy-one will assuredly go to hell.

I observed in my travels that the mass of Indian Muhammadans, who are ignorant and uneducated, have a tendency to deify either Muhammad himself, or his son-in-law Alī, or the innumerable Muhammadan saints (*Pīrs*), whose tombs are scattered everywhere throughout Hindūstān and the Dekhan. Many regard them as mediators.

Moreover, the Islām of India appears to have borrowed something not only from Hindūism but from Buddhism. I saw relics of Muhammad, including a hair from his head, preserved as sacred objects in Delhi and Lahore, and the impress of his foot is revered much as the Hindūs and Buddhists revere the footstep of Vishṇu and Buddha. When Islām thus lapses into too great exaltation of Muhammad, it may fairly be called Muhammadanism.

The attitude of a Muhammadan towards Christianity is far more hopelessly hostile than that of a Hindū, and it is generally believed that, although Indian Muslims in some parts of India are more active and intelligent than Hindūs, the teaching of the Kurān has a tendency to make them more intolerant, more sensual and inferior in moral tone. They are certainly more proud and bigoted, and are often left behind by the Hindūs for the simple reason that they refuse to avail themselves in the same way of the educational advantages we offer.

With regard to Christianity, I have no hesitation in declaring my conviction that it has more points of contact with Hindūism (notwithstanding the hideous idolatry encouraged by that system) than with Buddhism, Jainism, or even Islām. For example—Hindūs are willing to confess themselves sinful. They acknowledge the necessity of sacrifice. They admit the need of supernatural revelation, and they have a doctrine of inspiration even higher than our own. Their sacred scriptures are not the work of one mind like the Kurān, but represent a process of gradual accretion and progressive expansion like the sixty-six books of our own Holy Bible. They are familiar with the ideas of a divine trinity, of incarnation, and of the need of a Saviour, however perverted these ideas may be. Their Gāyatrī, a prayer repeated morning and evening by every Brāhman throughout India, might with slight alteration be converted into a Christian prayer. They believe in the 'vanity' of all earthly concerns. They affirm that the Supreme Being is a Spirit, omnipotent and omnipresent, and their dogma that 'God is existence, thought, and bliss,' is only inferior to the Christian assertion that 'God is love.'

With regard to the progress of Christianity in India, I will only at present record my opinion that the best work done by the missionaries is in their schools. In some important places, such as Benares, the missionary schools are more popular than those of the Government, although the Bible is read and religious instruction given in the former, and not in the latter. Education is, indeed, causing a great upheaving of old creeds and superstitions throughout India, and the ancient fortress of Hindūism is in this way being gradually undermined. The educated classes look with contempt on idolatry.

In fact, the present condition of India seems very similar to that of the Roman Empire before the coming of Christ. A complete disintegration of ancient faiths is in progress in the upper strata of society.

Most of the ablest thinkers become pure Theists or Unitarians. In almost every large town there is a *Samāj*, or society of such men, whose creed would be well expressed by the first part of the first Article of the Church of England. They retain the name Brahma as applicable to the Supreme Being, but they regard him as a personal god, to be addressed by prayer as well as praise. No sooner, however, is a Samāj formed than, as is usual in India, it splits up into subdivisions, some founding their theism on the Veda, others partially appealing to it, and others rejecting it altogether. Even great leaders like Keshab Chandra Sen, of Calcutta, are unable to unite all Indian Theists into one body. Christianity has made most progress among people of low caste and with some of the aboriginal tribes, and will probably gradually work its way upwards as it did on its first propagation by our Lord and His disciples. The religion of conquerors is never likely to be popular with either the higher or lower classes, if it offers no political or social advantages; and controversial discussion, though it may convince the head, will not touch the heart. It should always be borne in mind that, unlike the Muhammadans and Roman Catholics, we have abstained, as a conquering government, from enforcing our religion by government influence and authority. Hence conversions to Christianity bear no adequate proportion to the teeming millions of India (as indeed the Indian Bishops themselves allow in their circular of November 27th, 1873). Nor will conversions, in my opinion, be more common until our religion is presented to the Hindūs in a more Oriental form,—that is, in a form more like that which belonged to it on its first foundation at Jerusalem; and by more Orientalized missionaries,—that is, by men who will consent to live among the natives and become themselves half Indianized. It is even a question whether certain caste-customs might not be tolerated among Indian converts.

At any rate, an Indian ought not to be expected to have less caste-prejudices than a European. He ought to be allowed, as a convert to Christianity, to retain such of his caste-customs as may not be inconsistent with his submitting to the test of baptism, and meeting other converts on terms of perfect equality at the communion table.

Our Administration of the Country.

No one can travel in India and shut his eyes to the benefits conferred on its inhabitants by English rule. In fact, our subjugation of the country affords an exemplification of the now trite truth that the conquest of an inferior race by a superior, so far from being an evil, is one of the great appointed laws of the world's progress and amelioration.

We are sometimes accused of governing India in the interest of England and English commerce—of making India the *corpus vile* of political, social, and military experiments, of thinking more of what is called the maintenance of our prestige than of the welfare of the country. Yet the traveller has only to look around to see everywhere conspicuous monuments of the good intentions, integrity, and efficiency of our administration. I believe that in no part of the world is so much work done, and so well and conscientiously done, and with such a single regard to the discharge of duty, as by the Queen's servants in India. Even men of inferior energy and mental calibre, who, in England, would do little to benefit society, are, by the circumstances of their position in India, drawn out and developed into useful officers and able administrators.

And what are the results? The picture once presented to our view was that of a country devastated by intestine wars, oppressed by despotic rulers, depopulated by famine, and left to succumb unresistingly to the attacks of pestilence or to the destructive energy of physical forces. Instead of which, what do we now find? The same forces tamed and controlled, steam and electricity made to subserve the purposes of traffic and intercourse, good roads, canals, and waterworks constructed, rights of all kinds secured, justice impartially administered, education actively promoted, and everywhere a thriving, law-abiding, rapidly increasing population.

Yet our very anxiety to do all we can for India may sometimes lead to our doing too much. The extension of the telegraphic system has necessarily caused greater centralization of Government authority at Calcutta. But India is a collection of countries which differ so essentially, and require such varied treatment, that each would probably be better governed by carefully-chosen men of strong will and judgment, if more power of independent action were conceded to them.

And now, again, submarine telegraphy has led to further centralization, so that India is at present more governed from the central terminus of Queen, Lords, and Commons, than by those who are at the Indian end of the wires. Formerly the ignorance and apathy of Parliament were of little importance; now its interposition may often complicate our difficulties.

Moreover, the possibility of conveying a message backwards and forwards between the India Office and Calcutta in a few hours fosters a forgetfulness of the enormous distance dividing the Western from the Eastern Empire, and of the vast gulf separating the condition of England and of English society and habits of thought from those of India. Hence it is often supposed that Western ideas may be suddenly transfused into an Eastern mind, and English institutions abruptly transplanted to an Indian soil, when neither the one nor the other is prepared to receive them. It may certainly be questioned whether we are not prone to too much and too frequent legislation, and whether, in many places, we are not fifty, or even a hundred, years too early with some of our laws and regulations, with our civil courts and trials by jury, with our appeals to supreme tribunals, and our modern municipal institutions.

The Collector of a large district assured me that, as chairman of a municipal board in a large town, he could make native members vote in any way he chose to direct. Clearly that town is not advanced enough for the ratepayers to elect their own municipal authorities. Yet India has for centuries been accustomed to a form of municipal self-government in its village corporations. What is wanted is a wise and cautious progress, a zeal according to knowledge, a discreet adaptation of legislation to varying conditions of time and place.

Our Connection with the Native States.

Few persons are aware that the number of native States and Principalities still remaining in India exceeds 460. Some frontier countries, like Nepāl, merely acknowledge our supremacy; others pay us tribute, or provide military contingents. Some have powers of life and death, and most of them are obliged to refer capital cases to English Courts. Nearly all are allowed to adopt on failure of heirs, and their continual existence is thus secured. In fact, we are bound by treaty to maintain them, provided they govern well. Some think that in case of a rising in our own territories, the native States will increase our risks and weaken our position, instead of becoming havens of refuge and sources of strength. No doubt, in such a case, most of the Mahārājas would be individually eager to aid us, because they know that their own existence is bound up in ours. Few of them would survive the anarchy that would inevitably follow if we were cruel enough to leave India to govern itself. Hence they would strive to help us. But very few have sufficient personal authority and influence with their own people, and even with their own troops, to control their hostility to us. I fear that the people generally prefer maladministration and a limited amount of oppression under their own rulers to good government under ours.

I ought here, however, to remark that it is naturally considered rather surprising that we only employ an army of 190,000 men (65,000 Europeans and 125,000 Natives) for the government of the 190 millions of people under our own direct administration, while native states with a population of only fifty million are allowed by us to employ armed men to the amount of nearly 315,000. Of these men the troops of the Nizām and of Sindia are the best disciplined; and in case of a mutiny among our own native army they would probably add very seriously to our difficulties instead of helping us out of them.

Granted that of the others some troops would be controlled by loyal chiefs and ministers (as the Nizām's soldiers formerly were). Granted, too, that a vast number would be simply contemptible either as allies or as opponents. Yet the expediency of permitting the native feudatory princes to organize and equip, at the expense of their impoverished people, unnecessarily large forces, is certainly a matter which has not yet awakened the attention it deserves.

The external and internal security of the native states is guaranteed by our administration; and all they need is an effective police force, the maintenance of which would not drain the resources of their territories as standing armies do.

I believe that the gross revenue of all the feudatory states subject to our rule is about sixteen millions, and that out of that amount a sum of only three quarters of a million sterling is annually contributed towards the Imperial administration which guarantees to them complete immunity from foreign invasion and from internal rebellion. Surely a portion of the money now wasted on needless armaments and senseless military show, might reasonably be compelled by us to flow into channels which would improve and enrich the condition of the people. In this manner each particular state would be enabled to make an adequate return for the protection it receives, both indirectly and directly—indirectly by augmenting the general prosperity, directly by paying an equitable contribution to the Imperial Treasury.

At Calcutta, and other places in India, during the Prince's tour, I had unusual opportunities of becoming acquainted with the principal Mahārājas, and occasional interesting conversations with them and their Ministers. Some are enlightened men. Many have been brought up under our superintendence with great care. But I fear the truth about many of them is this. On coming of age they are allowed to manage their kingdoms, under the eye of our Residents and political Agents, who watch them without direct interference. At first they give great promise, but soon become surrounded by designing Ministers, who, to serve their own interests—which are better promoted by bad government than by good—encourage the young Rājas in a life of dissipation. Very few resist the evil influences of their surroundings for any length of time. By degrees they succumb and degenerate. In the end they fall into excesses and become debilitated in body and mind. Then their feeble sons, if they have any, generally die early, and an heir is adopted. Happily, there are exceptions to this rule, and examples might be given of good native princes who devote themselves to the welfare of their territories.

As an illustration I may state that, when I was at Calcutta, I accepted the invitation of the Mahārāja of Kaśmīr to pay him a visit at Jammu. He is a son of Gulāb Singh, a Rājput chief who served under the Sikhs, and to whom we made over the Dogra district, of which Jammu is the capital, and Kaśmīr, of which Srinagar is the capital, for a stipulated sum of money after the first Panjāb war. The present Mahārāja is most desirous of pleasing us, and opens his kingdom to our travellers for eight months in the year, providing them with accommodation at his own expense. He himself prefers living in the town of Jammu (probably named from the Jambu tree common in the neighbourhood), because it commands the entrance to his territories, which altogether cover an area larger than England. The town most picturesquely crowns one of the undulations which, rising abruptly from the Panjāb plains, are succeeded by wave after wave of higher ranges till they terminate in the white crests of the Himālayas. From the King's palace a grand view of the Tavī Valley, shut in at the further end by snowy ranges, may be obtained. Another palace, very like a large railway station, was built the other day for the occupation of the Prince of Wales at an alleged expense of £60,000.

The Mahārāja, whose appearance is handsome and soldierlike, is unwearied in his royal duties. He rises early, is strict in his devotions, and temperate in his habits, and every morning for several hours may be seen in a room overlooking the courtyard of his palace, surrounded by able advisers, and diligently superintending the affairs of his kingdom. What chiefly deserves mention as distinguishing him from the generality of native Sovereigns is his encouragement of literature. He is the Augustus of Indian Princes. Not only has he established the best native schools I have seen in India for the teaching of Sanskṛit, Arabic, Persian, and English, but he has also set up a press, with a type foundry, and keeps around him a large staff of Pandits and other learned men who are constantly engaged in translating the best European works into the dialects of the country. This dialect is a modification of Panjābi—called Dogra, as belonging to the Dwigarta district, between the Rāvī and the Chenāb. Translations have already been made of works on grammar, history, geography, mathematics, surveying, architecture, medicine, and several of the physical sciences. A dictionary has also been commenced in six languages. Moreover, a standard alphabet has been constructed with much skill by employing the Devanāgarī to improve the imperfect graphic system formerly current in the country. The King's zeal for learning was rather curiously exhibited for my benefit. He had a detachment of soldiers manœuvred before me that I might listen to the words of command, which were all in Sanskṛit. The spread of education and knowledge in the Mahārāja's dominion during the last ten years is most remarkable.

There are other examples of well-governed States, notably that of the Mahārājā of Travankor; but the description of one must here suffice.

Our Education of the People.

It is commonly alleged that if we go on educating on our present plan we shall soon loose India. No one will dispute that whatever the consequences may be our duty is to continue educating. Whether, however, our system is altogether wise admits of question. I can certify that a vast work has been effected and is still proceeding. Everywhere there are schools—primary, intermediate, middle, and high—besides Colleges and Universities—and every year witnesses an increasing number of scholars and students. At Bombay I saw 12,000 children—all under education—assembled to greet the Prince of Wales. I also saw 1,263 candidates being examined for matriculation, and among them some young Princes. At Calcutta I saw even a greater number, and the standard of proficiency seemed higher than in England. Yet we have merely penetrated the outer fringe of society. Very little impression has yet been made on the masses of the people, and the chasm separating the educated from the uneducated is enormous. India cannot be said to possess a real middle-class, so that any middle education like that in England is impossible. Even in the case of those supposed to be under the higher form of education, I fear the work effected is rather information than education—rather informing the mind than forming the character and raising its tone.

This sort of education is, in some cases, better than nothing, but too often it inflates young men with conceit, unhinges their faith in their own religion without giving them any other, leads them to despise the calling of their fathers, and to look upon knowledge as a mere stepping-stone to Government situations which they cannot all obtain. I heard it stated (possibly with some exaggeration) that not long ago there were 500 applications for a municipal post at Kurnoul, worth only Rs. 15 per month. Those who are unsuccessful in gaining appointments will not turn to manual labour, but remain discontented members of society and enemies of our Government, converting the little real education they have received into an instrument to injure us by talking treason and writing seditious articles in native journals. I believe the defects of our present system are beginning to be acknowledged. Many think we shall be wiser to educate the generality of natives in their professions and callings rather than above them—to make a good mechanic a better one, a good carpenter more skilful in his own craft—and only to give higher forms of education in exceptional cases.

With regard to female education, although its bearing on the moral and intellectual and even physical progress of India can scarcely be overrated, little, I fear, has yet been effected. Scattered efforts are made with much energy and some success, but too often they show signs of languishing. The truth simply is that, before we can raise the women of India, we must first raise the men. We must do more than inform their minds—we must form their whole characters and cast them in a higher mould; and if we cannot convert them to the dogmas of Christianity, we must instil into them Christian ideas and ways of thinking. When we have thus elevated the men, we may safely leave the women to their keeping. The women will then be raised to the level of the men by the act of the men themselves without our interference. At present Hindū women are generally faithful wives and devoted mothers, and have great influence with their families, but they are grossly ignorant; and to their ignorance, bigotry, and subjection to the Brāhmans, the maintenance of superstition and idolatry, which would otherwise rapidly lose ground among the men, is, I suspect, mainly due.

Disposition and Attitude of the Natives towards us and our Rule.

In the first place, how are they disposed to us personally? I am sorry to say that my travels in India have revealed to me that between the ruler and the ruled in India there is a great gulf fixed, which, since the Mutiny, has widened and is becoming more and more difficult to be bridged over. The very arrangement of every large town bears witness to the truth of this statement, the European residences being collected in a quarter of their own quite distinct from the native town. Another significant fact is that on railways Europeans and natives are never seen together in the same carriages.

The causes which lead to this separation are mostly patent, but a remedy is not easily applied. First, there is what is called the race feeling, by which is meant the natural antipathy between races of different coloured skins—a feeling which, however manifestly unreasonable, is difficult to overcome. Then there is the caste feeling, which we have quite as strongly in our own way as Indians. With us, however, it is of a different kind. It is not part of our religion. In the case of the Hindūs the principal result of caste, in relation to us Europeans, is that although they may be of the same rank as ourselves they will not consent to eat with us, or to drink water touched by us or our servants. We, on the other hand, are accustomed to regard dining together as essential to social intercourse, and are apt to resent their declining to sit at meat with us, as if we were personally insulted. But we ought to bear in mind that eating and drinking is, with a Hindū, bound up with his religion, or rather with its system of purificatory rites;

and that the killing of animals (especially oxen) for food is regarded as an impious act, so that the absence of Hindūs from our tables ought not to offend us more than their absence from our churches.

Then there is the feeling naturally springing up between governors and governed. A commanding tone of voice may often be necessary for the maintenance of authority, but I fear we rulers are sometimes unnecessarily imperious. We are naturally conscious of our superiority, but need our bearing towards those we are ruling make them feel their inferior position too keenly? An advanced native, of independent character, once complained to me that most Englishmen appeared to him to walk about the world with an air as if God Almighty intended the whole universe to be English. He had probably been thrown with young civilians recently imported from England. Few others would think of lording it over their Indian brethren in any offensive manner. A reaction in this respect has set in all over India. I could enumerate many cases in which the mild Hindū is not a whit milder in manner than those who are set over him.

Then there are other feelings springing from early training, habits, and association. It is difficult for a European, who has never been in the East, to estimate the difference in ideas and ways of thinking arising from this source. Not only is there a different standard of taste as shown in dress, music, &c., but even to a certain extent of right and wrong. For instance, if a Hindū thinks it wrong to kill animals for food, much more does he object to destroying life of any kind for sport. Again, an Asiatic, whether Hindū or Musalmān, thinks it highly improper for women to mix familiarly with men who are not relations, much more to dance with them. Then there are differences in nearly every common custom. For example, a Hindū uncovers his feet when a European uncovers his head. In a few cases assimilation of habits has been effected, but when this has occurred the Indian has become more Europeanized than the European has become Indianized. It would be foolish to expect these differences to cease. What is really to be regretted is the estrangement they produce.

And now, in the last place, what is the attitude of the natives of India towards our Government? The most intelligent are quite ready to admit that they enjoy greater benefits under our rule than they would under any other; and the wiser, who know that universal disorder would follow its cessation, even pray for its continuance; but the mass of unthinking people would rather be badly governed by their own chiefs than well governed by us. In the native States they will acquiesce in exactions which in our territories would be regarded as intolerable. Of course nothing will conciliate those who are determined to dislike us. But even the wiser, who value our rule, consider that they have certain grievances. Why—I have often been asked—are we treated as if in mental capacity and moral tone we were all inferior to Europeans? Why are we never allowed to rise to the highest executive appointments? Why are those of us who compete for the Civil Service forced to go to England for examination? Supposing we are not yet fit for representative government, why are we not allowed deliberative assemblies, like the Houses of Convocation in the English Church, that our opinions may be made known before fresh laws are enacted? Why cannot justice be administered more cheaply and directly, and with fewer delays? Why does the Government spend so much of the revenues on public works and give us no new serais and tanks? These are a few of the complaints I have heard.

Perhaps some of them are not real, and others are in course of redress. I believe our Government admits that when natives can show themselves mentally and morally fit for the highest administrative offices they must be allowed to fill them. We are certainly doing our best to redress political grievances. Let us also endeavour to do more than we have hitherto done towards bridging over the social chasm that at present separates the two races and complicates the difficulties of our position in India. Our great English Universities may contribute something towards this important object if they will make facilities for the reception of young Indians and for their intercourse with young Englishmen. I believe that the young men of England and India may learn useful lessons from each other and yet preserve their separate nationalities. We must of course be conscious of our own superiority in religion, morality, and general culture; but let us give our Indian fellow-subjects credit for such excellences as they possess, and condescend to admit that good may accrue from some interchange of ideas and mutual attrition between the two races. Assuredly a better feeling between them must result from consciousness of reciprocal benefits bestowed.

One thing at least is certain, that India is given to us to conciliate as well as to elevate, even if she offers us nothing to imitate. In my opinion the great problem that before all others presses for solution in relation to our Eastern Empire is, how can the rulers and the ruled be drawn closer together? How can more sympathy and cordial feeling be promoted between them?

GENERAL IMPRESSIONS OF SOUTHERN INDIA.

BOMBAY, FEBRUARY 14, 1877.

LET me first note, for the benefit of those who have hitherto given little heed to the progress of our Eastern Empire, that the old tripartite separation of India into three Presidencies gives an inadequate, if not inaccurate, idea of its present political divisions.

The term Presidency is still retained for Bombay and Madras (whose governments correspond directly with the Secretary of State, and not through the Governor-General), but cannot now be suitably applied to the twelve divisions[1]

[1] Mr. Trelawny Saunders in commenting on my *Times*' letter, June 14, 1877, enumerated these twelve divisions, and gave an official explanation of the present political divisions of India, part of which I here extract as useful and instructive, though his description of what he states ought still to be called the Bengal Presidency is likely to bewilder the general reader: 'Ever since the reduction of the lower Provinces of Bengal from being the chief Presidency to the position of a Lieutenant-Government, it has been the fashion in certain official quarters to deny the existence of the Bengal Presidency, and, indeed, of the Presidencies altogether. As, however, the officials of Madras and Bombay have not suffered any detraction from their rank as Presidencies, the fashion which prevails in Calcutta does not appear to have extended to Madras and Bombay; and thus the Professor allows that "the term may be conveniently retained" in their cases.

'But the Presidency of Bengal (or, technically, Fort William in Bengal), so far from having been abolished, has become so largely extended as to require that the local Government of the original Presidency should be delegated by the Governor-General of the extended Presidency to a Lieutenant-Governor, just as other parts of the Presidency have been. The honours of the Bengal Civil Service are now, therefore, no longer confined to the area under the Lieutenant-Governor of Bengal, but are disseminated throughout India, excepting Bombay and Madras. A reference more immediately under the Viceroy, and generally supplied with officers from the Bengal Civil Service.

It would be better, I think, to speak of Modern British India as divided into eight Provinces, each under its own Government. These are :—1. Bengal (sometimes called the Lower Provinces, consisting of Bengal, Behār, and Orissa); 2. the North-West (so called from its position relatively to Bengal); 3. the Panjāb; 4. the Central Provinces; 5. British Burmah; 6. Assam; 7. Bombay; and 8. Madras.

Till quite recently the province of Oudh formed a ninth division under a separate Government, but is now attached to the North-West Provinces.

There are also eight principal native territories surrounded by, or contiguous to, these eight British Provinces; and of course protected and controlled by us through Residents and Political Agents, viz. 1. Rājputāna; 2. Central India (including the dominions of Sindia and Holkar); 3. the Bombay Marāṭha States (especially that of the Gaikwār of Baroda); 4. Hyderabad or the Nizām's

to the "India List" will prove that, as a rule, it is Members of the Bengal Civil Service who are employed, not only in (1) the Lieutenant-Government of Bengal Proper, but also in (2) the North-Western Provinces (of Bengal) and Oudh, (3) the Punjab, (4) Rājputāna and Ajmir, (5) Central India, (6) the Central Provinces, (7) Hyderabad and Berar, (8) Mysore and Coorg, (9) Assam, (10) Manipur, a little state, east of Assam, on the frontier of Burmah, (11) British Burmah, (12) the Andaman and Nicobar Islands. All these distinct governments, whether under Lieutenant-Governors, Commissioners, Superintendents, or Native Princes, with political agents as their advisers, are supplied with British officials of the Bengal Civil Service, and are subject to the superior control of the Governor-General in Council. The Presidencies of Madras and Bombay cover the remainder of India, and have their own distinct Civil Services (making in all fourteen great political divisions). The tripartite organization of India is also determined by this fact—that, although there are fourteen separate governments in India, including Madras and Bombay, the twelve divisions of the Bengal Presidency have no correspondence with the Secretary of State except through the Governor-General. Bombay and Madras, as separate Presidencies, retain that distinction.'

territory; 5. Mysor; 6. Travankor; 7. Kaśmīr; 8. Nepāl.

Of these the last two (especially Nepāl) are outlying countries and practically independent of us [1], though both, of course, acknowledge our supremacy, while Hyderabad (where we have a Resident), though completely environed by British territory, is the largest and most powerful of all the native states. It is the only great Muhammadan power that has survived the dissolution of the Moghul empire in India. It has an area of 100,000 square miles, and a population of eleven millions, and maintains an army of 50,000 men. No other native state approaches it either in area or population, Mārwār (Jodhpur) in Rājputāna, which is the next largest, having an area of only 36,000 square miles, and a population of less than two millions.

There are, however, five minor Muhammadan states, viz. Khairpur, bordering on Sindh; Bhāwalpur, contiguous to the Panjāb; Rāmpur in the North-West; Bhopāl in Central India; and Tonk in Rājputāna.

Of course some of the eight principal native territories include an immense number of separate states and principalities. For example, there are nineteen Rājputāna states, of which the three chief are (1) Jodhpur, or Mārwār, (2) Jaipur, and (3) Udaipur, or Mewār [2]. These (especially the last) are the most ancient sovereignties of India. Central India includes the state of Gwalior (with more than 33,000 square miles, a population of nearly three millions, and an army of more than 22,000 men), ruled by Sindia; and that of Indore (with little more than 8,000 square miles and half a million population, and, according to Colonel Malleson, an army of 8,500 men), ruled by Holkar.

[1] Afghānistān is another outlying country even more independent of us than Nepāl, and less entitled to be included under the term India.

[2] Sometimes written Maiwār, and said to be a contraction of *Madhya-wār*, central region.

The Bombay Marāṭha states include (besides that of the Gaikwār of Baroda in Gujarāt) a large number of minor principalities in Kāthiāwār, and in the South, so that the grand total of native states and feudatories great and small, throughout India, is not far short of five hundred.

Having endeavoured to give some idea of the present divisions of India, I must, before proceeding further, explain what I mean by Southern India.

Southern India may be regarded as embracing all India below the twenty-second parallel of latitude—that is to say, speaking roughly, all within the northern tropical line. It will, therefore, include that part of the Bombay Presidency south of the Narbadā, of which Bombay and Poona are the capitals; that portion of the Central Provinces of which Nāgpur is the chief town; Orissa; the Nizām's territory, of which Hyderabad is the capital; Mysor, and the whole Madras Presidency, with Travankor as far as Cape Comorin. To these may be added the island of Ceylon, the south point of which is within six degrees of the Equator.

Climate of Southern India.

I described my experience of a winter in the Northern parts of India as delightful, and now a winter passed in the South has not changed my opinion as to the superiority of the Indian climate to our own for at least five months in the year. Indeed, I am satisfied that to those who can retire to the Hills for a time in the hot and rainy seasons, residence in India all the year round is attended with less risk to the health than residence in England.

But India is like a continent which offers every variety of sanitary condition, and it must not be forgotten that the whole of Southern India is within the Tropics. It has places which are correctly described as deadly in their effect on the health of Europeans, and in certain jungly districts, where there is no lack of moisture and the temperature is persistently high, rank deciduous vegetation generates fever as a matter of course. The rainfall on the western coast is the greatest, and with abundant tropical rain, and abundant tropical vegetation, comes inevitable malaria. It must be admitted, too, that so far as my experience has gone during the past winter, I found the climate of the whole of Southern India more trying to the health than that of the districts north of the Narbadā river and Vindhya hills. It is true that there is not the same intensity of summer heat in the South, and the temperature from one year's end to the other is more equable, but there are no intervals of bracing cold either in the winter or in the night time. I believe it may be proved by statistics that cholera is always more prevalent in the South than in the North. Certainly, this winter a bad type of the disease prevailed in some of the districts through which I travelled, and I heard of many Europeans being attacked. Probably, however, the drought, famine, and badness of the water may have caused an exceptionally unhealthy season.

Physical Features of Southern India.

What strikes one most in travelling through any part of India is the vastness of the country. No sooner does one land in Bombay than one's whole ideas of distance have to be cast in a new mould. You are told that an old acquaintance is residing close to your hotel, and you find to your surprise that a visit to his house involves a drive of ten miles. The sense of vastness is not so overpowering in Southern India as in Northern, and yet the Nizām's territory alone embraces an area little less than that of the kingdom of Italy.

Perhaps the most remarkable physical feature of Southern India is the existence of an immense triangular plateau of table-land caused by the circumstance that the high ranges of hills on the western coast slope down gradually, but with numerous irregular depressions and isolated elevations, towards the eastern coast, where the plateau breaks up into lower ranges, leaving much level land between the heights and the sea. The two eastern and western coast ranges, which come to a point near Cape Comorin, are called Ghāts because they recede like steps (Sanskṛit *Ghaṭṭa*) from the seashore, and the triangle of table-land formed by their junction with the two extremities of the Vindhya range which traverses the centre of India, is called the Deccan, from Prakrit *Dakkin*, for Sanskṛit *Dakshin*, 'the south country.' The great Indian Peninsula Railway from Bombay to Jabalpore and Raichore conducts to this plateau by a wonderful piece of engineering skill up the Bhore Ghāt. Poona, the capital of our part of the Deccan, is nearly 2,000 feet above the sea; so is our military station of Secunderabad, close to Hyderabad, the capital of the Nizām's portion of the Deccan; and our station of Bangalore, in the Mysor country, is about 3,500 feet above the sea level. There is an extensive tract of ugly flat country round Maḍras, along the Coromandel coast and Northern Circars. But there is no lack of grand scenery on the Western Ghāts, especially towards their southern extremity, on the Nīlgiri, Animalli, Pulney, and Asambhu hills, some of which rise to an altitude of more than 8,000 feet. The ascent to Ootacamuṅd is quite equal to the finest Swiss pass I ever saw. What it loses by the absence of snow is counterbalanced by the glories of its tropical vegetation. Moreover, all Europe cannot boast such waterfalls as the Gairsappa Falls, on the Malabar coast, and those of the River Kāverī in Mysor. The former even in the dry season present a perpendicular fall of a large mass of water 900 feet high. I have heard this called the third sight of India, the Himālayas coming first, and the Tāj at Agra second.

As to the chief town of the Madras Presidency, a situation more unsuited to a great capital can hardly be conceived. Madras has no harbour and no navigable river, and the ships anchored in its roads are in constant danger of being driven ashore, as the 'Duke of Sutherland' was the other day. Its drainage—if any is possible where the ground is often below the sea level—is so bad that cholera is never absent. Indeed, so far as my experience goes, Madras is inferior to Bombay and Calcutta, not only in a sanitary point of view, but in nearly every other partiular, except perhaps in the one point that more English is spoken by the native servants. Its inhabitants are now making a great effort to improve its trade, and the present Governor, who has a decided penchant for engineering, is developing his taste in the interest of the merchants by promoting the construction of an artificial harbour, the cost of which is to be defrayed out of the revenues of India. Untold sums of money are being thrown into the sea in the shape of huge blocks of concrete, each of them about 12 feet long by 10 feet in breadth and 8 feet in thickness, for the formation of a breakwater, which is to encircle the present pier with two projecting arms. But the difficulty of enclosing a sufficient area of water, and the perpetual drifting of sand along the coast, make the success of the undertaking highly problematical. Under any circumstances, Madras, though large enough to attract a trade of its own, will never overcome its own natural disadvantages of position, so as to compete with either Bombay or Calcutta, the former of which is destined to become the great commercial emporium and capital of all India (if not of all Asia), the wealth and importance of which will be vastly increased so soon as the Baroda Railway is connected with Jeypore, Agra, and the North-West. Calcutta, too, is likely to continue the political capital of India, both from the convenience of its situation on the Ganges, in the midst of a naturally peaceful and law-abiding population, and from the obstacles its position offers to an attack from the sea.

Animal and Plant Life.

Perhaps the most striking point of difference between Northern and Southern India is due to the circumstance that the South possesses all the characteristics of the Tropics in the greater exuberance of all kinds of life and vegetation. To realize this exuberance fully, one must go to the extreme South and Ceylon. There one may come across almost every animal, from a wild elephant to a firefly. There, as one strolls through a friend's compound or drives to a neighbouring railway station, one passes the choicest plants and trees of European hothouses growing luxuriantly in the open air. As to animals, they seem to dispute possession of the soil with man. They will assert with perfect impunity their right to a portion of the crops he rears and the food he eats, and will even effect a lodgment in the houses he builds as if they had a claim to be regarded as co-tenants. This is a good deal owing to the sacredness of animal life in India. Not only is there an absolute persuasion in the mind of a Hindū that some animals, such as cows, serpents, and monkeys, are more or less pervaded by divinity, but most Indians believe that there are eighty-four lakhs of species of animal life through which a man's own soul is liable to pass.

In fact, any noxious insect or loathsome reptile may be, according to the Hindū religion, an incarnation of some deceased relative or venerated ancestor. Hence, no man, woman, or child among the Hindūs thinks it right to kill animals of any kind. Hence, too, in India animals of all kinds appear to live on terms of the greatest confidence and intimacy with human beings. They cannot even learn to be afraid of their enemies the European immigrants. Musquitoes will settle affectionately and fearlessly on the hands of the most recent comer, leeches will insinuate themselves lovingly between the interstices of his lower garments, parrots will peer inquisitively from the eaves of his bedroom into the mysteries of his toilet, crows will carry off impudently anything portable that takes their fancy on his dressing-table, sparrows will hop about impertinently and take the bread off his table-cloth, bats will career triumphantly round his head as he reads by the light of his duplex lamp, monkeys will domesticate themselves jauntily on his roof, and at certain seasons snakes will domicile themselves unpleasantly in his cast-off garments, while a whole tribe of feathered creatures will build their nests confidingly under the trees of his garden before the very eyes of the village boys who play near his compound. I have heard it said in England that the tigers of India will soon be exterminated; yet I looked down from the heights near Ootacamund on a tract of country swarming with tigers and wild animals of all kinds. Such animals are on the increase in these and other similar localities, notwithstanding the active hostility of rifle-armed English sportsmen. The truth is that those Europeans who venture into such jungles to shoot down tigers are themselves struck down, like Lord Hastings, by jungle fever; and before we can induce the natives to wage a war of extermination against beasts of prey, we must disabuse them of the notion that men are sometimes converted into wild beasts, and that the spirit of a man killed by a tiger not unfrequently takes to riding about on the animal's head [1].

With regard to plant life, it must be borne in mind that in the creed of the Hindūs even plants may be permeated by divinity or possessed by the souls of departed relatives. No Hindū will cut down the divine Tulsī, or knowingly

[1] See Sleeman's 'Rambles and Recollections,' p. 162.

injure any other sacred plant. As to the holy Pīpal, it may indulge its taste for undermining walls and houses, and even palaces and temples, with perfect impunity. Happily, there is a limit to even the most pious Hindū's respect for plant life. Perhaps the most demonstrative and self-asserting and, at the same time, most useful of tropical trees is the palm. Palm trees are ubiquitous in Southern India, and yet the eye never wearies of their presence. One hundred and fifty different species may be seen in Ceylon, among which the most conspicuous are the cocoa-nut, the palmyra, the date, the sago, the slender areca, and the sturdy talipot—often crowned with its magnificent tuft of flowers, which it produces only once before its decay, at the end of about half a century. Avenues of palm trees overshadow the roads and even line the streets of towns. The next most characteristic tree of Southern India is the banyan. The sight of a fine banyan tree is almost worth a voyage from Southampton to Bombay, and it can only be seen in perfection in the South. One I saw in a friend's compound at Madura was 180 yards in circumference, and was a little forest in itself. Then there is the beautiful plantain, with its broad, smooth leaves, rivalling the palm in luxuriance and ubiquity. Then one must go to Southern India to understand how the lotus became the constant theme of Indian poets, as the symbol of everything lovely, sacred, and auspicious. Space indeed would fail if I were to tell of groves of mangoes and tamarinds, clumps of enormous bamboos, gigantic creepers in full blossom, tree ferns, oranges and citrons, hedges of flowering aloes, cactus, prickly pear, wild roses, and geraniums, or even if I were to descant at large on such useful plants as coffee, cinchona, tea, and tobacco.

With regard to these last I will merely say that our thriving colony of Ceylon is the true home of the coffee plant, and that I found coffee-planting there in a peculiarly flourishing condition. Nearly £6 per cwt. is now given for coffee which formerly realized only £2 10*s*. The island owes much of its present prosperity to Sir William Gregory's energetic Governorship. Coffee in great quantities is also grown on the Nīlgiris, the hill districts of Mysor, the Wynaad, Travankor, and the Asambhu hills. Cinchona (yielding quinine) is being cultivated with great success in Ceylon, Sikkim, and some hill stations of Southern India. As to tea, ever since the tea-plant was found to be indigenous in Assam and Kachār, its cultivation has gone on increasing so rapidly that it is likely to become one of the staple products of India, and will vie as an export with rice, opium, cotton, and jute. It is said that 357,000 chests were exported last year from Assam, Kachār, and Darjīling—the three chief tea districts—alone. Tea cultivation is also carried on in other hill stations of Northern and Southern India. I am told that a great future is in store for tobacco, and that it will take the place of opium as a source of revenue should the Chinese demand for the latter cease. All that is wanted is skill in its cultivation, and more delicate manipulation in the rolling of the leaves of the plant for the manufacture of cigars. Its success in British Burmah is remarkable. But enough of plants; let me now turn to men.

Character of the People in Southern India.

If the most apathetic traveller is astonished by the nature of the climate, by the vastness of the country, by the diversity of the scenery, by the exuberance of animal and plant life in Southern India, much more is his wonder excited by the multiplicity of races which constitute its teeming population, by the variety of their costume, manners, social institutions, usages, religious creeds, and dialects. Biologists, ethnologists, archæologists, and philologists, will find here (as in Northern India) a rich banquet set before them, from which they may always rise with an appetite for more. The inhabitants of Bombay, whose number exceeds that of any other city in the British Empire (except London and Calcutta), may be said to belong partly to Gujarāt, partly to the Konkan, and partly to the Marāṭha country. When we have ascended the Bhore Ghāt and are in that part of the Deccan of which Poona is the capital, we are fairly among the Marāṭhas, who are the principal representatives of the Āryan race in Southern India. The Brāhmans and higher classes of this race are often fine intelligent men, and sometimes great Pandits, but withal proud and bigoted. Their women are kept less secluded, and are far more independent than the women in Northern India, where Muhammadan influences are much stronger. It is common to see Marāṭha ladies walking about in the streets of large towns and showing themselves in public without any scruple.

The rest of Southern India, not including the Āryan portion of Orissa, is peopled first by the great Drāviḍian races (so called from Drāviḍa, the name given by the Sanskrit speakers to the Southern, or Tamil, part of the Peninsula), whose immigrations into India in successive waves from some part of Central Asia immediately preceded those of the Āryans. These Drāviḍians are of course quite distinct from the Āryans; their skin is generally much darker, and the languages they speak belong to what is called the South Turanian family. They may be separated into four distinct peoples, according to their four principal languages—Telugu, Kanarese, Tamil, and Malayālam. Secondly, Southern India is peopled by the wild primitive races, some of them Negroid in complexion, and others Negrito, of a type similar to the savages of Australia. They are now usually called Kolarians. Their irruptions preceded the advent of the Drāviḍians, and they are still found in the hills and other outlying localities. Of the Drāviḍians the Telugu and Tamil speakers are by far the majority, each numbering fifteen or sixteen millions. The Tamil race, who occupy the extreme south from Madras to Cape Comorin, are active, hard-working, industrious, and independent. Their difficult and highly accentuated language reflects their character and possesses quite a distinct literature of its own. The Telugu people, inhabiting the Northern Circars and the Nizām's territory, are also remarkable for their industry, and their soft language, abounding in vowels, is the Italian of the East. The Kanarese of Mysor resemble the Telugu race in language and character, just as the Malayālams of the Malabar coast resemble the Tamils. I noticed that the seafaring Tamils of the Southern coast near Rāmnād, Rāmeśvaram, and Tuticorin are much more able-bodied and athletic than ordinary Hindūs. Numbers of them migrate to Ceylon, and at least half a million form a permanent part of the population of that island. They are to be found in all the coffee plantations, and work much harder than the Sinhalese.

Indeed, all the races of South India seem to me to show readiness and aptitude for any work they are required to do, as well as patience, endurance, and perseverance in the discharge of the most irksome duties. The lower classes may be seen everywhere earning their bread by the veritable sweat of their brow and submitting without a murmur to a life of drudgery and privation. But they are not, as a rule, physically strong, and their moral character, like their bodily constitution, exhibits little stamina. They have, so to speak, little solidity of backbone, either to keep them upright when they are brought into collision with stronger races, or to enable them to rise to the high standard of European morality. It must be borne in mind, too, that Europeans are sometimes strong in vices as well as virtues; and that, as the Hindū rarely has the power of assimilating himself to our best qualities, he is apt to copy our worst. Even our Administrative Government, with all its moral purity, has introduced temptations which are to him a stone of stumbling. Yet I have been told by officers of long experience, who have witnessed the growth of much of our Indian Empire, that on the acquisition of newly-acquired territories, the inhabitants have never shown any immediate disposition towards deceit, litigiousness, subtlety, and avarice, or any of the faults they have afterwards displayed so conspicuously in our Courts of Justice, and in their dealings with us as rulers. The plain fact is, that the people of India are simply human beings with very human infirmities; and that, if the professing Christian finds it difficult to bear up against the tide of human care, crime, and trial which ever follows in the track of advancing civilization, much more does the non-Christian Hindū. I doubt, however, whether the worst Indians are ever so offensive in their vices as the worst type of low, unprincipled Europeans. At any rate, their vices are more subtle. As servants, they are faithful, honest, and devoted, and will attach themselves with far greater affection than English servants to those who treat them well. They show greater respect for animal life than Europeans. They have more natural courtesy of manner, more filial dutifulness, more veneration for rank, age, and learning, and they are certainly more temperate in eating and drinking. I once asked a Peninsular and Oriental captain whether he preferred a crew of ordinary Indian or ordinary English sailors, and he unhesitatingly gave the preference to Indians, 'because,' said he, 'they are more docile, more obedient, less brutish in their habits, and can be trusted not to get drunk.'

Another point to be noted in comparing Indians with Europeans is that the rich among them are never ashamed of their poor relations, and, what is still more noticeable, neither rich nor poor are ever ashamed of their religion.

Religions of Southern India.

Religion is even more closely interwoven with every affair of daily life, and is even more showily demonstrative in the South of India than in the North. Unhappily, it is not of a kind to strengthen the character or fortify it against temptation. Yet its action on social life is so potent, that to make clear the condition of the people, I must briefly explain the nature of their creeds. And here a distinction must be pointed out between Brāhmanism and Hindūism. Brāhmanism is the purely pantheistic and not necessarily idolatrous creed evolved by the Brāhmans out of the religion of the Veda. Hindūism is that complicated system of polytheistic doctrines, idolatrous superstitions, and caste usages which has been developed out of Brāhmanism after its contact with Buddhism and its admixture with the non-Āryan creeds of the Drāviḍians and Aborigines of Southern India. Brāhmanism and Hindūism, though infinitely remote from each other, are integral parts of the same system. One is the germ or root, the other is the rank and diseased outgrowth. It is on this account that they everywhere co-exist in the same localities throughout the whole of India. Nevertheless, the most complete examples of both creeds are now to be looked for in Southern India, because the North has been always more exposed to Muhammadan influences. In fact, it was the South which produced the three great religious revivalists, Śankara, Madhva, and Rāmānuja.

The followers of Śankara (who lived about the seventh or eighth century of our era, and whose successors reside at Śringeri, on the Mysor Ghāts) are usually strict Brāhmans. They call themselves Smārtas, as observers of Smṛiti or traditional ceremonies, and their creed is generally pure

Brāhmanism. In other words, they are pure Pantheists, though some profess a predilection for Śiva, identifying that god (as the Dissolver and Reproducer of Creation) with the One Omnipresent Spirit of the Universe.

The adherents of Madhva, on the other hand, call themselves Vaishṇavas—as worshippers of the god Vishṇu, whom they identify with the Supreme Spirit when he assumes incarnation for the preservation of his creatures, and they maintain an eternal distinction between the human and Supreme Soul. This is a form of Hindūism which has more common ground with Christianity than any other. I have met with many excellent and intelligent Brāhmans and others in the South of India who profess it.

But the great majority of South Indian Vaishṇavas are followers of Rāmānuja, who led the Vaishṇava revival in the twelfth century. These illustrate the operation of a law which appears essential to the vitality of every religious and political system. They have separated into two grand antagonistic parties—the Tengalais, or followers of the Southern doctrine, and the Vadagalais, or followers of the Northern, whose opposition is very similar to that which prevails in Europe between Calvinists and Arminians. Their quarrels, however, relate more to the external mark of their sect than to differences in fundamental doctrine, the one party contending that this mark—made with a kind of white paint on the forehead—should represent both Vishṇu's feet and should extend halfway down the nose, while the other maintains that the mark should only represent one foot of Vishṇu and that the nasal organ is not entitled to be honoured with any paint at all.

Besides these three principal sects there is another, called Lingavats (vulgarly Lingaits), who are the followers of a leader Basava (= Vṛishabha). They are worshippers of Śiva (symbolized by the lingam worn round their necks); but abjure all respect for caste distinctions and observance of

Brāhmanical rites and usages. A great part of the Kanarese population below Kolapore and in Mysor is Lingait.

In short, Vaishṇavism and Śaivism (or the worship of Vishṇu and Śiva) constitute the very heart and soul of Southern Hindūism. As to Brahmā—the third member of the Hindū Triad, and original creator of the world—he is not worshipped at all except in the person of his alleged offspring, the Brāhmans. Moreover, Vaishṇavism and Śaivism are nowhere so pronounced and imposing as in Southern India. The temples of Kanjīvaram (Kānćī-puram), Tanjore, Trichinopoly, Madura, Tinnevelly, and Rāmeśvaram are as superior in magnitude to those of Benares as Westminster Abbey and St. Paul's are to the other churches of London.

Furthermore, it must not be forgotten that, although a belief in devils, and homage to *bhūtas*, or spirits, of all kinds, is common all over India, yet what is called 'devil worship' is far more systematically practised in the South of India and in Ceylon than in the North. And the reason may be that as Drāviḍians and Āryans advanced towards Southern India, they found it peopled by wild aboriginal savages, whose behaviour and aspect appeared to them to resemble that of devils. The Āryan and Drāviḍian mind, therefore, naturally pictured to itself the regions of the South as the chief resort and stronghold of the demon race, and the dread of demoniacal agency became more rooted in Southern India than in the North. Curiously enough, too, it is commonly believed in Southern India that every wicked man contributes by his death to swell the ever-increasing ranks of devil legions. His evil passions do not die with him. They are intensified, concentrated, and perpetuated in the form of a malignant and mischievous spirit. Moreover, the god Śiva is constantly connected with demoniacal agencies, either as superintending and controlling them, or as himself possessing (especially in the person of his wife Kālī) all the fierceness and malignity usually attributed to demons.

In fact, in the South of India, even more than in the North, all evils, especially drought, blight, and diseases, are attributed to devils. When my fellow-travellers and myself were nearly dashed to pieces over a precipice by some restive horses on a ghāt near Poona, we were told that the road at this particular point was haunted by devils, who often caused similar accidents, and we were given to understand that we should have done well to conciliate Gaṇeśa, son of the god Śiva, and all his troops of evil spirits, before starting. Of all gods Gaṇeśa is, perhaps, the most commonly conciliated, not, in my opinion, because he is said to bestow wisdom, but simply because he is believed to prevent the obstacles and diseases caused by devils. Homage, indeed, may be rendered to the good God, or Supreme Spirit pervading the universe, but he is too absolutely perfect to be the author of harm to any one, and does not need to be appeased. Devils alone require propitiation. Happily, the propitiating process is generally easy. It is usually performed by the sacrifice of certain common animals such as fowls, or goats, or by offerings of food or other articles supposed to be peculiarly acceptable to disembodied beings. For example, when a certain European, who was a terror to the district in which he lived, died in the South of India, the natives were in the constant habit of depositing brandy and cigars on his tomb to propitiate his spirit, supposed to roam about the neighbourhood in a restless manner and with evil proclivities. The very same was done to secure the good offices of the philanthropic spirit of a great European sportsman, who, when he was alive, delivered his district from the ravages of tigers.

Indeed, it ought to be mentioned that all evil spirits are

thought to be opposed by good ones, who, if duly propitiated, make it their business to guard the inhabitants of particular places from demoniacal intruders. Each district, and even every village, has its guardian genius, often called its mother. If smallpox or blight appear, some mother (especially the one called Mārī Amman) is thought to be angry, and must be appeased by votive offerings. There are no less than 140 of these mothers in Gujarāt. There is also one very popular male god in Southern India called Ayenār (*Harihara-putra*), son of Śiva and Vishṇu, to whom shrines in the fields are constantly erected. A remarkable point is that these guardian spirits (especially Ayenār) are supposed to delight in riding about the country on horses. Hence the traveller just arrived from Europe is startled and puzzled by apparitions of roughly-formed terra-cotta horses, often as large as life, placed by the peasantry round rude shrines in the middle of fields as acceptable propitiatory offerings, or in the fulfilment of vows during periods of sickness.

Another remarkable circumstance connected with the dread of demoniacal agencies is the existence in the South of India and Ceylon of professional exorcisers and devil-dancers. Exorcising is performed over persons supposed to be possessed by demons in the form of diseases. The exorciser assumes a particular dress, goes through various antics, mutters spells, and repeats incantations. Devil-dancing is performed by persons who paint their faces, or put on hideous masks, dress up in demoniacal costumes, and work themselves up into a veritable frenzy by wild dances, cries, and gesticulations. They are then thought to be actually possessed by the spirits and to become, like spiritualist mediums, gifted with clairvoyance and a power of delivering oracular and prophetic utterances on any matter about which they may be questioned. There seems to be also an idea that when smallpox, cholera, or similar pestilences are exceptionally rife, exceptional measures must be taken to draw off the malignant spirits, the supposed authors of the plague, by tempting them to pass into these wild dancers and so become dissipated. I myself witnessed in Ceylon an extraordinary devil dance performed by three men who were supposed to personate or represent three different forms of typhus fever.

With regard to Buddhism, although its importation into Ceylon must have been effected to a great extent from Southern India, where its images still occasionally do duty as Hindū gods, yet it no longer exists there. In Ceylon it is a cold, negative, undemonstrative, sleepy religion, contrasting very remarkably with the showy, positive, and noisy form of Hindūism prevalent on the other side of the Straits. Its only worship consists in presenting flowers before images and relic shrines of the extinct Buddha, and in meditating on his virtues and on the advantages of doing nothing beyond aiming at similar extinction.

In times of sickness and calamity, the Sinhalese, having no Divine protector to appeal to, betake themselves, like the Hindūs, to the appeasing of devils or to the worship of idols borrowed from the Hindū Pantheon, whose temples often stand near their relic-dagobas. I myself saw several such temples near the celebrated dagoba erected over Buddha's eye-tooth at Kandy.

As to the South Indian Muhammadans, they are, of course, worshippers of one God, but I believe that even more than in the North they have made additions to the simplicity of Islām by the adoration of Pīrs, or saints, by the veneration of relics, and by conforming to Hindū customs and superstitions. In the Nizām's territory alone homage is paid to hundreds of Pīrs. The great Aurangzīb is buried near the tomb of a celebrated saint at Rozah, and crowds of pilgrims annually throng the shrine of a popular

Pīr at Gulburga. In times of sickness I have seen the lower orders of Muhammadans resort to Hindū deities, especially to the goddess of smallpox. By far the majority are like the Turks, Sunnīs (not Shī'as), but from conversation I had with several learned men, I feel convinced that they have no idea of acknowledging the Sultan of Constantinople as their spiritual head, and that the existence of sympathy between India and Turkey (except perhaps in towns like Bombay) is a figment of political agitators.

The question now arises how far these creeds have tended to degrade the character and condition of the people of India. And here we must guard against confusing cause and effect. In my opinion, the present low intellectual and moral condition of the masses of the Hindū people is as much the result of their social usages as it is the cause of their own superstitious creeds. It is very true that these social usages, enforced by what are called caste rules, are now part and parcel of their religious creeds, but they do not properly belong to the original pure form of the Hindū religion. They are merely one portion of its diseased outgrowth, and they are, in my opinion, the true cause of that feeble condition of mind in which the later superstitions have naturally taken root and luxuriated.

Not that the rules of caste have been an unmixed evil. On the contrary, they have done much good service to India. Each caste has been a kind of police to itself, keeping its own members in check and saving them from lawlessness. But the advantage thus gained has been far outweighed by the irreparable harm done to the physical, mental, and moral constitution of the Hindū people by the operation of caste in three principal particulars—first, in making early marriage a religious duty; secondly, in enforcing endogamy—that is to say, in obliging castes, and even subdivisions of castes, to marry within themselves; thirdly, in surrounding family and home life with a wall of secrecy. The evils of early marriage are too manifest to need pointing out. I have sometimes examined the upper classes of Indian high schools in which half the boys have been fathers. In fact, the chief solicitude in the minds of parents is, not the education of their children, but their early marriage. When girls of twelve are mothers, and boys of sixteen fathers, it is surely too much to expect vigour of mind or body, and strength of character, either in parents or offspring. The children of mere children will probably remain children all their lives. They may have precocity and intelligence, but are very unlikely to develope manly faculties. Moreover, the universality of early marriages tends to increase population in a way which adds greatly to our difficulties in times of drought and famine. As to the evils of endogamy they are too well known to need pointing out. I believe that physiologists are agreed that when first cousins and other blood relations marry, the resulting offspring must be of a feeble type. In the India of the present day polygamy is scarcely known, but endogamy is beginning to be common, and I firmly believe that with increasing subdivisions of caste into mere groups of families, and inhibition of marriages out of these families, serious deterioration of brain-tissues is likely to take place among certain classes.

The weakness entailed by the two pernicious caste rules I have named might, perhaps, be partially overcome or counterbalanced if it were not for the third pernicious rule —namely, the seclusion of women and the surrounding of family life with an impenetrable wall of secrecy. All nations are but a collection of families, and as are the homes so will be the condition of the people. In truth, the welfare of a country radiates from its homes—one might almost say from its nurseries. But no one knows what is going on in an Indian home, much less can any one, except a member of the family, enter there. It is so shut in by the close shutters of caste that healthy ventilation is impossible. The fresh air of heaven and the light of God's day have no free entrance. Weakly children are brought up by ignorant, superstitious, narrow-minded mothers in a vitiated atmosphere. Hence, in my opinion, the present deteriorated character and condition of a large majority of the people of India.

What, then, is the chief hope for the future? It seems to me to lie in a complete reorganization of the social fabric, in a new ideal of womanhood, and an entire renovation of family life. Before the people of India can be much elevated by their connexion with England they must learn from us to abolish caste regulations about early marriage; Indian fathers must keep their daughters under education as long as we do, and members of different castes must intermarry, as peer and commoner do in Great Britain. This, it will be said, amounts to an upheaving of the whole social fabric. Yet it is not, in my opinion, a work of such hopeless magnitude as some would make it out to be. Symptoms of impatience under caste-restrictions are already observable among the wealthier, better-educated, and more Europeanized classes of natives, and social reform is openly advocated in some quarters. A great advance may be expected when the increasing contact of Indians with English social institutions, in England itself, becomes still more common, when the visits of influential men to our shores are oftener repeated, and when the Baniyahs, or wealthy traders of the old Vaiśya class (some of whom, nevertheless, are the incarnate curses of India by the facilities they offer for borrowing money), succeed, as they appear likely eventually to do, in interposing a strong middle class and a firm barrier of public opinion between the Brāhmans and the lower grades of society.

All honour, too, to those noble-hearted missionaries who, like Bishop Sargent and Mrs. Sargent at Tinnevelly, are seeking, by the establishment of female schools, to supply India with its most pressing need—good wives and mothers; or, like Mr. and Mrs. Lash, are training girls to act as high-class schoolmistresses, and sending them forth to form new centres of female education in various parts of Southern India.

But let our missionaries bear in mind that more than mere preaching, more than mere education, more than the alteration of marriage rules, is needed for the regeneration of India. The missionary bands must carry their ark persistently round the Indian home, till its walls are made to fall, and its inner life exposed to the fresh air of God's day, and all its surroundings moulded after the pattern of a pure, healthy, well-ordered Christian household whose influences leaven the life of the family and the nation from the cradle to the grave. My belief is that until a way is opened for the free intercourse of the educated mothers and women of Europe, trained to speak and understand the Indian vernaculars, with the mothers and women of India, in their own homes, Christianity itself, or at least its purer forms, will make little progress either among Hindūs or Muhammadans.

For Christianity is a religion which, before it can dominate over the human heart, requires a clear apprehension of certain great facts, and a manly assent of the reason to the doctrines and practice they involve. Although we Christians are required to be children in guilelessness, we are told to be men in understanding. That, indeed, is not true Christianity which does not make a kind of religion of manliness of character, healthiness of body and mind, and soundness of judgment. Now, it is certain that although exceptional cases of men of vigorous intellect exist in India, and its races differ considerably in physique, yet the ordinary Indian has hitherto inherited such a feeble condition of brain, such a diseased appetite for mental stimulants, such unhealthy biasses and habits of mind from his ancestors, that he is almost incapable of grasping plain facts, much less of incorporating them, like plain food, into the texture of his moral constitution. Nor is he generally at all capable of appreciating the importance of their bearing on daily life and practice. Hence the absence of all history in India, and hence the difficulty of obtaining any accurate, unexaggerated, or undistorted narrative of common occurrences. Here, too, in my opinion, lies the principal difficulty of convincing a Hindū of the superiority of the plain story of the Gospel to the wild exaggerations of the Rāmāyaṇa. The chief successes of Christianity in India have been hitherto achieved by Roman Catholics, who offer to the Hindū mind a kind of Hindūized Christianity, or, at any rate, present him with the images, symbols, processions, decorations, miraculous stories, marvellous histories of saints, and imposing outward ritual of which his present mental condition appears to stand in need.

Our Administration of the Country.

I am confirmed in my opinion (expressed on a previous occasion) that the points we have most to guard against in the administration of our Indian Empire are, first, a desire to advance too rapidly and too uniformly; secondly, a tendency towards the over-centralization of authority.

India is a poor country saddled with a costly Government. Very naturally, therefore, we Englishmen who form that Government are sensitively anxious to do work that shall really be worth the money we cost. Hence we are ever striving to benefit the people by fresh legislative measures, for which the country is not always sufficiently prepared, and which we are inclined to apply too uniformly. Yet England's worst enemies cannot shut their eyes to the good our administration has effected. Indeed, my travels have convinced me that the Natives of India have no cause whatever to complain of our excluding them from their equitable share in the administration of their own country. Our Government is ever zealous for their interests, and ever on the watch to find competent Indians to fill responsible posts. For all the lower grades of executive offices they are now selected before equally competent Europeans.

In law courts, in police courts, at railway stations, post and telegraph offices, and in every department of the public service one meets with Indian functionaries doing the work which was formerly done by Europeans. English barristers and attorneys are now driven out of the field by Indian Wakeels. The same applies to the Educational Department. Headmasterships of High Schools, which were once reserved for Englishmen, and even filled by Oxford and Cambridge graduates, are now assigned to the ablest Native teachers. Even the highest judicial offices are now being filled by Natives who have gained admission to the Civil Service through the competitive examinations. The Judge of Ahmedabad, Mr. Satyendranāth Tagore, whose guest I was for a few days, is an Indian of a well-known family at Calcutta. He has been elevated to a higher position in the Service than competition-wallahs of his own year, and of at least equal ability. Another Indian gentleman, Mr. Gopāl-rāo Hari Deshmukh, whom I met frequently at Bombay—a man of great energy and ability, and a well-known social reformer—has lately been appointed joint Judge at Tanna, with the personal title of Rāo Bahādur. The title was conferred the other day at a public meeting, and Judge Gopāl-rāo, in acknowledging the honour, is reported in the *Times of India* (September 4, 1877) to have said:—

'This Sanad is given to me for loyalty and services. I am sure that every sensible and well-informed man in this country is loyal. This country for many past centuries had no Government deserving the name. There was neither internal peace nor security from foreign invasion. There was no power in India which could put a stop to the evil practices of satī, infanticide, religious suicide, and human sacrifices. The whole nation presented a scene of stagnation and ignorance; but the case is now different. Under the auspices of a beneficent, civilized, and strong Government we have become progressive. Light and knowledge are pouring in upon the country. Old prejudices and errors are vanishing. We therefore count it a great privilege to be loyal subjects of the Empress of India. There is now security of life and property, as perfect as human institutions can make it. Those who are old enough are aware of the plundering excursions of Pindāris, who, descending from the ghauts, spread terror in the Concan. These professional robbers have been extirpated by the British Government. We enjoy liberty of speech, petition, and press. We enjoy the blessings of education, useful public works, internal peace, and freedom from foreign invasions.'

Possibly, we are inclined to go beyond our duty in our appreciation of Native merit. It is certain that much bitterness of feeling is being excited among Anglo-Indians by the present laudable desire to do justice to Native ability. Everywhere I heard Englishmen complaining that their interests are set aside and their claims overlooked in favour of Natives. Language like the following is commonly used by members of the Civil Service:—'In thirty years,' say they, 'we English Judges and collectors will be swept out of India. The Natives we have educated are gradually "crowding us out" of the country. Even our own Government is inclined to make light of our merits. We have harder work than ever laid on our shoulders; but we get neither thanks nor additional pay. If we were Hindūs we should be flattered and honoured, but, being Englishmen, we are snubbed and reprimanded.' Such language, though obviously too strong, may have elements of truth which call for careful consideration.

In the matter of over-centralization it seems to be now generally admitted that it results from an undue passion for what may be called administrative symmetry in an Empire far too vast, varied, and composite in its races, customs, religions, and climates, to admit of uniformity of treatment by means of telegraphic messages radiating from a central secretariat. Lord Lytton, who is supposed from his seat in the Viceregal council chamber of Calcutta and Simla to command the manipulation of the whole telegraphic system, was reported not long ago by one of *The Times*' Correspondents to be in favour of more decentralization in regard to taxation. I heard intelligent Natives in Madras complain that, although their ryotwary land tenure and their system of cultivation and irrigation bring in a larger revenue than the systems prevailing elsewhere, yet no benefit accrues to any particular districts in their Presidency, because their surplus goes to make up the deficit in other Provinces.

Nevertheless, it must be confessed that, if decentralization is carried too far, it will remove some salutary restraints on the eccentricities of inexperienced Provincial governors. If the strings of Government are pulled a little too strongly from the India Office and from the secretariats at Calcutta and Simla, they are also handled a little too freely by the array of secretaries at other central stations. In short, the India of the present period is becoming a little too secretariat-ridden. High functionaries, recently imported from England, are obliged, in their blank inexperience, to trust to their secretaries, and these, again, being often new to their work, have to trust to their under-secretaries, while these, again, are a good deal dependent on their head clerks. Thus the Government of a great Empire has a tendency to place too much power in the hands of a few clever under-secretaries' clerks, and to become, if I may be allowed to coin a new phrase, too much of a clericocracy. Half the time of a Collector is now occupied in replying to the inquiries of inquisitive under-secretaries. Every post brings piles of official documents and demands for reports and written statistics on every conceivable subject, while, in return, piles of foolscap find their way from the Collector's cutchery into the pigeon-holes of the Under-Secretary's office. There these precious bundles of foolscap are forthwith entombed, and from these graves there is seldom any resurrection to the light of day.

It is said that a Collector in the North-West Provinces was required, not long ago, to write a report on the habits of the Gangetic porpoise. Certainly it is not uncommon to hear language like the following from Collectors and Commissioners of long standing:—'It is impossible for me to get through my work as I did formerly. For instance, I cannot ride off 30 miles to the other end of my district to see that order is kept at a large religious fair now going on. I am no longer master of my own movements. I have to serve a dozen masters. I am compelled to furnish returns to the head of the Public Works Department, to Sanitary and Revenue Commissioners, to superintendents of police, to directors of public instruction, and to archæological and scientific surveyors. Then I have lately been politely requested to compile a complete Gazetteer of my own district, with an exhaustive account of its fauna and flora.

In short, I am buried in piles of paper from morning till night.' There is certainly exaggeration in such language. Without doubt the writing of reports and compiling of gazetteers by some able civilians has already produced most valuable results, but the exaggerated language is an indication that in some directions we are attempting too much. At any rate, we are laying too great a burden on shoulders already overcharged.

In other directions we might do more. For example, we might carry on a more systematic defensive warfare against drought and famine by the storage of water in tanks, and its distribution by irrigation. India is blessed with abundant rivers. Why are not more anicuts, reservoirs, and canals made? Why should the water of any manageable river be allowed to lose itself in the sea? More might also be done in forest-management, in encouraging emigration, in developing the agricultural and mineral resources of the country; though judgment is here needed, especially in regard to agricultural improvements. For India is too poor and populous a country, and not sufficiently advanced, for the introduction of steam-ploughs, expensive machinery, and chemical manures. In some localities the land is so subdivided that its cultivation amounts to mere spade husbandry.

One thing requires instant attention. The connexion between agriculture, meteorology, and astronomy is now admitted on all hands, and no country in the world would be benefited more than India by systematic meteorological and astronomical observations carried on under Government direction. Much is already being done in this way. Yet I could only find one effective astronomical observatory, and that not adequately supported by Government, though I travelled from Kaśmīr to Cape Comorin. It is not generally known that from his observations of the present condition of the disk of the sun, in connexion with various atmospherical phenomena, the Madras astronomer, Mr. Pogson, prophesied in 1876 a recurrence of the drought and famine in 1877.

Again, more efforts might be made to promote the development of those industrial arts in which the natives are already skilled, and to teach them new trades and industries, such as printing, paper-making, book-binding, sugar-refining, and tobacco-curing.

One crying evil requires immediate redress. A limit should be put by law to the increase of native pleaders. If Indian money-lenders are metaphorically called incarnate curses, Indian Wakeels are rapidly earning a title to the same flattering appellation. I have heard natives complain of what they call the oppression of our Law Courts, with their elaborate machinery of expensive processes and appeals. What they mean is not that injustice is done, but that justice is overdone. They might, with more reason, complain of the oppression of their own Wakeels, who live by promoting quarrels, prey upon litigants, and drain the very life-blood out of their own fellow-countrymen.

Our Connexion with the Native States.

Under this head let me merely say that I visited three most prosperous and well-managed States of Southern India—Travankor, Cochin, and Hyderabad. Travankor and the little State of Cochin are both on the Malabar Coast. The former has a wise and enlightened Mahārāja, and his Prime Minister is a sensible high-minded man of large acquirements and great administrative ability. I sailed along the coast of Travankor from Cape Comorin to Cochin, and was much struck by the constant succession of thriving villages clustering under beautiful groves of palm trees close to the water's edge. Nearly all were overlooked by the lofty façades of substantially-built Roman Catholic churches, which are conspicuous objects everywhere on the Malabar coast, testifying to the almost superhuman energy and devotedness of the great missionary Xavier. The interior of these churches presents an appearance very like a Hindū Temple. They all contain images of the Virgin Mary, dressed up and decorated much in the same way as the idols of the Indian goddess Bhavānī. In every direction Roman Catholic churches force themselves on one's notice. On saints' days they are brilliantly illuminated, while displays of fireworks and Bengal lights, with explosions of crackers and guns, are made in front of the churches, much to the delectation of the native converts. I was told, too, that their priests endear themselves to their flocks by living among them very much like Indian Gurus, and by attending to their bodily as well as spiritual needs. Those who come from Europe set our Protestant missionaries a good example in at least two particulars. They are satisfied with wonderfully small salaries, and never think of going home.

There are also two very singular colonies of Jews at Cochin. The one set are quite white in complexion, and the other quite black. I was present at the service in a synagogue, and saw the richly-decorated rolls of the Books of Moses carried round in procession and kissed by the congregation, after the law had been read by the Rabbis from a central reading-desk.

My visit to Sir Richard Meade, our able Resident at Hyderabad, enabled me to judge of the condition of the Nizām's territory, which occupies the central plateau of the Deccan, and has a population of 10,000,000 or 11,000,000. It owes its present prosperity, as most people know, to the excellent administration of Sir Sālār Jung, who delivered it from a condition of chronic mismanagement. Our large military station at Secunderabad, six miles from the capital, contains 40,000 inhabitants, and is under our own jurisdiction. We also hold Berār (commonly called the Berārs) in trust for the payment of the Nizām's contingent. It was taken by us from the Marāṭhas, and we have administered it since 1853. It has thriven wonderfully under our management; but as we gave it to the Nizām in 1803, the surplus revenue goes to his treasury. We restored to him the Raichore Doāb, between the Kṛishṇa and Tungabhadra rivers, in 1860. Whether Berār ought to be so restored is another matter. Some authorities think we did wrong to give up our claim to Mysor, and that we might with as good reason give up Berār. Probably Berār would not suffer much by being given back so long as the continuance of so able a Minister as Sir Sālār Jung at the helm could be secured. But India is not likely to produce two such men as Sir Sālār Jung and Sir T. Mādhava Rāo more than once in two or three centuries. I conversed with both these great Ministers not long since in their own houses (one at Hyderabad, and the other at Baroda) and found them capable of talking on all subjects in as good English as my own.

Sir Sālār Jung (whose person is familiar to many of us from his recent visit to England) showed me his everyday working-room—a room not so large as an Oxford graduate's study, plainly furnished with a few book-cases filled with modern books of reference, chiefly English. He has an extensive library in an adjoining gallery, with a window commanding a courtyard, where those who have to transact business with him assemble every day. I may mention as an evidence of his enlightened ideas that on hearing that a deserving young Indian, now at Oxford, was in need of assistance, he at once assigned a scholarship for his support, stipulating that he should be trained for the Nizām's educational service. He has other young Indians under training in London, similarly supported.

I was told that I should see numbers of armed ruffians and rowdies in the city of Hyderabad, and that I could not possibly traverse the streets unless lifted above all chances of insult on the back of an elephant. Yet I can certify that I saw very few armed men and no signs of disorder or lawlessness anywhere in the city, and that I dismounted from my elephant and walked about in the throng of people without suffering the slightest inconvenience, molestation, or rudeness. Of course, a town of 400,000 inhabitants is liable to disturbances, and it is certain that during my stay an Arab, whose father died suddenly, made a savage attack with his dagger in a fit of frenzy on the doctor who attended him. Nevertheless I am satisfied that the stories about murderous brawls in the streets are much exaggerated. Without doubt it must be admitted that the 7,000 armed Arab mercenaries, who form part of an army of 50,000 men, and the numerous armed retainers of the nobles, all of whom are allowed to roam about without much discipline, are generally ripe for turbulence and mischief. It is, moreover, a significant fact that about three-fourths of the wealth of Hyderabad is concentrated within the limits of the Residency, held to be British territory. These limits are carefully marked off from the rest of the city by walls and lines of streets; and here a population of 20,000 persons, including the chief rich bankers and merchants of the Nizām's dominions, cluster under the ægis of British jurisdiction and authority.

Our Education of the People.

South India is not behind the North in its zeal for education. Indeed, if advance of education is to be measured by its promoting among natives of all ranks the power of speaking English with fluency, the palm will have to be given to the Colleges and Schools of Madras. And here, as in other parts of India, missionary schools are, in my opinion, doing the best work. The education they impart is openly and professedly founded on a Christian basis. They teach the Bible without enforcing ecclesiastical dogmas on their pupils. Indeed, my second tour has impressed me more than ever with the benefits which India derives from the active efforts of missionaries of all denominations, however apparently barren in visible results those efforts may be. Moreover, I think that the part that they have hitherto played is as nothing compared with the *rôle* they are destined to fill in the future of our Eastern Empire. The European missionary is daily becoming a more important link between the Government and the people. He is confided in by natives of all ranks, and is often able to do what the Government with its wise professions of neutrality cannot effect. Missionary schools attract the children of parents of all creeds, though they openly aim at permeating their minds with a spirit hostile to those creeds. It may be very true that their bible-teaching tends to destroy without necessarily reconstructing, but it is gradually and insensibly infusing principles incompatible with the pantheistic ideas with which the Indian mind is generally saturated. If it does not always build up the true creed in place of the false, yet it lays the foundation of a future belief in a personal God. It substitutes for the slippery sands of Pantheism a basis of living rock, which may be afterwards thankfully occupied by evangelizing missionaries as a common standpoint, when the Gospel is confronted in argument with the Veda and Kurān.

My conviction is that the vast work of Christianizing India will not be accomplished entirely through missionary instrumentality, but rather through the co-operation of divine and human agencies, working in a great variety of ways. Yet I am equally convinced that it will be principally effected, and far more slowly, gradually, and insensibly than is commonly expected, through impressions made on the minds of children by a process of education like that our missionaries are carrying out in their schools. Of all such schools visited by me, in Southern India, there were two, the merits and effectiveness of which struck me very forcibly. They were those of the Free Church of Scotland at Madras, under Mr. Miller and Mr. Rae, where about 1,000 pupils are under education; and the Church Missionary schools, under Bishop Sargent, at Tinnevelly, in which latter district there are about 60,000 converts to Protestant Christianity. I regret I was unable to visit Bishop Caldwell's excellent schools at Edeyengoody. I could name a hundred others if space and time were at my disposal. Those founded by a native named Pacheappah at Madras and Conjevaram are rendering good service to the community. The Basle Mission schools at Mangalore are also most efficient and useful, and its members most devoted and self-sacrificing. Their example deserves to be followed in their plan of teaching trades and industries, and of instructing their converts how to be independent and support themselves. The schools of the Pārsīs at Bombay are also conspicuously good. And let it not be supposed that the work done by our Government schools and colleges is insignificant. Its importance can scarcely be overrated. Nevertheless, it is generally admitted that our whole educational system needs revision and amendment. The great complaint that one hears on all sides while travelling in India is that we are over-educating. We cannot, however, be accused of over-educating if our education is of the right kind. Quality, not quantity, is what is wanted for India. Excellence of quality can scarcely be over-done.

Probably there are three principal points that call for amendment in our present system. 1. We want more real education. 2. We want more suitable education. 3. We want more primary education.

As to the first point:—To secure more reality of education we have to make our native teachers understand that the human skull, which is their field of operations, is not in childhood a mere rigid case, nor even a wholly empty cavity, to be crammed with a given amount of knowledge in a given time, but rather an assemblage of organs and capacities to be gradually and carefully shaped, moulded, and expanded. We in England sometimes require to be reminded that the duty of an educator ought to be in accordance with the etymology of the word—that it should consist in gently drawing out rather than in roughly hammering in. Indian educators of Indian children are still more forgetful of this truth. Nor do they sufficiently bear in mind that the most valuable knowledge is that which is self-acquired when the faculties are matured, and that teachers are doing their business most effectively when they are teaching their pupils to be their own future self-teachers. I am afraid our Indian colleges and schools are turning out more well-informed than well-formed men, more free thinkers than wise thinkers, more silly sceptics than honest enquirers, more glib talkers than accurate writers, more political agitators than useful citizens. I do not mean to imply that our European principals and professors and directors of public instruction, generally chosen with care from our English Universities, are not perfectly aware of the defects in our system. On the contrary, I believe they are doing their best to make Indian education a reality. I have met, too, with native schoolmasters who are really able educators. What I mean is that a larger number of good normal schools and a better system of teaching how to teach are urgently needed in India, and some security is required that the applicants for masterships have really received adequate training.

It is certain that assistant masters and subordinate teachers are too often found in positions for which they are not thoroughly qualified. Even in England the heads of our great public schools are beset with similar difficulties. Every one admits that national schoolmasters must be certificated as teachers, but no one dares to cast a suspicion on University first-class men, who would feel themselves humiliated at the bare suggestion that first-class scholarship and first-class teaching are two very different matters.

The next point is that we want more suitable education. The sons of persons of low social status ought not (except, of course, in special cases when they show evident signs of unusual ability) to receive an education above the rank of their fathers. Let their training be the best of its kind, but let it be suited to their position and prospects. Furthermore, greater efforts should be made to co-ordinate the education of daughters with that of sons. In brief, we ought to aim at educating children in their stations, rather than above their stations—at making the son of a potter a better potter, the son of a carpenter a better carpenter. To this end I submit that we should immediately raise our school and college fees for high-class education. Not that I would place obstacles in the way of the lower castes elevating themselves, but I would at once correct the mistake of putting too low a price on the highest form of education. No parent of inferior rank will then be ambitious of a University degree for his son unless he is likely to repay with interest the outlay necessary to secure it. When I was at Poona, I found, on inquiry, that a student at the great central Deccan College there could obtain a first-class education by paying 16*s.* per month for his room-rent, 10*s.* per month for his tuition, and 18*s.* or 20*s.* per month for his board. Of course, Indian students are much more simple in their habits than Oxford undergraduates. They are satisfied with one chair, one table, and a mattress on the ground. They make free use of the college library, and they eat little except rice, with perhaps once a day a modicum of curry-powder. But even for Indians, the present charge for room-rent, board, and tuition at a first-class college is ridiculously small.

Further, I submit that in all our Indian colleges and schools we pay too much attention to the linguistic and literary element in education, and too little to the practical and scientific. A great improvement, however, is observable in this respect in some parts of India.

With regard to languages I cannot help thinking that a great mistake is committed—a mistake which calls for the immediate consideration of the directors of public instruction. We do not sufficiently encourage the vernaculars. The classical languages receive due respect and attention, but the vernacular dialects of India, which ought to be stimulated to draw fresh vitality and energy from Sanskṛit, are everywhere showing signs of serious deterioration. Be it observed, however, that they are by no means dying out. It would be simple folly to suppose that we can impose English on 240 millions of people. But by enforcing English as a *sine quâ non* at our matriculation examinations, and by making a knowledge of it the only road to employment in the public service, we are dealing a fatal blow at the purity of the vernacular languages. My conviction is that unless more is done to encourage their cultivation, some of them will soon lapse into vulgar hybrid dialects. A highly-educated Marāṭha gentleman told me that he scarcely knew a man among his own fellow-countrymen who could write good Marāṭhī. Even the right spelling of the words derived from the Sanskṛit, which ought to be carefully preserved, is becoming hopelessly corrupted. A vicious style of verbose and inflated composition, copied from Dr. Johnson's 'Rambler,' is becoming common, and English words are ostentatiously imported into it, when far more suitable expressions might be drawn from a Sanskṛit source. Such great native poets as Tukarām and Morapant are becoming neglected, and intelligent men, who might do much to develope and improve their own languages, waste their time in concocting, and even printing and publishing, wretched English verses which no Englishman can read without a smile. The result of such a mistaken system is that India is flooded with conceited and half-educated persons who despise and neglect their own languages, and their own religious and political systems, without becoming good English scholars, good Christians, or good subjects of the Queen. And hence we are confronted with a difficulty which, even if it does not endanger our rule in India, is becoming more embarrassing every day—the difficulty of providing suitable employment for the thousands of young men we have educated badly and unsuitably. For excessive and misdirected education cannot be carried on with the same impunity in India as in England, where we have the safeguard of our Colonies and an outlet in India itself.

The third point is that we do not everywhere pay sufficient attention to Primary Education. It is superfluous to remark that no system of education can be satisfactory which does not begin at the right end, and rise from the lower to the upper strata of the community. In the villages and the indigenous rural schools a good system of teaching the vernacular dialects, with reading, writing, and arithmetic, is needed. And here is another reason for encouraging by every possible means the cultivation of the vernaculars, and their development and improvement by means of Sanskrit. I have seen a few excellent village schools, conducted in the open air under trees, where the children are taught to write on palm leaves, and can repeat the multiplication table up to a hundred times a hundred, and even multiply fractions together in their heads. The difficulty is to secure good village teachers. Sir George Campbell, and Sir Richard Temple, following his predecessor's lead, did admirable service in this way and started an excellent plan of primary instruction by trained teachers in Bengal. Much has been effected in the same direction all over India. In 1873 there were 30,477 primary schools, with 963,000 pupils. These seem sufficiently large figures, but remembering the increasing density of the population we have to deal with, we ought not to be satisfied till our system of primary instruction has really penetrated to the remotest corner of the lowest stratum of Indian society.

The Disposition and Attitude of the Natives towards us and our rule.

I confess that in travelling through Southern India it seemed to me that there is even less social fusion between the rulers and the ruled in Madras than in Bombay and Calcutta. Doubtless there are faults on both sides. The longer we continue to hold the country, the more its condition before we took it in hand is forgotten. In those parts of the Madras Presidency which have been longest under our rule, the people, having had no personal experience of the evils from which their fathers were delivered through our intervention, are unable to cherish a due sense of gratitude towards us. I fear that Englishmen, unless they are plainly and sensibly benefactors, are not otherwise liked for their personal qualities. They are thought to be proud, cold, and reserved. Very much the same, however, might be justly said by us of the natives of India. The Hindūs, we might fairly allege, are even more exclusive than we are. They have little sympathy with any one outside their own caste. The impenetrable barrier with which they surround their homes and their refusal to sit at meat with Europeans are fatal to mutual friendliness and sociability. On the other hand, Englishmen, by reason of a concurrence of changed conditions, are certainly living in India more like strangers and pilgrims who have no abiding resting-place there. Increased facilities of communication between Europe and Asia, which ought to have drawn the two races closer together, have only tended to widen the separation between them. In former days it was not uncommon for a civilian or military officer to remain a quarter of a century in India without going home. He had then time and opportunity to identify himself with the people, and interest himself in their interests—to form friendships among them and win their affection. Now, if he has only three months' leave, he rushes to England, *viâ* Brindisi, in three weeks, and undergoes inordinate fatigue, that he may spend six weeks in the old country, and then rush as quickly back to the land of his exile.

The competitive system, too, has had a bad effect in severing some of the ties which once bound the two races together. It has deprived India of the successive generations of Outrams, Prinseps, Macnaghtens, and other old families who were drawn towards it by a long train of inherited associations, who were inspired with goodwill towards its people by the example of their forefathers, and who imbibed Indian tastes, ideas, and predilections with their earliest education.

Let no one, however, from this time forward, accuse us of want of sympathy with our Indian fellow-subjects in their hour of trial and affliction. There may be increasing race-antagonism, less social blending, and more frequent misunderstandings between the governing and the governed in India, but the best practical proof has now been given of our disinterested desire for the well-being of the great country committed to our charge. The voluntary subscription of more than half a million pounds sterling in a few months for the relief of the famine-stricken districts, and the self-sacrificing courage, zeal, and energy displayed by every one of the Queen's officers, from the Viceroy downwards, in their efforts to alleviate the sufferings of the people, have for ever wiped away the reproach that the attitude of Great Britain towards its Eastern Dependency is cold and unsympathetic. I believe there have been no less than four Indian famines during the past ten years, and these have finally culminated in a period of distress the like of which has not afflicted the land since 1833. Yet this last famine, however deplorable in the present suffering it is causing, will have effected a great benefit, if it opens our eyes to India's needs and to our own shortcomings; if it convinces our Indian subjects of England's devotion to their welfare; if it evokes feelings of gratitude in return for the active sympathy displayed; if it helps to draw the rulers and the ruled closer together by bonds of mutual kindliness, confidence, and cordiality.

Let me, in conclusion, point out one or two causes of discontent which, so soon as the remembrance of our present efforts for the relief of the country has passed away, are likely to bring our rule into increasing disfavour with certain classes of the population. One cause is the constant necessity we are under of revising the land assessment. On the acquirement of any new territory, we have been obliged, of course, to settle the land revenue, and the first settlement has always been very judiciously a mild one. At the end of thirty years a new assessment has generally been made, and the necessary increase in the rate of payment has been demanded from the cultivators. Very naturally, this has always caused an outbreak of great discontent. Of late years a still more microscopic and, perhaps, occasionally vexatious revision of the assessment has led to still further irritation. The cultivators cannot be made to understand that with an increase in the value of land a higher rate of tax is justly due, and they will not be convinced that the Government is not breaking faith with them. There can be no doubt that Lord Cornwallis's permanent settlement of the Government demand in Bengal, Behār, and Orissa, though it has proved a lamentable loss to the Indian revenue, has had its advantages, and nothing would tend to conciliate the whole population of India more than if a similar principle could be applied everywhere. This, however, in present circumstances, is, I fear, almost an impossibility.

Another source of dissatisfaction is now looming in the horizon. The maximum age for competing for the Indian Civil Service will be fixed in 1878 at nineteen, and the minimum at seventeen. Many Indians have complained to me that this lowering of the age will practically exclude natives from the competition. 'How can we send mere boys,' say they, 'on a long voyage at a great expense to a place like London to prepare for an examination of such difficulty? The risks will be too great. A certain number of appointments ought to be set aside for India—say six every year—and the printed questions might then be sent out under seal to the local Governments, who would appoint examining committees.' There is, doubtless, much justice in this proposal, and I hope it will receive due consideration. If it is eventually adopted, all selected native candidates ought to be positively compelled to go to England for two years' probation. I fervently hope, too, that the Government scholarships which were formerly founded to enable deserving young Indians to complete their education in England, but which were for some inscrutable reason abolished before they were fully tried, will be reestablished. In this regard our Government ought to follow the example so wisely set by Sir Sālār Jung. Let the residence of Indians among us be encouraged by all means, and let them return to India—not, indeed, de-nationalized—but imbued with some of our most refining and purifying home influences, elevated by intercourse with some of our best men and women, and penetrated with an earnest desire to aid in the regeneration of their country by assimilating, as far as possible, its social institutions to those of England.

THE SOUTH INDIAN FAMINE OF 1876–77.

Having recently passed through the famine districts, I here record a few particulars which have come under my observation. Most persons think that Southern India is now merely passing into the first shadow of a period of distress the like of which has not darkened the land since 1833. At least 15,000,000 human beings will have to struggle for existence, if they are not actually struck down by famine, or by the diseases which famine brings in its train. Of course, this estimate has reference only to the poorest classes.

The area of the scarcity and famine is immense, stretching, as it does, from the neighbourhood of Poona, not far from Bombay, to Tinnevelly, near the extreme south of the Madras Presidency. But it must not be supposed that the drought has been equally severe everywhere. Although in many places, where the usual rainfall is thirty-five or forty-five inches, only fifteen or twenty have fallen, yet other parts of the country have been more favoured. Moreover, all the belts of land reached by the grand system of irrigation, which stretches between the Godāvarī, Kistna, and Kāverī rivers—fertilizing the soil wherever it penetrates, and forcing even haters of the English rule to admit that no other Rāj has conferred such benefits on India—present a marvellous contrast to the vast tracts of arid waste which meet the eye of the traveller as he journeys by the Great Indian Peninsula, Madras, and South Indian Railways.

A sad feature in the spectacle is the condition of the cattle. As I travelled from one place to another, often diverging from the neighbourhood of the railway to less frequented outlying districts, I saw hundreds of lean, half-famished kine endeavouring to eke out a doomed existence on what could only in mockery be called herbage. When it is remembered that the cow is a principal source of sustenance to Hindūs of nearly all castes, and that no such animal as a cart-horse is to be found in India—all agricultural labour depending on the ox—some idea may be formed of the terrible calamity involved in a mortality among cattle. Even the cows and oxen that survive will be almost useless. Utterly enfeebled and emaciated, they will have little power left either to yield milk or to drag a plough through soil caked and indurated by months of unmitigated sunshine.

But the saddest feature of all is the condition of the human inhabitants of this great peninsula. I will simply recount what I know and testify of what I have seen with my own eyes in the capital of this Presidency. Only a fortnight ago, I saw many thousands of poor famine-driven creatures from the villages round Madras collected on the shore and on the pier. They were crowding round the sacks of rice-grain, with which the sands for at least a mile were thickly covered and almost concealed from view, the grain-bags being often piled up in mounds to the height of fifteen or twenty feet. Yet no onslaught was made on the grain. A few men scattered about, armed with canes, were guarding the sacks for the merchants who owned them, and were sufficient to prevent any attempts at depredation, though here and there I detected surreptitious efforts, not so much to make incisions, as to enlarge any happy defects already apparent in the material which enclosed the coveted food. What generally happened was this:—Very few of the grain-bags were so well made as to make any leakage impossible, and sprinklings of rice were thus scattered about everywhere. The knowledge of this circumstance was the cause of the vast concourse of miserable, half-starved, emaciated creatures who had walked many miles to the spot. Men and women, old and young, even cripples, mothers with infants on their hips, and naked children—all more or less pitiable in their leanness and in their hard-set aspect of misery—were earnestly engaged in gleaning up every grain that escaped from the sacks on the pier and on the shore. Many were provided with coarse sieves, by means of which a few rice-grains were, with infinite pains, separated from bushels of sand. On the pier every crevice was searched, and every discoloured grain eagerly scraped up, mixed as it was with dirt, ejected betel-juice, and filth of all kinds. This is a brief and imperfect description of what I saw with my own eyes.

And now it will be asked, what measures are being taken to meet and mitigate the impending calamity? My answer is that, so far as I have observed, the Governments of Madras and Bombay are fully alive to their duty. They are organizing relief as speedily as possible. Before I left Madras, I saw thirty ships laden with grain at anchor in the roads. Large surf-boats were continually plying between the ships and the shore; heavily laden trucks were passing and repassing on the pier; and dozens of huge cranes, worked by countless coolies, were refilling the trucks as they returned empty. Thirty-five thousand human beings were daily being fed at Madras with cooked food or supplied with raw rice, but of these about two-thirds were taken in hand by benevolent rich natives. Kuddapah, Bellary, Kurnool, and other towns were also feeding a large number; some as many as 2,000 every day. As I left Madras the rail was blocked with trucks laden with grain. Indeed, all the districts near the railway are tolerably certain of being adequately relieved. But how is it to be conveyed to distant corners of the famine-stricken land? And, worse still, how is the 'water-famine' likely to ensue two or three months hence to be met? There is a large tank near here which usually contains fifteen feet of water, and is now nearly dry. Possibly partial showers of rain may yet fall in particular districts. At Trichinopoly, where I have recently been staying, more than three inches of rain fell on Sunday and Monday last. This downpour will, I trust, check the cholera already gaining ground there. Here at Madura scarcely any rain fell, while the adjoining district was being drenched.

It is evident, indeed, that the most severe trial has yet to come, and a hard task lies before the Collectors and Deputy-Collectors everywhere. They must not intervene with aid before the proper time, and they must by no means intervene too late. They have to inquire when and where and how relief is to be given, and they ought to provide work for all who are relieved. Many Collectors are at work from morning to night in their offices deciding these difficult questions.

Surely, then, I may be allowed to close this imperfect account of the distressing scenes through which I have lately passed by adding a tribute to the energy and devotion of our fellow-countrymen—the rulers of this land—who are everywhere exerting themselves to the utmost in the present crisis. Numbers who had a right to furlough, or were looking forward to a holiday at Delhi, are remaining cheerfully at their posts.

Indeed, my second visit to India has impressed me more than ever with the desire shown by the Queen's officers in this country to govern India righteously and to make our rule a blessing to the people. Evidences of the benefits we have conferred, and are still daily conferring, meet one at every turn. But I crave permission to add a word or two of warning. In our anxiety to conciliate the natives, let us beware of alienating our own officers. Let the Central Governments balance the scales evenly between the two. Our hold of India depends mainly on the personal influence of the representatives of those Governments in the several districts, and the personal influence of these representatives depends mainly on the degree of support they receive from the central seats of authority. Every Commissioner and Collector is a little Viceroy in his own territory. He has vast responsibilities laid upon him, and he ought to be trusted by his superiors. It is right that the British public should be made aware that while the Queen is being proclaimed Empress at Delhi, and the loyalty of her Indian subjects is being evoked by the holding of Darbārs and the distribution of rewards to deserving natives in every Collectorate, much irritation of feeling is apparent among her European subjects. Over and over again I have heard able officers exclaim, 'I dare not act on my own responsibility in this emergency. Cholera may break out; symptoms of serious riots may show themselves; people may be dying of famine; instant action is needed, but I dare not trust to my own life-long knowledge and experience of India—I must telegraph for instructions.' There can be no doubt that the energy of the most successful administrator will be paralyzed if he is made to feel that a single blunder or an act of indiscretion will be visited by a formal reprimand, which is sure to find its way into every native newspaper and become the talk of all the bazaars throughout his district. I much fear that the benefits which have accrued to India from the trust reposed by the old East India Company in its officers are in danger of being sacrificed to the present mania for the centralization of authority.

FURTHER ACCOUNT OF THE SOUTH INDIAN FAMINE OF 1876–77.

MADRAS, JANUARY 24, 1877.

IN my previous description of the famine now, unhappily, prevalent in the Deccan and Southern India, I expressed a doubt as to whether any organization for the relief of the sufferers, however complete, would be able to reach every corner of the immense area over which the drought and dearth extend. Now that I have travelled in various directions over a great part of the country from Bombay to Cape Comorin, and noted with my own eyes what is being done to spread a network of this organization over every separate district, so as to embrace the most remote places, I am bound to admit that my fears were unfounded. Indeed, it would be difficult to use exaggerated language in speaking of the zeal, ability, and devotion displayed by Indian civilians and other executive officials in the present emergency.

I have recently been staying with the energetic Collector of Salem (Mr. Longley), and early one morning I visited with him one of the Relief Camps now being constructed in the large district over the welfare of which he presides. The spot chosen for this Camp is an elevated piece of ground beautifully situated near a spring of excellent water, close under some chalk hills (supposed by the natives to be formed of the bones of the mythical bird Jaṭāyus, killed by Rāvaṇa when carrying off Sītā), and not far from the base of the Shervaroy Hills—the sanatarium of this part of India. On this ground nearly twenty long huts or sheds—each capable of accommodating forty persons—had already been constructed with bamboo poles, coarse cocoa-nut matting, and palmyra leaves. I was told that as only three months of the famine have passed, and at least four months have still to be provided for, it will be necessary to erect about 100 similar huts in this one Camp, with accommodation for 4,000 or 5,000 people.

In fact, these Relief Camps may be described as *temporary workhouses* with wards for the old, feeble, and infirm, where the famine-driven inhabitants of outlying districts will take refuge, and where they will be comfortably housed, fed, and, if strong enough, made to work, till better times arrive.

In Mr. Longley's camp the two classes of workers and non-workers into which every camp-community will be divided were plainly distinguishable from each other. The former were engaged in making new huts, breaking stones for a road, clearing the environs of the Camp, and keeping the whole place clean; while the non-workers were sitting on the ground in three rows, exposed, by their own choice, to the heat of a tropical sun for the sake of the warmth which insufficient food made necessary to them. It was piteous to see the emaciated old men and shrivelled old women, many of them blind or crippled, whose existence is being prolonged for a few months by the minimum of nourishment they are now receiving at the hands of a paternal Government; but still more sad to look upon the unclothed skeletons of young men, boys, and little children with drawn features, shoulder bones standing out, legs like thin sticks, and ribs enclosing the feeble organs of their shrunk bodies, like bony cages, every bar of which was visible.

Yet I was told that the great difficulty in Indian famines is not so much the effective distribution of relief as the effective application of any proper method of detecting the vast number of undeserving applicants who ought not to be relieved at all. We were informed that about 300 applicants for food, without work, ought to have been present on the day of our visit, but that more than half had run off during the night, either because they disliked the confinement to which they had been subjected, or because they had heard of the intended visit of the Collector and other Sahibs, and were filled with vague suspicions and fears of being questioned too closely. Yet no one is admitted to the Camp without a ticket, which is supposed to be given to deserving objects only. Those who were seated on the ground in our presence had empty earthenware bowls before them, in each of which about a pound of good boiled rice was placed while we looked on. This, with another meal administered in the evening, is held to be sufficient to keep the body and soul of a non-worker together. The workers are, of course, better fed. It was curious to observe the cleverness with which some of the recipients of the dole of boiled rice quietly pressed down the eagerly accepted ration with their hands, hoping thereby to be served with a little more than the due allowance. Each recipient then made a hole with his hands in the centre of his mess, and waited patiently till the half-pint of pepper-water (*mulliga tanir*), to which every one was entitled, had been poured into the cavity. Finally, by means of the spoons, with which every man was naturally provided, and in a manner which those only can understand who have seen a low-caste native seated on his hams with head bent back, mouth expanded to its utmost limits, and all four fingers and thumb converted into a convenient scoop for introducing into the aperture as much rice as a human being is capable of swallowing at once, every grain was disposed of before our eyes—in most cases with the utmost avidity and apparent satisfaction.

It is intended, I understand, that caste prejudices shall

be, as far as possible, respected. Those of the same caste will be grouped together in separate companies, and cooks of sufficiently high caste will be provided. But no genuine Brāhman is ever likely to enter a Relief Camp. He will rather starve than submit to the chances of pollution, which to him would be worse than death. Starving Brāhmans, who in some parts of the country may be even more plentiful than starving Śūdras, will have to be cared for by their own richer caste-fellows. I am sorry to have to add to this brief narrative that pestilence is following closely in the track of famine. Here at Madras three Europeans have recently succumbed to attacks of cholera, and the number of fatal cases among the natives is increasing every day. In some country towns and villages I have visited I have been cautioned to beware of a bad type of the disease prevalent all round. Of course, I could go into further details, but what I have written will, at least, give an idea of how the six or seven millions sterling which the present famine is likely to cost will be spent.

PĀRSĪ FUNERAL RITES AND THE PĀRSĪ RELIGION.

OBSERVANT European travellers, when they first arrive at Bombay, cannot fail to be struck with the interesting contrasts which everywhere meet the eye. Perhaps the most remarkable of such contrasts is that afforded by the different methods adopted by the adherents of different creeds for the disposal of their dead.

There in Bombay one may see, within a short distance of each other, the Christian cemetery, the Muhammadan graveyard, the Hindū burning-ground, and the Pārsī Dakhmas, or Towers of Silence. The latter, five in number, with a sixth—which is square instead of circular—used for criminals, are, as most Anglo-Indians know, at the summit of Malabar Hill, in a beautiful garden, amid tropical trees swarming with vultures. I obtained leave to visit these towers in the autumn of 1875, and again shortly after my second arrival in India last year.

A correct model of the principal tower was then kindly presented to me by order of Sir Jamsetjī Jījībhai, and a careful examination of its structure enables me to describe it with more accuracy than was possible after my first visit. I also obtained the correct dimensions from the Secretary. The chief tower may be described as an upright cylindrical stone structure, in shape and solidity not unlike a gigantic millstone, about fourteen feet high and ninety feet in diameter, resting on the ground in the centre of the garden. It is built, as I before stated, of solid granite, except in the centre, where a well, ten feet deep and about fifteen across, leads down to an excavation under the masonry, containing four drains at right angles to each other, terminated by holes filled with either charcoal or sand. Round the upper and outer edge of this circular structure, and completely hiding its upper surface from view, is a high stone parapet. This is constructed so as to seem to form one piece with the solid stone-work, and being, like it, covered with chunam, gives the whole erection, when viewed from the outside, the appearance of a low tower. Clearly, one great object aimed at by the Pārsīs in the construction of these strange depositories of their dead is solidity. We saw two or three enormous massive stones lying on the ground, which had been rejected by the builders simply because they contained almost invisible veins of quartz, through which it was possible that impure particles might find their way, and be carried, in the course of centuries, by percolating moisture, into the soil. Earth, water, and fire are, according to Zoroaster, sacred symbols of the wisdom, goodness, and omnipotence of the Deity, and ought never, under any circumstances, to be defiled. Especially ought every effort to be made to protect Mother Earth from the pollution which would result if putrefying corpses were allowed to accumulate in the ground (*Vandidād* iii. 27). Hence the disciples of Zoroaster spare neither trouble nor expense in erecting solid and impenetrable stone platforms fourteen feet thick for the reception of their dead. The cost of erection is greatly increased by the circumstance that the towers ought always to be placed on high hills, or in the highest situations available (*Vand.* vi. 93). I was informed by the Secretary that the largest of the five towers was constructed at an outlay of three lakhs of rupees.

The upper surface of the massive granite column is

divided into compartments by narrow grooved ridges of stone, radiating like the spokes of a wheel from the central well. These stone ridges form the sides of seventy-two shallow open receptacles or coffins, arranged in three concentric rings[1]. The ridges are grooved—that is, they have narrow channels running down their whole length, which channels are connected by side ducts with the open coffins, so as to convey all moisture to the central well and into the lower drains. The number three is emblematical of Zoroaster's three moral precepts, 'Good thoughts, good words, and good deeds' (*Vand.* v. 67), and the seventy-two open stone receptacles represent the seventy-two chapters of his Yaśna, a portion of the Zand-Avastā.

Each concentric circle of open stone coffins has a pathway surrounding it, the object of which is to make each receptacle accessible to the corpse-bearers. Hence there are three concentric circular pathways, the outermost of which is immediately below the parapet, and these three pathways are crossed by another conducting from the solitary door which admits the corpse-bearers from the exterior, and which must face the east, to catch the rays of the rising sun. In the outermost circle of the stone coffins, which stands for 'good deeds,' are placed the bodies of males; in the middle, symbolizing 'good words,' those of females; in the inner and smallest circle, nearest the well, representing 'good thoughts,' those of children. Each tower is consecrated with solemn religious ceremonies, and after its consecration no one, except the corpse-bearers—not even a high-priest—is allowed to enter.

On the occasion of my second visit I was accompanied,

[1] I hear from Mr. Cursetjee Rustamjee Cāma (who is a great authority on all points connected with his own religion) that all the Dakhmas have not seventy-two receptacles. Smaller towers have fewer receptacles. The number is not a fixed one, but depends on the needs of the place where a Dakhma is erected.

as before, by the courteous Secretary of the Pārsī Panchāyat, and was permitted to witness the funeral of a Mobed, or one of the second order of priests, whose flowing white costumes (supposed to be emblematical of purity) are everywhere conspicuous in the Bombay streets. I may here mention parenthetically that I believe the word Mobed is merely a corruption of a Zand word equivalent to Sanskṛit *Maga-pati*, 'chief of the Magians.' Dastūr, the name of the high-priest, is a modern Persian word, the best equivalent for which would perhaps be 'chief ruler.' The lowest order of priests, named Herbad[1], are not allowed to officiate at ceremonies. In the Zand-Avastā the whole priestly class are called Athravan (in Pāzand Athornan). In the present day the rest of the community—the laymen in fact, who are neither Dastūrs nor Mobeds nor Herbads—are styled Behadīn or Behdīn, that is, 'followers of the best religion.'

I reached the garden surrounding the towers about half an hour before sunset. At that time the funeral procession was already winding up the hill. The deceased man had died early in the morning, and a rule of the Pārsī religion requires that no corpse shall be exposed on the platform of the towers, to be consumed by birds of prey, unless the rays of the sun can first fall on it. Foremost in the procession walked a man carrying a loaf or two of bread wrapped up in a cloth. Then came the bier, which was flat and made of iron bars[2], having the body of the deceased stretched out upon it, covered only with a white

[1] Mr. Cāma informs me that Herbad properly means a religious teacher. Another name for a Herbad is Nāvar, which may possibly mean a new member of the ecclesiastical fraternity. The son of a priest is generally a Herbad. But he sometimes adopts a secular profession, discarding the white turban for a black one. In that case he generally abandons the name Herbad. In fact, priestly denominations have fallen into disrepute. The title Dastūr is applied ironically to every one with a white turban.

[2] In the case of a child it is a curved metal trough.

sheet, and borne by four bearers, followed by two assistants. These corpse-bearers are called *Nasasalār*. They are, of course, Pārsīs, but from the nature of their occupation are supposed to contract impurity, and are not associated with by the rest of the community. They are, however, well cared for and well paid.

After the bearers, at an interval of a few yards, followed a man leading a white dog, and behind him a long procession of at least a hundred priests in their robes of spotless white, besides relations of the deceased, also in white garments, walking in pairs, each couple following closely on the other, and each man connected with his fellow by a handkerchief held between them in token of sympathy and fellow-feeling. The procession advanced to a point about thirty yards distant from the portal of the largest tower. There it stood still for a minute while the dog was brought towards the corpse, made to look at the features of the dead man, and then fed with bread. This part of the ceremony is called *sag-dīd*. Meanwhile all who followed the bier turned round, and walked back to the *sagrī*, or house of prayer containing a fire-sanctuary, which is erected near the entrance to the garden. There they chanted prayers while the corpse-bearers entered the tower with the dead body, and exposed it naked in one of the receptacles on the stone platform. Their appointed task being then completed, they instantly quitted the tower, and were seen to repair to a reservoir of water near at hand, where they went through a process of thorough ablution, changing all their clothes, and depositing the cast-off garments in an open stone pit, almost hidden from view, on one side of the garden.

It is noteworthy that the fire-sanctuary of the *sagrī* has a window or aperture so arranged that, when the sacred fire is fed with sandal-wood fuel by the veiled priest, just before the corpse-bearers enter the tower, a ray from the flame may be projected over the dead body at the moment of its exposure. The theory is that the light of the sun and the light of the sacred fire ought to consecrate the mortal remains of the deceased before they are consumed by the birds. There is, at any rate, some poetical if not true religious sentiment in this hypothesis, and the bereaved relations appear to derive consolation from it; but whether the position of the sun and fire made this double consecration possible is doubtful. To us spectators on the occasion I am recording, it was evident that a beam from the setting sun and a ray from the sacred fire had barely opportunity to fall on the corpse at all; for scarcely had the bearers left the tower and closed the portal ere forty or fifty vultures, before seated motionless on the stone parapet, swooped down on their prey. In ten minutes they all flew back again. They had finished their work. The body was reduced to a skeleton before the mourners in the *sagrī* had finished their prayers. It should be mentioned that in three or four weeks after the funeral the bones are removed from the open coffin and reverently placed in the central well, where the dust of the dead, whether of high or low degree, is left to commingle undisturbed for centuries.

When I enquired about the meaning of the dog, I was told that, according to the teaching of Zoroaster, dogs as well as birds are regarded as sacred animals[1], and were formerly allowed to consume the dead bodies of Pārsīs. In the present day a representative dog kept for the purpose accompanies the corpse, and is fed with bread as a substitute for the flesh of the dead body. Moreover, dogs are supposed to possess some mysterious power in preserving the spirits of men from the attacks of demons[2];

[1] See *Vandidād* vii. 75, viii. 28; Bleeck's *Avesta*, Vol. I. pp. 104–109; Wilson's *Pārsī Religion*, pp. 325–328, 330.

[2] *Vandidād* (Bleeck) xiii. 25; Wilson's *Pārsī Religion*, pp. 49, 252.

and if the funeral dog is not fed, and made to look at the corpse, the soul of the deceased will assuredly be assailed by evil spirits during the three days which intervene between death and judgment.

I should state here that in the belief of the Pārsīs the soul of the deceased man is supposed to hover about in a restless state for the three days immediately succeeding death, in the neighbourhood of the Dakhmas, where also swarms of evil spirits congregate[1]. On the morning of the fourth day the soul is taken to judgment, which is passed on it by Mithra and the angels. It has then to pass a narrow bridge called *Chinvat-peretum*, 'the bridge where decision is pronounced.' The souls of the sinful, being unable to pass this bridge, imagined to be sharp as a razor, fall into hell on endeavouring to cross over. The Zand-Avastā even gives the names of certain dogs believed to protect the souls of men from the assaults of evil demons before crossing the bridge. The *Vandidād* (viii. 41, 42), moreover, states that the devil called Naśus is frightened away by a yellow dog with four eyes, and that such a dog ought to be led along the road of a funeral procession three times.

It is on this account, as was explained to me by a learned Pārsī, that the funeral dog is supposed to be four-eyed—that is to say, it is supposed to have two real eyes and two round spots like eyes, just above the actual eyes. I was told, too, that many yellowish-white dogs in India have this peculiarity, and that the Pārsīs try to procure such dogs, and keep them for their funeral processions. I observed nothing of the kind in the funeral dog on the occasion of the particular funeral I have here recorded;

[1] So at least says the Avastā, but according to Mr. Cāma the Pārsīs of the present day do not believe in the presence of evil spirits near the Dakhmas. He informs me that the Dakhmas of the Avastā were subterranean vaults and tombs, not towers.

but it struck me (before I knew that the same idea had occurred to German scholars) that the singular practice of leading a white dog at the head of the procession points to the common origin of the Pārsī and Hindū religions. For in the latter system the god of death, Yama, has two four-eyed brindled watchdogs, children of Saramā[1], who guard the road to his abode, and whose favour and protection against evil spirits are invoked every day by pious Hindūs when they perform the *kāka-bali*, or offering of rice to crows, dogs, and animals at the end of the *vaiśvadeva* ceremony before the midday meal. The mantra recited is as follows:—*Dvau śvānau śyāma-śabalau Vaivasvata-kulodbhavau tebhyām piṇḍo mayā datto rakshetām pathi māṃ sadā*, 'May the two dogs, dark and brindled, born in the family of Yama, protect me ever on the road! To them I present an offering of food.'

Having thus attempted to give some idea of the nature of a Pārsī funeral, and of the unique arrangements by which the Pārsīs endeavour to carry out the precepts of their prophet Zoroaster in the disposal of their dead, it will not be inappropriate if I add a brief account of Pārsī doctrines and of the initiatory ceremonies performed on admission of young Pārsīs to the Zoroastrian religion, and on their incorporation as members of the Pārsī society.

I may first mention that according to the pure form of the Zoroastrian faith—as propounded by learned Pārsīs of the present day—Ormazd (sometimes written Hormazd, contracted from the full expression Ahura Mazda) is the name of the Supreme Being, to whom there is no equal, and who has no opponent. It is a mistake to suppose

[1] Saramā is the dog of Indra, and is represented in *Ṛig-veda* X. 14. 10 as the mother of Yama's dogs, called in the *Mahābhārata*, *Ādi-parvan* 671, Devā-śunī. In the *Ṛig-veda* this dog is said to have tracked and recovered the cows stolen by the Paṇis. Saramā is even said to be the authoress of part of the *Ṛig-veda*, X. 108.

that Ormazd is opposed to a being called Ahriman, commonly regarded as the spirit of evil. The true doctrine is that Ormazd has created two forces in nature, not necessarily antagonistic, but simply alternating with each other—the one a force of creation, construction, and preservation; the other a force of decay, dissolution, and destruction. The first of these forces is named Spenta-mainyus, while the second or destructive power is commonly called Ahriman, or Hariman, for Anhra-mainyus (or *Anhro-mainyus*=Sanskṛit *Anho-manyu*). It is interesting to observe the analogy between the Hindū and Zoroastrian systems, Vishṇu and Rudra (Śiva) in the former being equivalent to Spenta-mainyus and Anhra-mainyus in the latter, while Brahma (neuter) corresponds to Ormazd. In later times the purity of the original doctrine became corrupted, and Ahriman was personified as a spirit of evil. In fact, all the evils in the world, whether moral or physical, are now attributed to Ahriman, while Ormazd is erroneously held to be the antagonistic principle of good.

It is contended that the Pārsī religion, in spite of its apparent dualism, is properly pure Monotheism, and that the elements and all the phenomena of Nature are merely revered as creations of the one God, and as symbolical of his power.

There can be little doubt, however, that with the majority of Pārsīs the elements are regarded as simple manifestations or emanations of the Deity, and that which is called Monotheism is really a kind of Pantheism very similar to that of Brāhmaṇism. The absence of all image-worship, however, is very refreshing after the hideous idolatry of the Hindū system.

So much for the Pārsī creed; and now for a few words as to the form of admission into the charmed circle of the Pārsī community.

It is a controverted point whether if any outsider

wished to become a Pārsī it would be possible, even in theory, to entertain the question of his being admitted to membership by his making public confession of his faith in the Zoroastrian system. As a matter of fact no one is at present allowed to become a Pārsī unless he is born a Pārsī. No provision seems to exist for the reception of converts, and the only form of admission is for the children of Pārsīs, though occasionally the children of non-Pārsī mothers by Pārsī fathers are permitted to become members of that community. Nevertheless it is certain, from a particular form of prayer still used by Pārsī priests, that Zoroaster himself enjoined on his disciples the duty of making proselytes, and had in view a constant accession of fresh adherents, who were all to be received as converts, provided they were willing to go through certain prescribed ceremonies.

With regard to the children of Pārsī parents, every boy is admitted to membership as a disciple of the Zoroastrian religion some time between the age of seven and nine, but more usually at seven years of age, in the following manner. He is first taken to one of the fire-temples, and in a room outside the sanctuary made to undergo a kind of baptism,—that is to say, he is placed nearly naked on a stone seat, and water is poured over his head from a loṭā by a Mobed appointed to perform the rite. Next, the child is taken out into an open area, made to sit on another stone seat, and required to eat one or two leaves of the pomegranate tree—a tree held very sacred by the Pārsīs, and always planted in the precincts of their fire-temples, for use in purificatory ceremonies (*Yaśna* viii. 4). After eating the leaves he is made to drink a small quantity of the urine of a bull—also kept at fire-temples, and held in high estimation for its purifying properties. This completes the first portion of the ceremony. The concluding act is performed in an apartment of the fire-temple, and consists in investing the child with the sacred shirt or under-garment (called *sadara*), and sacred girdle (called *kustī*). Several Mobeds, presided over by a Dastūr, are necessary to the due celebration of this part of the rite, which is very like the Hindū *upanayana*, or induction into the condition of a twice-born man by means of the *yajňopavīta*. They sit on the ground in a group, and the child is placed in the midst of them nearly naked. The sacred shirt is then put on, and the white woollen girdle fastened on around it, while the boy is made to repeat word by word the form of prayer which he is required to say ever afterwards, whenever the girdle is taken off or put on again (*Khurdah-Avastā* iv.). The sacred shirt and girdle are the two most important outward signs and symbols of Pārsīism, and an impostor laying claim to the privileges of the Zoroastrian religion would be instantly detected by the absence of those signs, or by his wrong use of them. But they are far more than outward signs,—they are supposed to serve as a kind of spiritual panoply. Unprotected by this armour a man would be perpetually exposed to the assaults of evil spirits and demons, and even be liable to become a demon himself. The shirt is made of the finest white linen or cambric. It has a peculiar form at the neck, and has a little empty bag in front to show that the wearer holds the faith of Zoroaster, which is supposed to be entirely spiritual, and to have nothing material about it. The second shirt has also two stripes at the bottom, one on each side, and each of these stripes is separated into three, to represent the six divisions of each half-year.

It has also a heart, symbolical of true faith, embroidered in front. The *kustī* or girdle is made of seventy-two interwoven woollen threads, to denote the seventy-two chapters of the Yaśna, but has the appearance of a long flat cord of pure white wool, which is wound round the body in three coils. Each end of the girdle is divided into three, and these three ends again into two parts. Every Pārsī ought to take off this girdle and restore it to its proper position round the body at least five times a day. He has to hold it in a particular manner with both hands; and touching his forehead with it to repeat a prayer in Zand invoking the aid of Ormazd (*Ahura-Mazda*) for the destruction of all evil beings, evil doers—especially tyrannical rulers—and imploring pardon for evil thoughts, evil words, and evil deeds. The girdle must then be coiled round the body three times and fastened with two particular knots (said to represent the sun and moon), which none but a Pārsī can tie in a proper manner. Every Pārsī boy is taught the whole process with great solemnity at his first initiation. When the ceremony is concluded the high-priest pronounces a benediction, and the young Pārsī is from that moment admitted to all the rights and privileges of perhaps one of the most flourishing and united communities in the world.

INDIAN AND EUROPEAN CIVILIZATION IN THEIR RELATION TO EACH OTHER AND IN THEIR EFFECT ON THE PROGRESS OF CHRISTIANITY.

THE kind of civilization to which I shall first advert is not that which we Englishmen have introduced into India, but that which has existed in India for at least three thousand years.

Of course very different ideas may be attached to the word civilization, and some may doubt whether, if religion is an ingredient of civilization, the Hindūs have ever possessed any true civilization at all. But when a people have a refined language, an extensive literature, an organized social system, fixed forms of government, with elaborate religious and philosophical systems, however false such systems may be, and have, moreover, made some progress in the arts and sciences, they may surely be called civilized, though their civilization may be very different in kind from that of other ancient peoples, or from that of modern Europe.

Doubtless every civilized nation is inclined to pride itself in its own institutions and to despise other countries. The Chinese, for example, look down with contempt on Europeans, and distinguish Englishmen in particular by epithets equivalent to foreign devils and uncivilized barbarians. Similarly, the Greeks called all other nations barbarians, and in the same way the Indians call us *Mleććhas*. This was originally a contemptuous term applied by the Indo-Āryans to those who could not pronounce their sacred Sanskṛit. It is now commonly applied by learned Hindūs to Europeans. But this term by no means represents the amount of disrespect in which the rulers of India are held by Brāhmans of the old school. I have met with bigoted Pandits, whose contempt for us and our boasted civilization, notwithstanding they travel by our railways, use our telegraphs, and live in security under our rule, and albeit they take pains to conceal their real estimate of our character, is, I am convinced, quite as great as the contempt of their forefathers for any non-Āryan savages, whether styled Dasyus or Nishādas.

I may mention, in illustration, that I often wondered, when in India, why certain great Pandits preferred calling on me very early in the morning, till I found out accidentally that, by coming before bathing, they were able afterwards to purify themselves by religious ablutions from the contamination incurred by shaking hands and talking with me.

Nor have the Muhammadans, as a rule, any greater respect for us, for our social institutions, or for our religion. When they are less scornful than usual they confine themselves to calling us *Kāfirs*, unbelievers. But in India this epithet scarcely represents the amount of contempt with which we are commonly regarded by bigoted Muslims. Many of them have been seen to spit on the ground on leaving the houses of eminent civilians, after interviews in which the most courteous expressions had been interchanged.

The point, then, which I wish to bring out strongly on the present occasion is, that the chief hindrance to the progress of Christianity among the people of India is their intense pride in their own supposed moral, religious, and even intellectual superiority. What says a member of the Brahma Samāj, in a letter written about a year ago to the editor of the *Times* newspaper—

'I am convinced,' he says, 'that the state of the poor in the Christian countries of Italy, France, and England (all of which countries I have visited), especially in the large towns, is infinitely more wretched, godless, degrading, and barbarous than it is in heathen India.'

The fact is, that the Hindūs believe that their whole national life and civilization, far from being heathenish, have been favoured above all countries with the special superintendence of the Supreme Being. Divine interposition commences with their very alphabet.

We in England think our A, B, C a very human invention, which we owe to the Phœnicians, whereas to a Hindū every stroke of his complicated characters is thought to be due to direct supernatural inspiration. His Devanāgarī alphabet, as its name implies, came directly from the gods.

In the same way all the other elementary processes which lay the foundations of knowledge are divinely superintended. The whole of a Hindū's education is regulated directly by his god's guidance. We are accustomed to regard our European grammars as very human, and mostly very imperfect productions, whereas to a Hindū the great grammar of Pāṇini—the source of all other grammars—is not only the perfection of linguistic analysis, but Pāṇini himself is an inspired sage, who did not compose his own grammar with the painful thought with which such works are commonly elaborated, but *saw* it supernaturally, the opening rules having been directly revealed to him by the god Śiva.

Then, when we pass on to language and literature, we in England take a pride in the gradual welding together of our native tongue into one compact whole by Saxon, Dane, and Norman, but a Hindū prides himself on the alleged fact that the divine Sanskṛit came ready-made from the goddess Sarasvatī.

Moreover, in matters of literature our ideas are far behind those of a pious Hindū. We admit a human element even in our most sacred Scriptures, whereas to a Hindū, not only is the Ṛig-veda believed to have issued like breath from the Self-Existent, but every one of a hundred other works, constituting what may be called the canon of Hindū revelation, is either attributed directly to his god, or is thought to be more or less written under special Divine superintendence.

For example, the moral and political code propounded by Manu was revealed to that inspired sage by Brahmā himself.

Then, as to social institutions, it is difficult for us Europeans, notwithstanding our own peculiar caste feelings, to understand how the pride of caste, as a Divine ordinance, interpenetrates the whole being of a Hindū. He believes that his god created men different in caste, as he created different kinds of animals. Nay more, in the Ṛig-veda the Brāhman is declared to be the *actual mouth* of Brahmā, soldiers are his *actual arms*, husbandmen his *actual thighs*, and Śūdras, or servants, issued from his feet. No wonder, then, that a Hindū looks upon his caste as his veritable god; and those very caste-rules which we believe to be a hindrance to his adoption of the true religion are to him the very essence of all religion, for they influence his whole life and conduct. And the lower the caste, the more do its members appear to regard the observance of its rules as an essential part of all religion and morality. To violate the laws of caste is the greatest of all sins.

For example, marriage is a Divine institution closely connected with caste. It is declared to be a *Sanskāra*, or sacramental purificatory rite. Every man, as soon as he is old enough, is under absolute religious obligation to have his own wife, and every woman her own husband. For a man not to marry, or to marry out of his caste, is, with rare exceptions, a positive sin, fraught with awful consequences in a future state. Husband and wife are sacramentally united. The wife is half her husband's body. They ought not to be parted, even by death.

Furthermore, all the caste-rules about food, its preparation, and the persons in whose company it may be eaten, are strictly a matter of religion. A Hindū abhors, as the most impious of beings, any one who allows himself unrestrained liberty in eating and drinking. Not only purity of blood, but religious purity also depends on purity of nutriment, and the distinction between lawful and unlawful food is even more observed as a Divine ordinance than it was with the Jews. No high caste will eat with a lower caste, and not even a low caste will eat with Christians.

Then, finally, in regard to the dead, funeral ceremonies among the Hindūs are of course solemn acts of religion, as in all other countries. But far more than this—the bodies of deceased Hindūs must be burnt by certain near relatives according to carefully prescribed rites, on pain of bringing misery on the disembodied spirits; and such rites must be repeated periodically. To maintain the perpetual memory of the dead, to make periodical offerings to the spirits of fathers, grandfathers, and great-grandfathers, is a peremptory religious duty.

But what are a Hindū's ideas about the nature of that God who thus superintends every act, and directs every step of his existence from the cradle to the grave? It is here that his pride in his own superiority may be said to culminate. The very point in which we think the Hindūs most mistaken is the very point in which they pride themselves most of all. We admit that they might, with reason, be proud of the perfection of their alphabet, of the symmetry of their language, of the poetry in their literature, of the subtlety of their philosophy, of the acuteness of their logic, of their invention of the ten arithmetical figures, of their advance in mathematics and science when all Europe was wrapped in ignorance, and even of the elevated sentiments in their moral code; but we cannot understand their being proud of their false ideas of the Supreme Being. The Hindūs, we affirm, have no knowledge of the true God. They have not one God, but many. They degrade their deities to the level of sinful creatures by the acts, characters, and qualities they attribute to them.

Yet the Hindūs themselves maintain that they are not polytheists at all, but worshippers of one God, who manifests Himself variously, and that they have conceived sublimer notions of this Deity than any other people, ancient or modern. 'Our sacred books,' say they, 'insist on the unity of the Supreme Being, and abound in the grandest descriptions of His attributes.'

He is 'the most Holy of all holies; the most Blessed of the blessed; the God of all gods; the Everlasting Father of all creatures; omnipotent, omniscient, omnipresent; He is the Life in all; the Father, Mother, Husband, and Sustainer of the world; the Birth, the Death of all; the Incomprehensible; the Ancient Sage, without beginning or end; the Universe's Maker; the one God hidden in all beings, and dwelling as a witness within their hearts.'

And are not we Christians bound to accept and approve such sublime descriptions of the attributes of the Deity, though we well know that in the books from which they are taken, abundant false conceptions are mingled with the true, and that a Hindū's boasted theïsm is simple pantheism, behind which, as behind an impregnable fortress, he retires whenever his polytheism and idolatry are attacked?

There is, however, one point left in which we think educated Indians must at last acknowledge themselves inferior to Christian nations. 'Your religion,' we affirm, 'leads to the grossest idolatry. Everywhere in India idol-worship and superstition are hideously rampant!' How great, then, is our astonishment when we are assured in India by the educated Hindūs that they are not really idol-worshippers. 'Worship *before* images, not *to* images,' say they, 'is practised by us as a condescension to weak-minded persons. The highest form of worship is the *Mānasa-pūjā* and the *Nirākāra-pūjā*—heart-worship and formless worship.'

Hear what Mr. Pramadā-Dās Mitra, of Benares, in a recent address delivered at the Benares Institute, replied to one who accused his fellow-countrymen of the grossest idolatry: 'If by idolatry,' he said, 'is meant a system of worship which confines our ideas of the Divinity to a mere image of clay or stone, which prevents our hearts from being elevated with lofty notions of the attributes of God—if this is what is meant by idolatry, we disclaim idolatry, we abhor idolatry, and deplore the ignorance and uncharitableness of those that charge us with this grovelling system.' And he then goes on to point out that, so far from worshipping material images, the Hindūs are too spiritual to believe even in the existence of matter, the only really existing essence being (according to a dogma of their philosophy) the one universal spirit, of which the numerous gods, represented by images, are but manifestations.

Clearly, then, the chief impediment to Christianity among Indians is not only the pride they feel in their own religion, but the very nature of that religion. For pantheism is a most subtle, plausible, and all-embracing system, which may profess to include Christianity itself as one of the phenomena of the universe. An eminent Hindū is reported to have said, 'We Hindūs have no need of conversion; we are Christians and more than Christians already.'

In short, it is the old story. Pride and self-complacency are the chief obstacles to the entrance of truth into the human mind. We go to the Hindūs with a true revelation and the good news of God's love and good-will towards them in becoming incarnate for their sakes, and we find that they claim to have possessed a true revelation of their own, incarnations of their own, and a more excellent way of salvation suited to themselves, long before Europe had any revealed religion at all.

I could proceed to point out other great hindrances in the Hindūs themselves, such as their peculiar mental constitution, their incapability of appreciating historical facts, their appetite for wild legends and monstrous exaggerations, their natural dislike to the doctrine of sanctification as the only evidence of regeneration; but it is time for me to come nearer home, and to direct attention to the hindrances arising from *our own self-complacency, our own pride in our own boasted civilization.*

Let me begin with the pride of race. It is now well known that, notwithstanding the recent demonstration of the original oneness of the Indo-Āryan and English races, there is at present little or no social blending between the rulers and the ruled in India. Both Indians and Englishmen may be equally in fault, and each lays the blame upon the other; but the simple fact is, that Indians and Englishmen keep as distinct from each other as oil and water. Even Christianity does not overcome this race feeling. It is, indeed, generally acknowledged that if a highly-educated Brāhman becomes a Christian, and thereby consents to sit at table with Christians, he ought to be admitted into the best European society, but the pride of race is generally too strong for the sense of duty, and I fear that, as a matter of fact, few English homes, except those of the missionaries, are really opened to high-caste converts.

Thus it arises that well-bred men, who are quite our own equals in rank and education, are deterred from an open profession of Christianity through the want of any respectable circle of society to which they can be admitted in the adopted religion. If the force of conviction compels them to seek baptism at any sacrifice, they are instantly excommunicated by their own community, and then, if no missionary family be near, have no choice except to live alone or put up with the society of low-born native converts, with whom, perhaps, they have nothing in common but their adopted faith.

Then there is the pride of knowledge. The English in India must, of course, be conscious of their superiority in civilization and scientific knowledge, but they bring discredit on Christianity and hinder the missionary cause when they take no pains to conceal their contempt for Hindūs and Muhammadans; and, forgetting that India was given to us to elevate rather than to humiliate, make them feel their own inferiority too keenly.

But perhaps the greatest hindrance arising from ourselves is the pride of religion. We cannot glory too much in our possession of the Gospel of Christ. God forbid that we should not glory in what we believe to be the only power of God unto salvation to Jew, Greek, Hindū, and Muhammadan! But if our love for our Gospel truth leads us to shut our eyes to the elements of truth that underlie all false religions, how are we even to approach those religions, much less bring any force of argument to bear upon them?

The missionary who goes to a believer in the Kurān or the Veda with the Holy Bible in his hand, has no choice but to search diligently for a common standpoint. 'Anything in your Bible,' the Mussulmān will say, 'which agrees with my Kurān I will accept, otherwise I will not even listen to it.' The same language will be held by the Hindū with regard to the Veda. It may, indeed shock Christians in this Christian country of ours to think of our missionaries placing the Bible on the same platform with the Kurān and the Veda; but there is really no alternative.

Young and enthusiastic missionaries must not be surprised, nor must we in England blame them, if they are forced to imitate St. Paul—to become Muslims to the Muslims, Hindūs to the Hindūs (without, however, giving up one iota of the truth which they themselves hold), in order that both Muslims and Hindūs may be won over to Christ.

And is there really no common ground for the Christian missionary, the Muhammadan, and the Hindū to stand upon? Are there not certain root-ideas in all religions which bear testimony to the original truth communicated to mankind? Hindūism, at any rate, may be shown to be a system which, on a solid basis of pantheism, has brought together almost every idea in religion and philosophy that the world has ever known. Even some of the greatest truths of Christianity are there, though distorted, perverted, caricatured, and buried under superstition, error, and idolatry.

And is it not a proof of the Divine origin of Christianity, and its adaptation to humanity in every quarter of the globe, that some of its grandest and most essential dogmas, and, so to speak, its root-ideas, do indeed lie at the root of all religions, and explain the problems of life which sages and philosophers in all ages of the world have vainly attempted to solve? Is it not the fact that all the gropings after truth, all the religious instincts, faculties, cravings, and aspirations of the human race which struggle to express themselves in the false religions of the world, find their only true expression and fulfilment—their only complete satisfaction—in Christianity?

When I began the study of Hindūism, I imagined that certain elementary Christian conceptions—such as the Fatherhood of God—the Brotherhood of God, and the indwelling of God in the human heart—were not to be found there, but a closer examination has enabled me to detect not only these, but almost every other rudimentary idea of our holy religion. They are nearly all to be found in Hindūism, like portions of adamantine granite beneath piles of shifting sedimentary strata, and they ought to be eagerly searched for by the missionary as a basis for his own superstructure.

Hindūism, in fact, is a mere general expression, invented by Europeans for all the innumerable phases of pantheistic worship which exist in India. And, verily, I believe that much has yet to be done before all the shapes, and, so to speak, dissolving views of this Protean system are thoroughly comprehended.

At any rate, we students of India (including missionary students) have not as yet produced, though we are trying to do so—witness the series of books just published by the Christian Knowledge Society—any thoroughly exhaustive and trustworthy account of Hindūism. We have not sufficiently studied it in its own sacred Sanskṛit. We under-estimate its comprehensiveness, its receptivity, its subtle compromising spirit, its recuperative hydra-like vitality; and we are too much given to include the whole system under sweeping expressions, such as 'heathenism' or 'idolatry,' as if every idea it contains was to be eradicated root and branch.

Again, our religious pride will operate prejudicially to the missionary cause if it leads us to expect a complete and universal adoption of our own form of English Christianity. We cannot indeed glory too much in our loved Church of England, in her organization and her Book of Common Prayer; but is our zeal altogether according to knowledge if we attempt to force the Act of Uniformity with too iron a hand on all our Indian fellow-subjects? Depend upon it, that when the fulness of time arrives, and the natives of India everywhere openly accept Christianity, they will construct for it a setting of their own. And bearing in mind that our religion originated in the East, and that the Bible itself is a thoroughly Eastern book, we shall not only expect, but joyfully acquiesce in an Indian framework for Indian Christianity.

I will merely allude to two other obvious hindrances which beset the missionary cause in India,—I mean our own divisions and our own inconsistencies. As to the first, after travelling from Kaśmīr to Cape Comorin, I am able to certify that I have found, as a general rule, Christians of all denominations working together harmoniously, and forgetting in their conflict with a common foe their own conflicts of opinion in unessential matters.

Still, grave differences have recently arisen in some localities; and I venture to submit that it may be well not to forget that in the first struggles of Christianity with the paganism of the Roman Empire, the one mark by which all Christians were singled out from the rest of the world was their love for each other. 'See how these Christians love one another.'

As to our inconsistencies, let me quote the same member of the Brahma Samāj. 'Why,' he says, 'do you not make more Christians among the respectable classes of society? Because there is little to recommend itself in your Christianity. Does it make your merchants honest men? Are their goods pure and unadulterated? Does it make your soldiers polite and moral?'

It is satisfactory, however, to note, as I have lately done, that although some professing Christians may still walk as if they were the enemies of the Cross of Christ, no glaring scandals are now common in India. Nor can it be said of us by the natives, as it was to Mr. Terry (the first English clergyman, I believe, who ever visited India) in 1616, 'Christian religion devil religion; Christian much drunk, Christian much do wrong, Christian much beat, Christian much abuse others.'

And surely there is comfort in the thought that our hindrances in India under our own friendly rule are not greater than the obstacles in Europe under the hostile Roman Empire: nor are they greater anywhere than they always have been everywhere and may be expected to continue. And is it not the case that a steadily advancing cause thrives best under impediments, and that success is only the last step in a series of failures, difficulties, and discouragements?

At any rate, it is certain that men may hinder and men may impede, but the living waters of the river of God's truth will flow on for ever. Nay more, it is certain that though barrier and embankment may obstruct their course, the heaped-up waters will only gather strength and volume, till, with accumulated force, they spread themselves irresistibly over every region of the habitable globe.

INDIAN MUHAMMADANISM IN ITS RELATION TO CHRISTIANITY, AND THE PROSPECTS OF MISSIONARY ENTERPRISE TOWARDS IT[1].

In my travels through India, I repeatedly passed from Hindū to Musalmān places of worship, and my spirit, troubled by the hideous idolatry witnessed in the temples of Vishṇu and Śiva, was instantly tranquillized by the severe anti-symbolism conspicuous in all the surroundings of Muhammadan mosques.

It is true that the transition was a little too abrupt. The atmosphere and aspect of the mosque seemed to strike me with a sudden chill; I appeared to have jumped from tropical glare to Arctic ice. But when I beheld the earnest bearing of Muslims prostrating themselves in adoration on the cold stone, and apparently worshipping God in spirit, if not in truth, I felt that there was nothing in the outward appearance of either building or worshippers incompatible with the spirit of Christian prayer. Nay more—I felt as I watched the devout Muslims, that I also might have prayed in the same place in my own way, and even learnt from them to pray with more solemnity and reverence of manner than I had ever before practised.

On such occasions I frequently asked myself the question—How is it that the attitude of Islām towards Christianity is far more hopelessly hostile than that of the other two great false systems of the world, Brāhmanism and Buddhism? Have we not read of hundreds and

[1] Speech at the Croydon Church Congress, October 1877.

thousands of Hindūs and Buddhists converted by Christian Missionaries? but where are the Muslims? Why is it that so few Muhammadans are found to give glory to God in the knowledge of Christ? We are verily guilty concerning forty-one millions of our Indian brethren; and we are bound to search and try our ways, and see where our fault lies.

In the first place, how do we meet the present intolerant bearing of Islām towards other religions? Our Government is wisely neutral, but in our Missionary efforts are we not inclined to fight Islām with its own weapon? do we not sometimes oppose intolerance by intolerance?

There is, I admit, a false and true tolerance. But do we bear with all that we can, and denounce as little as we can in a system whose founder, however fiercely intolerant of idolaters, never denounced the Founder of our own religion?

In an excellent work by a faithful Missionary, recently published[1], I find it advocated that the attitude of Christianity towards the religions of India, ought to be one of true intolerance. And what is his reason? 'Because,' he says, 'there is none other name under heaven but one, given among men, whereby we must be saved.'

But need we give up one iota of this precious truth, because we welcome everything good in Muhammad's system, and because we hold that we can best overcome the uncompromising intolerance of modern Muslims by confronting it with the charity and forbearance of our Lord Himself, and the first Missionaries, His Apostles?

Let us not forget, too, that however bitter the feelings of hostility now displayed by the followers of Muhammad towards the followers of Christ, the attitude of Muhammad himself towards Christ Himself and the Gospel, as exhibited in the Kurān, was not only tolerant, but friendly

[1] Robson's 'Hindūism, and its relation to Christianity,' p. 297.

and reverential[1]. Indeed, the more I have reflected on the present want of success in winning Musalmāns to our own most holy faith, the more surprise have I felt that we do not oftener advance to meet them on the common ground which belongs to the Bible and the Kurān—that we do not oftener remind them that the Kurān itself exalts Christ above humanity and teaches a manifold connexion between Islām and the Gospel.

We ought to bear in mind that the people we call Muhammadans call themselves Muslims, that is, persons who were taught by Muhammad to believe that salvation consists in holding as cardinal doctrines the Unity of God, and resignation to His Will. Muhammad himself never claimed to be the originator of these doctrines, and never allowed them to be called by his name. He was, in his own view of his own mission, the latest of four prophets (the others being Moses, Elias, and Christ), who were all followers of Abraham, the true founder of the doctrine of Islām[2], and were all Muslims, because all preached the Unity of God and submission to His Will.

O for more of the wisdom and courage of the great

[1] Sir William Muir (p. 157 of his excellent work, 'The Life of Mahomet') shows that no expression regarding either the Jewish or Christian Scriptures ever escaped the lips of Muhammad other than that of implicit reverence. Both Jews and Christians, however, are repeatedly accused of having falsified certain texts (see Kurān, Sūra II. 39, 134).

Islām was really an illegitimate child of Judaism, and Muhammad owed much of the sternness of his monotheism to the teaching of the Jews. Christians as well as Jews are styled in the Kurān 'people of the Book.' The Pentateuch, and sometimes the whole Old Testament, is called Taurāt, and the New Testament Injīl. All three—the Law, the Gospel, and Kurān—are spoken of as the Word of God, and belief in them is enjoined on pain of hell, but the Kurān, according to Muhammad, was the latest revelation. See Kurān, Sūra III. 2; V. 52. The miraculous birth of Christ is asserted in Sūra III. 40-42.

[2] Muhammad always called Abraham the first of Muslims. Islām and Muslim are from the same Arabic root *salama* signifying 'to submit to God's Will,' 'to trust in God.'

Apostle of the Gentiles! Were he at this moment unfolding before Muslims the unsearchable riches of Christ, would he not begin by saying, 'I also, like Abraham, am a Muslim. I believe as strongly as you do in the Unity of God. I resign myself as submissively as you do to the Will of God. Whatsoever things are good, are true, are lovely, are of good report in your system, I think on them, I accept them, I welcome them, nay more, I call on you to hold them fast'?

And ought not every Missionary to begin by meeting the Muslim on the ground of his own Kurān, for the very reason that he may more effectually combat its soul-destroying errors.

I fear that the present position of the Church Militant on earth is making cowards of us all. We shrink from Unitarian Islām as if we dreaded the infection of a disease easily communicated. We are living in the midst of malarious influences—some outside, some inside our camp. Every man suspects the soundness of his neighbour's religious opinions. What excites especial alarm in our Indian Mission-fields is the spread of theistic and pantheistic ideas among educated natives. Even the religious atmosphere of Europe is believed to be largely impregnated with the subtle germs of many forms of deistic and materialistic philosophy. In our dread of wandering unguardedly into the neighbourhood of these contagious errors we are doubtless rightly careful to take our stand firmly on the sure foundation of the divinity of God the Son. But ought we on that account to insist less forcibly on the doctrines of God's Fatherhood and of Christ's humanity which equally lie at the very foundation of sound Christianity?

I trust I shall not be misunderstood if I venture as a layman deferentially to inquire why it is that nearly every sermon I have heard for many years, whether in

India or England, has been eloquent of God the Son—few sermons of God the Father, and God the Holy Spirit? Why is Christ so constantly held up to believers and unbelievers as the one God—so rarely as the Man Mediator leading us by one Spirit unto the Father?

We cannot, indeed, wonder that deeply religious Christians should concentrate their affections on the Saviour of the world. Nor can they render to the world's Redeemer more love than is His due. Yet it seems to me that in combating Unitarianism in our Indian brethren we may possibly ourselves be fairly charged with lapsing into a subtle form of Unitarianism, if we habitually place the One Mediator in the position of the One God.

Let me not be mistaken. I trust no one believes more firmly than I do in the necessity for insisting on Christ's Divine nature. But I am persuaded that if we would achieve more success in our Missionary dealings with Muhammadans, our first care should be to convince them that Christianity alone satisfies the yearnings of the human heart for mediation and atonement, because Christianity alone presents us with the One perfect Mediator between God and men, the Man Christ Jesus.

For if Muslims admit that their own prophet believed himself to be an imperfect man who needed every day to pray for the pardon of his own sins[1], they are on that very account more likely to be impressed with the contrast, when we set before them Christ as the One perfect Representative of our race,—the One divine Mediator whose atonement was efficient, because He was in all points tempted like as we are, yet without sin.

Depend upon it that in seeking to win Muslims to the true faith, we require to cultivate more of the wisdom of the serpent. We require to creep into their hearts by

[1] See Kurān, Sūra XLVIII. 2.

a frank admission of the Unity of the Godhead, and of the excellence of Muhammad's teaching in regard to this and other doctrines. We may then perhaps induce them to meet us half-way—to relax a little of their stern monotheism—to concede that sinful man's necessity may have acted, like a prism on light, to exhibit a triple manifestation of the One God; and so may cautiously, tenderly, gradually, lead them on to a full sense of the complex existence of the Almighty Being Who created us in His own Image, and to an unqualified acceptance of the great central dogma of our Church. But even when we have brought the need of an everliving Mediator and eternal Paraclete home to their hearts, we may wisely hesitate to force upon them, before they are able to bear it, the acceptance of merely ecclesiastical terms not found in our Bible.

I know that we members of the Church of England are rightly jealous for the term Trinity. I know that half the Sundays of the ecclesiastical year remind us of our Trinitarian creed. I know, too, that we rightly fence round our great central doctrine with every possible ecclesiastical safeguard. But in our first efforts for the conversion of Muslims, we shall be equally right to bear in mind that the language of the Bible preceded the Book of Common Prayer, that Christ Himself declared the first of the commandments to be, 'The Lord our God is One Lord,' that in the first Article of our Church, and in all our Creeds, the Unity of the Godhead is asserted before the triple Personality.

Before I conclude let me express a doubt whether we Christians, who claim divine inspiration for the Bible, believed by us to be the only true Word of God, delivered through the minds of men, are quite as fair as we ought to be towards the book believed by Muhammadans to be a record of the actual words of the Almighty.

In travelling from Kaśmīr to Cape Comorin, I scarcely met a single Missionary who professed himself conversant with the language in which the Kurān is written. His chief knowledge of the book, held to be the direct word of God by forty-one millions of our Indian fellow-subjects, is derived from translations made by Christians who utterly disbelieve even its partial inspiration.

Moreover, although innumerable commentaries on the Kurān have been written in Arabic by pious Muslims, not a single one is generally studied by our Missionaries, nor has a single one ever been translated into English[1], nor do our Missionaries think of accepting any other interpretations of difficult passages than those given by unbelieving Christians.

I ask then what should we think of Indian Musalmāns if, after organizing a mission to convert England to Islām, they were to send us Missionaries who judged of our Bible not from their own knowledge of the original text, or even of our own English translation, but from translations into Indian languages made by unbelieving Muslims?

Or again, if Musalmān controversialists were to interpret all the difficulties of our sacred Scriptures, not from the point of view of such Christian writers as Butler, Pearson, or Hooker, but from that of hostile Muslim commentators?

One reflection more before I conclude. If the self-deluded but fervent-spirited Muhammad, whose whole soul was stirred within him when he saw his fellow-townsmen wholly given to idolatry, had been brought into association with the purer forms of Christianity—if he had ever

[1] The two Arabic Commentaries of highest repute, and indispensable for a right understanding of the Kurān, are those of Zamakhsharī and Baidhāwī, the latter especially valuable for grammatical and historical explanations. There are excellent editions of these Commentaries by Lees and Fleischer, but no English translation. Two other well known Commentaries are by the two Jalālu 'd-dīns.

listened to the true ring of the Gospel—if, from the examples which crossed his path he had formed a correct ideal of the religion of Christ, he might have died a martyr for the truth, Asia might have numbered her millions of Christians, and the name of a Saint Muhammad might have been recorded in the calendar of our Book of Common Prayer.

As it was, alas! the only Christianity presented to the Arab enthusiast, thirsting for the well of living water, was that adulteration of the truth prevalent in the seventh century, which he believed it his mission to supplant by a purer system. It has somewhere been affirmed that the religion of Jesus, and the precepts of the Gospel, may be found scattered piecemeal through the pages of the Kurān. What should rather be alleged is that the religion of a spurious Jesus, and the precepts of a spurious Gospel, may be extracted from such parts of Muhammad's pretended revelations as were communicated to him by the followers of a debased form of Christian doctrine.

Think, then, of the difference in the present condition of the Asiatic world, if the fire of Muhammad's eloquence had been kindled, and the force of his personal influence exerted on the side of veritable Christianity.

Ought not this thought to intensify the sense of responsibility in those of us who are living among Muhammadans? What examples are Christians setting in Muhammadan countries? What ideal of Christianity are they presenting to millions of Muslims in our own Indian territories?

If the pages of the Kurān are ever submitting to the pious Musalmān, who yearns like ourselves for a perfect Mediator, the image of a counterfeit Christ and a counterfeit Gospel, the spuriousness of the copy will not be so clearly manifested by argument and controversy as by the exhibition of a true reflection of the Divine Original in the lives, acts, and words of Christian men.

THE THREE RELIGIONS OF INDIA COMPARED WITH EACH OTHER AND WITH CHRISTIANITY.

LET me begin by declaring my conviction that the time is approaching, if not already arrived, when all thoughtful Christians will have to reconsider their position, and, so to speak, readjust themselves to their altered environments.

Be it observed, I do not say readjust their most holy faith—not the faith once for all delivered to the saints, which cannot change one iota with changing circumstances—but readjust themselves. All the inhabitants of the globe are being rapidly drawn together by facilities of communication, and St. Paul's grand saying, that God has made all nations of the earth of one blood, is being brought home to us more forcibly every day.

Steam-presses, railroads, electric telegraphs, telephones, are producing effects quite without a parallel in the records of the past, and imposing on us Englishmen, the principal colonizers of the world, new duties and responsibilities.

A mighty stir and upheaving of thought is shaking the foundations of ancient creeds to their very centre; and those not reared on the living Rock are tottering and ready to fall. Thinkers, speakers, and writers, Christian and anti-Christian, throughout Europe, America, and Asia, are eagerly interchanging ideas on all the unsolved problems that have for ages baffled the powers of the human mind.

Christians, whether they will or no, are forced to regard the most sacred questions as admitting of other points of view besides their own. Christianity itself is tested like everything else—its time-honoured records placed (so to speak) in the crucible; its cherished dogmas submitted to that potent solvent—Reason.

Muslims, Brāhmans, Pārsīs, and even Buddhists and Confucianists, no longer ignore our Bible, presented to them in their own languages. Intelligent and educated adherents of these creeds are found to look upon Christianity with respect, though they regard it from their own respective stand-points, and examine it by the light of their own hereditary knowledge and traditional doctrines.

In fact, a conviction is everywhere deepening in men's minds, that it is becoming more and more the duty of all the nations of the world to study each other; to inquire into and compare each other's systems of belief; to avoid expressions of contempt in speaking of the sincere and earnest believers in any creed; and to search diligently whether the principles and doctrines which guide their own faith and practice rest on the true foundation or not.

And thus we have arrived at an important epoch in the history of the human race. Thoughtful men in the East and West are fairly trying to understand each other's opinions, and impartially weighing all that can be said in favour of every religion opposed to their own.

And we Christians are taking the lead, and setting the example. We are labouring to translate our own Holy Scriptures into all the languages of the world. We are sparing no expense in printing and distributing them lavishly. We are saying to unbelievers everywhere: 'Read, mark, learn,' judge for yourselves.

But this is not all. We are doing for the adherents of other religious systems what they are slow to do for themselves. We are printing, editing, translating, and publishing the ancient books which claim to be the inspired repositories of their several creeds. And thus to us Christians is mainly due that now, for the first time, it is possible for the adherents of the four chief antagonistic systems prevalent in the world—Christianity, Brāhmanism, Buddhism, and Islām—to study each other's dogmas in the books held sacred by each.

Here, then, we have before us four sets of books. First, and in the forefront, our own *Holy Bible.* All honour to our 'Bible Society!' this sacred book, which we hope may one day be carried into every corner of the globe, has already been translated into 210 languages; and if we include the labours of other societies, 296 different versions of it exist. Secondly, the *Veda*, a word meaning *knowledge*, on which Brāhmanism rests. There are four Vedas (namely, Rig, Yajur, Sāma, and Atharva, written in an ancient form of Sanskṛit), each containing three divisions—*Mantra*, *Brāhmaṇa*, and *Upanishad*—nearly all of which have been edited and nearly all translated. Besides the four Vedas there are the eighteen Purāṇas which constitute the bible of popular Hindūism. Thirdly, we have the *Tri-piṭaka*, or three baskets, that is, the three collections of writings on which Buddhism rests (written in an ancient language of the Sanskṛit family, called Pāli). Three important portions of these collections have been edited by European scholars, and recently translated into English. They are called the *Dhamma-pada*, 'Precepts of Law;' *Sutta-nipāta*, 'occasional discourses;' *Jātaka*, 'previous births of the Buddha.' Fourthly, we have the *Kurān*, in Arabic, a word meaning '*the book to be read by all*,' on which, as every one knows, Islām rests, and of which Sale's excellent English translation has been long available.

I now give specimens of select passages from the Veda and Purāṇas, from the Tri-piṭaka, and from the Kurān.

From the Atharva-Veda (IV. 16).

The mighty Varuṇa, who rules above, looks down
Upon these worlds, his kingdom, as if close at hand.
When men imagine they do ought by stealth, he knows it.
No one can stand, or walk, or softly glide along,
Or hide in dark recess, or lurk in secret cell;
The God detects him, and his movements spies.
Two persons may devise some plot, together sitting
In private and alone, but *he*, the king, is there—
A third—and sees it all. This boundless earth is his,
His the vast sky, whose depth no mortal e'er can fathom.
Both oceans find a place within his body, yet
In that small pool he lies contained. Whoe'er should flee
Far, far beyond the sky, would not escape his grasp,
His messengers descend, for ever traversing
This world and scanning with a thousand eyes its inmates.
Whate'er exists within this earth, and all within the sky,
Yea, all that is beyond, the mighty king perceives.

From the Kaṭha Upanishad (Vallī 2).

The good, the pleasant, these are separate ends.
The one or other all mankind pursue,
But those who seek the good, alone are blest.
The careless youth, by lust of gain deceived,
Knows but one world, one life; to him the Now
Alone exists, the Future is a dream.
The highest aim of knowledge is the soul;
This is a miracle, beyond the ken
Of common mortals, thought of though it be,
And variously explained by skilful teachers.
Who gains this knowledge is a marvel too;
He lives above the cares—the griefs and joys
Of time and sense—seeking to penetrate
The fathomless unborn eternal essence.
The slayer thinks he slays, the slain
Believes himself destroyed, the thoughts of both
Are false, the soul survives, nor kills, nor dies;
'Tis subtler than the subtlest, greater than
The greatest, infinitely small, yet vast,
Asleep, yet restless, moving everywhere
Among the bodies—ever bodiless—
Think not to grasp it by the reasoning mind;
The wicked ne'er can know it: soul alone
Knows soul, to none but soul is soul revealed.

From the Vishṇu-purāṇa (V. 23).

Lord of the Universe, the only refuge
Of living beings, the alleviator
Of pain, the benefactor of mankind,
Show me thy favour and deliver me
From evil; O creator of the world,
Maker of all that has been and will be,
Of all that moves and is immovable,
Worthy of praise, I come to thee, my refuge,
Renouncing all attachment to the world,
Longing for fulness of felicity—
Extinction of myself, absorption into thee.

From the Tripiṭaka (*Dhamma-pada*).

Conquer a man who never gives, by gifts;
Subdue untruthful men by truthfulness;
Vanquish an angry man by gentleness;
And overcome the evil man by goodness.

The following is a prophecy from the Lalita-vistara of what the Buddha was to do for the world (translated by Dr. John Muir).

The world of men and gods to bless,
  The way of rest and peace to teach,
  A holy law thy son shall preach—
A law of stainless righteousness.

By him shall suffering men be freed
  From weakness, sickness, pain, and grief,
  From all the ills shall find relief
Which hatred, love, illusion, breed.

His hand shall loose the chains of all
  Who groan in fleshly bonds confined;
  With healing touch the wounds shall bind
Of those whom pain's sharp arrows gall.

His potent words shall put to flight
  The dull array of leaden clouds
  Which helpless mortals' vision shrouds,
And clear their intellectual sight.

By him shall men who, now untaught,
  In devious paths of error stray,
  Be led to find a perfect way—
To final calm at last be brought.

From the Tri-piṭaka (*Sutta-nipāta*).

How can a man who has fallen into a river, having bottomless water and a swift-flowing current, being himself carried away, and following the current, cause others to cross it?

As one, skilful, attentive, and acquainted with the mode of steering, going on board a strong ship provided with oars and rudders, causes by means of it many others to cross the ocean; even so he who has attained the knowledge of religious paths, being devoted to meditation, very learned, and of an unmoved nature, can teach others who listen with attentive ears to his preaching.

Drinking of the water of a life of seclusion and of the water of subjugating the passions, drinking also of the pleasant beverage called the perception of truth, one becomes freed from emotion and sin.

Thou art the Buddha, thou art the Teacher, thou art the Vanquisher of the evil one (*Māra*), thou art the Sage; having cut off all thoughts, and crossed the sea of repeated births, thou hast taken over these beings to the other shore.

From the Kurān (Chapters II, VIII).

To God belongeth the east, and the west; therefore, whithersoever ye turn to pray, there is the face of God; for God is omnipresent, and omniscient. And when he decreeth a thing, he only saith unto it, 'Be,' and it is.

The Jews say, The Christians are grounded on nothing, and the Christians say, The Jews are grounded on nothing; yet they both read the scriptures. But God shall judge between them on the day of the resurrection, concerning that about which they now disagree.

Verily the true believers are those whose hearts fear when God is mentioned, and whose faith increaseth when his signs are rehearsed unto them, and who trust in their Lord; who observe the stated times of prayer, and give alms out of that which we have bestowed on them. These are really believers. They shall have superior degrees of felicity with their Lord, and forgiveness, and an honourable position.

O true believers! answer God and his apostle, when he inviteth you unto that which giveth you life; and know that God goeth between a man and his heart, and that before him ye shall be assembled.

O true believers! deceive not God and his apostle, neither violate your faith, against your own knowledge. And know that your wealth and your children are a temptation unto you, and that with God there is a great reward.

Having, then, these books before us, it is clear that we ought not to despise documents held sacred by our fellow-creatures, as if they were too contemptible even to be glanced at from the elevated position on which we stand. Rather are we bound to follow the example of the great Apostle of the Gentiles—who, speaking to Gentiles, did not denounce them as atheists or idolaters, but appealed to them as Δεισιδαιμονεστέρους, very God-fearing; and even quoted one of their own poets in support of a Christian truth—and who, writing to Christians, enjoined them not to shut their eyes to anything true, honest, just, pure, lovely, and of good report, wherever it was to be found; but that if there was any virtue anywhere, or any praise anywhere, they were to think on these things.

And have not we Englishmen, in particular, to whose rule India has been committed, special opportunities and responsibilities, brought as we are there into immediate contact with these three principal religious systems—Brāhmanism, Buddhism, and Islām?

Let us look for a moment at any modern map of India. The first glance shows us that it is not one country but many. Nor has it one race, language, and religion, but many races, languages, and religions. Mr. R. N. Cust, late a distinguished member of the Bengal Civil Service, and a member of the Legislative Council at Calcutta, has recently published a map of India (including all the territories subject to British imperial authority) in which the boundaries of all the languages are marked out. It is accompanied by a table which classifies the languages under eight heads. These are as follow:—(1) Āryan, 20; (2) Drāviḍian, 12; (3) Kolarian, 7; (4) Tibeto-Burman, 56; (5) Khasi, 1; (6) Tai, 5; (7) Mon-Anam, 5; (8) Malayan, 33; in all, 139 distinct languages. At least 100 dialects are not included in the above classification. We may safely affirm, therefore, that the languages and dialects of India amount to at least 200.

Its population, according to the recent census, now exceeds 240,000,000.

Of these, about 185,000,000 are Hindūs, nominal adherents of Brāhmanism.

Then, secondly, nearly 41,000,000 are Muhammadans, adherents of Islām—so that England is by far the greatest Muhammadan power in the world, and the Queen reigns over about double as many Muslims as the representative of the Khalīfs himself.

Then, thirdly, there are about 3,000,000 Buddhists, including the Jains (whose peculiar tenets and sacred scriptures are described at p. 94). This will appear a small number to those who are aware that there are nearly 500,000,000 nominal Buddhists now in the world, the numbers of nominal Christians being far less—only about 360,000,000.

Nevertheless, the original home of Buddhism was India, which it did not finally leave till about the eighth or ninth century of our era. It is now found in Ceylon, Burmah, Nepāl, Assam, and scattered here and there throughout India in the form of its near relative, Jainism.

For what purpose, then, has this enormous territory been committed to England? Not to be the 'corpus vile' of political, social, or military experiments; not for the benefit of our commerce, or the increase of our wealth—but that every man, woman, and child, from Cape Comorin to the Himālaya mountains, may be elevated, enlightened, Christianized.

Let us now, therefore, briefly inquire what are the leading ideas which characterize these chief religions of the world, as represented in India; and in doing so let us rise from the false to the true.

1. To begin with Brāhmanism.

This has two sides—two aspects—and a vast chasm separates the two. One is esoteric, the other exoteric; one is philosophical, the other popular; one is for the few, the other for the many.

What, then, is the highest or philosophical form of Brāhmanism? Its creed, which rests on the Upanishad portion of the Veda, has the merit of extreme simplicity. It may be described in two words: Spiritual Pantheism; or, in the original Sanskṛit, Ekam eva advitīyam, *One only Being, no second*—that is, nothing really exists but the one self-existent Spirit, called Brahma (neuter); all else is Māyā, or *illusion*. In other words, nothing exists but God, and everything existing is God. You, he, and I are God. We do not know that we are God, because God wills for a time to ignore Himself. When this self-imposed ignorance ceases, all distinction of personality vanishes, and complete oneness of being is restored. This is true philosophical Brāhmanism—*the unity of all being.*

An enormous gulf separates this pure pantheism from the popular side of Brāhmanism, which may be called Hindūism, and which rests on the Purāṇas, and is practically polytheism. But the gulf is bridged over by the word emanation. In the philosophical creed, everything is identified with Brahma; in the popular, everything emanates from Brahma. Stones, plants, animals, men, superior and inferior gods, good and bad demons, and every conceivable object, issue from the one self-existent universal soul, Brahma, as drops from the ocean, as sparks from fire. Men emanate in fixed classes. They cannot alter their social status in each separate existence. Born Brāhmans, they must remain Brāhmans; born soldiers, they must remain soldiers; born tillers of the ground, they must remain tillers of the ground; born menials, they must remain menials.

But what of stones, plants, animals? The spirit of men may pass into any of these, if their actions condemn them to fall in the scale of being; or, on the other hand, it may rise to gods.

And what of gods? There have been direct emanations from the Supreme Being in the form of personal gods: and it is noteworthy that these divine personalities are generally grouped in threes or multiples of three. In the Veda we have sometimes three principal gods, sometimes thirty-three gods named. The Vedic triad consists of—1. *Indra*, or the atmosphere personified; 2. *Agni*, Fire; 3. *Sūrya*, the Sun. The latter and better known triad consists of—1. *Brahmā* (masculine), the Creator; 2. *Vishṇu*, the Preserver; 3. *Rudra-Śiva,* the Dissolver of the world, and its reproducer.

This leads to the doctrine of Incarnation. The god Vishṇu, as Pervader and Preserver, passes into men to deliver the world from the power of evil demons.

His most popular and best known incarnations are those of Kṛishṇa and Rāma. The history of Rāma is told in the great epic poem called Rāmāyaṇa.

Again, many stories of miracles worked by Kṛishṇa—the other principal incarnation of the god Vishṇu—are told in the second great epic, called Mahā-bhārata. He is there represented as fighting with and destroying many evil demons, notably one in the form of a serpent (Kāliya), on whose head he is sometimes depicted as trampling.

What, then, is the end of Brāhmanism? Men, animals, plants, stones, pass through innumerable existences, and may even rise to gods. But gods, men, animals, plants, and every conceivable emanation from the supreme Soul, aim at, and must end by, re-absorption into their source, Brahma. This is Brāhmanism.

2. Turn we now to *Buddhism.*

Buddha was the son of a king who reigned in Kapilavastu, a little east of Oudh and south of Nepāl. He was, therefore, of the royal caste. The name Buddha is merely a title meaning *the Enlightened One.* His other names are Gautama, Śākya, Siddhārtha. He lived about

500 years B.C.; that is, about contemporaneously with Pythagoras, Zoroaster, and Confucius—all wonderful men. He was a great reformer of Hindūism; but it is a mistake to suppose that he aimed at an entire abolition of Brāhmanism, with the philosophical side of which his system had really much in common. His mission was to abolish caste, to resist sacerdotal tyranny, to preach universal charity and love, and to enjoin self-mortification and self-suppression through perhaps millions of existences, as the only means of getting rid of the evils of life and self-consciousness by an extinction of all being. He was himself the model of a perfect ascetic. He never claimed to be a god, but only the ideal of that perfection of self-subjugation to which every man might attain.

The Buddha had himself passed through millions of births, and was about to become extinct; but before his own attainment of Nirvāṇa, or annihilation, was enabled, by perfect knowledge of the truth, to reveal to the world the method of obtaining it. He died, and exists no more. He cannot, therefore, be worshipped. His memory only is revered. Temples are erected over his relics, such as a hair or a tooth. The Dathāvanśa, a history of one of his teeth, has recently been translated from the Pāli. In the same manner every man must pass through innumerable existences, rising or falling in the scale, according to his conduct, until he also attains Nirvāṇa, and becomes extinct. The Buddha once pointed to a broom in a corner, which he said had, in a former birth, been a novice who had neglected to be diligent in sweeping out the Assembly Hall.

In Buddhism, then, there can be no God; and if no God, then no prayer, no clergy, no priests. By 'no God' I mean no real God. Yet action is a kind of God. Action is omnipotent. Action is all-powerful in its effects on future states of being. 'An evil act follows a man through a hundred thousand transmigrations, so does a good act.' By 'no prayer' I mean no real prayer. Yet there are two forms of words—*Om mani padme hūm*, 'Om! the jewel in the lotus;' *Amita Fo*, 'the immeasurable Buddha,' which repeated or turned in a wheel—either once or millions of times—must produce inevitable corresponding results in future existences by the mere mechanical law of cause and effect. By 'no clergy,' I mean no real clergy. Yet there are monks and ascetics by thousands and thousands, banded together in monasteries, for the better suppression of passion and attainment of extinction. Many of these are religious teachers but not priests.

Has Buddhism, then, no morality? Yes—a lofty system of universal charity and benevolence. Yet extinction is its ultimate aim. In this respect it is no improvement upon Brāhmanism. The more the depths of these two systems are explored, the more clearly do they exhibit themselves in their true light as little better than dreary schemes excogitated by visionary philosophers, in the vain hope of delivering themselves from the evils and troubles of life—from all activity, self-consciousness, and personal existence.

3. We now pass to *Islām*, sometimes called Muhammadanism, but not so called by Muhammad himself, who never claimed to be the founder of a religion. Its creed is nearly as simple as that of esoteric Brāhmanism. The one is stern pantheism; the other stern monotheism. The one says everything is God; the other says God is one, but adds an important article of belief—'Muhammad is the prophet of God.' In short, the mission of Muhammad (according to himself) was to proclaim the unity of God (*tawhīd*) and absolute submission to His will (*islām*). What is its end?

The Kurān promises to its disciples a material paradise (*jannat*) or paradises (for there are seven), with shaded gardens, fresh water—two great desiderata in Arabia—black-eyed Hūrīs, and exquisite corporeal enjoyments.

It also declares the existence of seven hells. The seventh and worst is for hypocrites; the sixth for idolaters; the third for Christians; the second for Jews.

Islām is plainly a corruption of Judaism and Christianity, and in point of fact began by admitting the truth of both.

The end or aim then of Brāhmanism is absorption into the one Soul of the universe; of Buddhism is extinction; of Islām is admission to a paradise.

4. So much, then, for the three great religious systems confronting Christianity. Now for Christianity itself, which, creeping onwards little by little, is gradually surrounding them on all sides—sometimes advancing on them by indirect approaches, sometimes pressing on them by direct attack. And here I desire to speak reverentially, deferentially, and with deep humility. But I have the highest authority for what I am about to state. Christianity is a religion which offers to the entire human race access to God the Father through Christ by one Spirit.

The end and aim, therefore, of Christianity is emphatically union with God the Father, but such a union—mark here my words—such a union as shall secure the permanence of man's personality, energy, and individuality—nay, even shall intensify these.

Let us now, the better to compare the four systems, inquire by what means the end of each is effected. And here let us change the order, and begin with the religion which we believe to be the only true religion in the world.

Christianity, then, asserts that it effects its aim through nothing short of an entire change of the whole man, and a complete renovation of his nature.

The direct means by which its end is accomplished may be described as a kind of mutual transfer, leading to an interchange and co-operation between God and man's nature, acting on each other.

Man—the Bible says—was created in the image of God. But the first representative man fell, and transmitted a taint to his descendants which could only be removed by suffering and death. Hence the second representative man, Christ, Whose nature was divine and taintless, voluntarily underwent a sinner's death, that the taint transferred to Him might be removed.

This is not all. The grand central truth of our religion is not so much that Christ died as that He now lives and lives for ever. It is Christ that died—yea rather, Who is risen again—that He may bestow, first, life for death: secondly, a participation in His own divine nature for the tainted nature He has removed.

This is the mutual exchange that marks Christianity—an exchange between the personal man descended from a corrupt parent, and the Personal God made man and becoming our Second Parent. We are separated from a rotten root and grafted into a living root. We part with a corrupt nature and draw re-creative force—a new nature—from the ever-living Divine stem of the Second Adam, to which by a simple act of faith we are united.

Other religions have their doctrines, their precepts of morality, which, detached from much that is worthless, may even vie with those of Christianity.

But Christianity has what other religions have not—a Personal God, ever living to supply the regenerating Spirit by which man, being re-created and again made God-like, and again becoming 'pure in heart'—yet still preserving his own personality—obtains access to God the Father, and fitness to dwell in His presence for ever.

Secondly, *Islām*. What are its means of effecting its end? Muhammad was the prophet of God, says the Kurān, but nothing more. He claimed no combination of Divinity with humanity. Even his human nature was not asserted to be immaculate. He made no pretensions to mediatorial or vicarious functions. He died like any other man, and certainly did not rise that his followers might find in him eternal springs of divine life and power. Even Muslims do not regard him as the source of any re-creative force, capable of changing their whole nature. Muhammad sets forth faith in Islām and in his own mission, repentance, the performance of prayer, fasting, alms, pilgrimages, and the constant repetition of certain words (especially parts of the Kurān), as infallible means of obtaining Paradise. In one place, suffering, perseverance, walking in the fear of God, and attachment to Him, are insisted on. Yet it must be admitted that the Kurān elsewhere maintains that good works have no real meritorious efficacy in procuring Paradise, and that the righteous obtain entrance there through God's mercy alone. Indeed, every action in Islām is done 'in the name of God, the merciful, the compassionate' (*b'ismillāh ar-rahmān ar-rahīm*). But it should be borne in mind that the Kurān is by no means systematic or consistent. It was delivered in detached portions according to the exigencies of the moment, and, being often confused and contradictory, had to be explained and developed by traditional teaching (*Sunnah*). It has some noble passages.

In one thing the Muslim sets the Christian an example—submission to the will of God. But can the submission enjoined in the Kurān bear comparison with the sublime example of the Redeemer in the Garden of Gethsemane? Is it the submission of a slave to the will of a master, or the dependence of a child on a loving Father for life and breath and all things?

Thirdly, *Brāhmanism.* What are its means of attaining its ends? In fairness we must allow that the lines of Brāhmanical and Hindū thought often intersect those of Christianity.

In the later Hindū system the end of union with a Supreme Spirit is effected by faith in an apparently personal God. But this seeming personality melts on scrutiny into a vague spiritual essence.

True, God becomes man, and interposes for the good of men. There is a seeming combination of the human and divine—an apparent interchange of action. Most remarkable language, too, is applied to Kṛishṇa (in the Bhagavad-gītā) as the source of all life and energy. But how can there be any permanent interaction and co-operation between divine and human personalities when both must ultimately merge in the Oneness of the Infinite?

Fourthly and lastly, *Buddhism.* What are its means of accomplishing its end? Extinction of being is effected by self-mortification, by profound contemplation, and by abstinence from action. The Buddha himself is extinct. He cannot therefore, of course, be the source of life—even if it were desired by those whose highest aim is to be blown out like a candle.

It is refreshing to turn from such unsatisfying systems —however interspersed with sublime sentiments and lofty morality—to the living, energizing Christianity of European nations, however fallen from its true standard, however disgraced by the inconsistencies of its nominal adherents.

One more observation before I conclude.

Brāhmanism is not a missionary religion, and from its very nature never has been nor can be. Trades may be associated in castes, and such associations are even now admitted into the modern caste-system of Hindūism; but trade combinations are no part of its true creed. Brāhmanism cannot make a Brāhman, even if it would; and so far from distributing in other countries the texts or translations of its own sacred Vedas on which its creed rests, prohibits the general reading and repeating of them by its own people, indiscriminately. As to printing and editing these books, even for philological purposes, orthodox Brāhmans regard them as too sacred to be defiled by printers' ink.

Had it not been for the labours of Christian scholars, their contents would have remained for ever a 'terra incognita' to the majority of the Hindūs themselves. Brāhmanism, therefore, must die out. In point of fact, false ideas on the commonest scientific subjects are so mixed up with its doctrines (in proof of which we need only refer to the description of the earth in some of its sacred works) that the commonest education—the simplest lessons in geography—without the aid of Christianity, must inevitably in the end sap its foundations.

Buddhism, on the contrary, when it first arose in India, was pre-eminently a proselyting system. Hence its rapid progress. Hence it spread as no other false system has ever spread before or since. But its missionary zeal has now departed, its philosophy has lapsed into superstition, and of real religion it has none, nor ever claimed to have. Hence its fate in India, and hence the fate that awaits it everywhere. Buddhism does not seem to have been driven forcibly out of India; it simply pined away and died out. It could not maintain a hold upon the Hindūs, who are essentially a religious people, and must have a religion of some kind. Take away Brāhmanism, and they cannot again become Buddhists. They must become Christians, Muslims, or Theists.

Young Calcutta, Madras, and Bombay, educated and Europeanized without being Christianized, may glory in Positivism; but these are not the real population of India. The masses will never be satisfied with mere European knowledge, or with systems of philosophy and oppositions of science falsely so called. Christianity has many more points of contact with their ancient faith than Islām has, and when the walls of the mighty fortress of Brāhmanism are encircled, undermined, and finally stormed by the soldiers of the Cross, the victory of Christianity must be signal and complete.

And how does the case stand with Islām? Here we have a system which is still actively proselyting, and therefore still spreading. Indeed, if Christians are too weak to stem the tide of its progress in Africa, the advancing wave of the Muslim faith—a faith attractive to uncultured minds from its simplicity—will rapidly flood that whole continent.

But of no other religion can it be affirmed so emphatically as of Christianity that the missionary spirit is of its innermost essence; for Christ, Who is the Life and Soul of Christianity, was Himself a missionary—the first and greatest of all missionaries. And if He had not ordained the Apostles to be His missionary successors, and if they had not ordained other missionaries, there would be no Christianity among us here, no Christianity anywhere in the world.

PROMOTION OF GOODWILL AND SYMPATHY BETWEEN ENGLAND AND INDIA[1].

A DISSERTATION on the promotion of goodwill between England and India may appear at the present moment somewhat ill-timed. Two nations in the East of Europe have been locked together for the last few months in a deadly embrace. Their struggle has been marked by worse incidents of savagery than ever disgraced the world's first periods of primeval barbarism. Raging passions have been let loose. A portion of this fair Europe of ours—the boasted home of true Christianity—has been converted into a scene of deplorable atrocities. We Englishmen, who have happily played no part in the dreadful tragedy, have nevertheless watched with a kind of fascination the ebb and flow of the blood-stained tide of war. We have allowed our minds to be engrossed with graphic narratives of military evolutions—our thoughts to run on fortresses and sieges—our curiosity to be directed towards the effectiveness of terrible instruments of destruction, Krupp guns, breech-loaders and torpedoes;—our imaginations to be rivetted by the horrors of the battle-field—by images of dead and dying soldiers, mangled bodies and stiffened corpses;—our hearts to be torn by tales of inhuman cruelty, borne with superhuman resignation.

At such a time, I may be told, it would be more appro-

[1] This was delivered as an address at a Meeting of the National Indian Association, held, December 12th, 1877, at the Langham Hall, London, the Earl of Northbrook in the Chair.

priate to discuss the best means of restoring peace and promoting goodwill between the two nations engaged in mortal strife. Or supposing it to be admitted that the exciting tragedy of the present war ought not to engross our attention to the exclusion of other topics, still I may be confronted, at the outset of my remarks, with a very natural enquiry;—Is this a suitable moment to talk of promoting sympathy between the people of England and the people of India?

England has just given a conspicuous proof of her profound sympathy with her Indian brethren. She has voluntarily subscribed more than half a million sterling in a few months for the relief of the famine-stricken population, and in India itself every member of our Government—from the Viceroy downwards—has displayed the most self-sacrificing zeal and energy in efforts to prevent death and alleviate suffering. All this is of course true. And yet, I am persuaded, there is no one in this room with any experience derived from actual residence in India, who will regard an address on the subject which constitutes the very *raison d'être* of the National Indian Association, as either out of place or out of time at a season like this. The sympathy of the English people has indeed been evoked by a terrible calamity. And deep down in the lowest depths of the great British heart there is always a spring of true sympathy ready to gush forth and flow at the cry of suffering, whether towards wounded Turks, mutilated Russians, or famine-driven, fever-stricken Indians. If it is a sad reflection that war and famine are never likely to cease out of the land, there is at least some comfort in the thought that the battle-fields of Europe and the famine-desolated fields of India are never likely to be cut off from the healing, quickening influences of the perennial stream of English sympathy and English charity.

Let me, however, remind my hearers that there is yet another field, which, though it gives forth no hurtling sound of shot or shell, no piercing cry of wounded soldiers or famished peasantry, is not the less a field of conflict, of suffering, of loss and gain, of defeat and victory. I mean the battle-ground of daily life and daily work—with its fightings within and its fears without, its grapplings with duties, its wrestlings with temptations, its struggles with opposing forces, wills and interests. It is on this arena that the people of England and the people of India are brought together, not as enemies fighting for the victory over each other, but as fellow-soldiers striving together for the mastery over every form of evil; as fellow-subjects yielding allegiance to the same sovereign; as fellow-men and brethren, members of the great human family, owing love and sympathy and tender consideration towards each other.

And is not mutual sympathy needed by all who meet together as fellow-labourers on this common working-ground of daily duties and monotonous occupations—needed all the more because too frequently believed to be uncalled for and superfluous? Is it not needed by members of the same household, however nearly drawn together by bonds of family relationship? Is it not needed by people of the same country, however closely bound together by ties of social union and interest? Much more then is it needed by two peoples of two widely different countries, thrown by the force of circumstances into intimate political association, though separated from each other as far as the East is from the West by diversities of language, religion, customs, habits of thought, and social institutions.

What then are the best means of promoting this much-to-be-desired goodwill and sympathy between the people of England and the people of India? This is the question

I have set myself to answer in the present lecture, and the answer is not difficult. I have nothing new to suggest, no special nostrum, no wonder-working panacea of my own to proclaim, no startling discovery to announce. I can only insist on principles well known to every one around me; I can add nothing to the trite truisms already familiar to all of us. How are goodwill and sympathy promoted between any collection of individuals of widely different characters who have to live in daily intercourse with each other? They must learn mutual forbearance, they must consider one another to provoke unto little acts of kindness—little abstinences and wise reticences—they must be charitable in judging of each other, in making allowance for each other's infirmities, in thinking no evil of each other, in bearing, believing, hoping and enduring all things. In a word, they must cultivate brotherly charity.

Are, then, the people of England and the people of India wanting in this most excellent gift of mutual charity? Let Indians look into their own hearts, and examine their own consciences. My business as an Englishman is to enquire particularly into our own shortcomings. The question is one which cannot be lightly set aside. For if we are wanting in common charity,—including, of course, in that term the exercise of kindly feelings towards the people committed to our rule,—then it is clear that all our doings in India are nothing worth. We may make laws, administer justice, preach the Gospel, educate the people, lay down railroads, telegraphs, and telephones, develope the resources of the country, tame and control the forces of Nature for the public weal,—nay, more, we may bestow all our goods to feed the famine-stricken poor,—but our rule will not be rooted in the hearts of the people, our legislation will be as hollow as sounding brass, our preaching and teaching as unmeaning as the tinkling of a cymbal, our Empire as insecure as a tower built on sand, which some great storm will suddenly sweep away.

Now I am not here to look at the black side of anything, not even of my own character as an Englishman. I believe there is no nation in the world so abounding in true charity as the great British nation. I appeal to obstinate facts. I appeal to stubborn statistics. Nevertheless, without agreeing with those who consider it their privilege as Englishmen to be ever finding fault with themselves, I desire to face the plain truth. I am ready for my own part to confess that we are not all of us as charitable as we ought to be in our everyday ordinary relations with our Indian brethren,—not as fair as we ought to be in our judgment of their character, our estimate of their capacities, our toleration of their idiosyncracies, our appreciation of what is excellent in their literature, customs, religions and philosophies. And I am persuaded that both our want of charity and our want of sympathy proceed from no innate incapacity for charitable and sympathetic feelings, which are always ready to show themselves on great occasions; nor from any real want of fairness, which is usually a conspicuous feature in our national character, but simply and solely from our insufficient knowledge of India, its people and its needs. To put the matter plainly, we are only unsympathetic and uncharitable when we are ignorant.

Certain Hindū philosophers assert that all the phenomena of the universe are caused by ignorance. We cannot, however, quite go with the Vedāntist to the length of affirming that this beautiful world, this wonderful city of London, this fine Hall and everything good in it owe their origin to ignorance. But thus much, I think, we may allow, that all sin and misery, all war and enmity, all evils great or small that mar the fairness of God's earth—doubtings, difficulties, jealousies, misunderstandings, envyings, wrath, seditions, heresies,—all these are rooted in ignorance, and in ignorance alone. And is it not the case that we Englishmen often go to India with minds more ignorant than they ought to be of India's condition and India's needs? Sometimes, I fear, we do not even know enough to know that we do not know, and when we commence work on Indian soil, the pressure of necessary duties makes the task of acquiring any thorough knowledge of the country and its people very difficult of accomplishment.

Let me not be misunderstood. I am quite aware that many of the Queen's Indian officers, in spite of insufficient early training, become able Indian statesmen, and accomplished Indologists. What I am speaking of is the general ignorance of India—of its moral, religious, and intellectual history and condition — which prevails among younger men on their first arrival, who nevertheless become in the end quite conversant with the affairs of their own districts. As to the ignorance of India and its wants, which is nearly universal in this country, and even conspicuous in some of our most distinguished University men,—our first-class men and Wranglers, our Professors and writers, our magistrates and legislators (happily, however, not in all),—I cannot do better than quote the words of Mr. Hurry-Chand Chintamon, who came from India to be present at the Congress of Orientalists held in London at the end of 1874. 'In my own experience among Englishmen,' he says, 'I have found no general indifference to India, but rather an eager desire for information. But I have found a Cimmerian darkness about the manners and habits of my countrymen, an almost poetical description of our customs, and a conception no less wild and startling than the vagaries of Mandeville or Marco Polo concerning our religion.'

I come, therefore, to what may be called the keynote of all I have to say in this lecture, namely, that if we wish to promote goodwill and sympathy between the people of England and the people of India, we must labour to promote *mutual knowledge*—that is—a correct knowledge of England in India, of India in England. And here, I may observe, that if want of sympathy is rooted in want of knowledge, it must not be assumed that the absence of knowledge is all on one side. The people of India are even more wanting in correct knowledge of England than we are in correct knowledge of India. Let Indians look to their own deficiencies. My present concern is to look at home and ask the questions:—What are *our own* shortcomings? What are *our own* needs?

Many they are, and of various kinds and in various degrees. Even our ablest Indian statesmen have to confess ignorance about many things. Such men would be the first to tell us that if we wish to promote a better knowledge of India among ourselves we ought to begin at the right end. We ought to introduce Indian studies as an element of education at our Schools and Universities.

I deeply regret that the study of Indian and Oriental subjects generally is practically under a ban at my own University, because Eastern acquirements are at present no avenue to a degree, but rather a hindrance. Any undergraduate who devotes himself to Oriental studies is likely to imperil his place in the class list, and if he remains in England, his future prospects in life. That we Englishmen, with our enormous Indian and Colonial Empire, our vast Eastern commerce, our increasing interest in Egypt, Turkey, Mesopotamia, Burmah, Tibet, and China should show such indifference to studies which other nations, with little interest in the East, regard as important branches of education, seems, indeed, wholly unaccountable. For the most superficial observer must be convinced that the political interdependence, and, so to speak, solidarity of England and India, are becoming every day more complete, the affairs and interests, the loss and gain, the honour and dishonour, of the two countries more and more interwoven. Witness the increasing space accorded to news from India in our leading journals. Witness the vacation speeches of our leading legislators. Witness the debates on India and the Eastern question in both our Houses of Parliament. In fact, the improvements in telegraphy are constantly causing increased centralization of authority, and India is at present more governed by mandates and influences emanating from the central terminus of Queen, Lords and Commons, than by orders and enactments issuing from the Council Chambers of Calcutta, Madras and Bombay.

Surely, then, we are bound to ponder our heightened duties, our deepening responsibilities. We are bound seriously to lay to heart the undoubted fact that our rule over two hundred and forty-one millions of the human race depends more than it has ever done before—not only for its excellence, but for its very continuance—on the promotion of a better knowledge of the history and condition of India among the few hundred individuals constituting our two legislative assemblies, most of whom have been educated at our public schools and Universities. It may be very true that the old ignorance and apathy of Parliament have passed away, and that the commencement of an Indian debate no longer acts like a dinner-bell on hungry members. Yet, I venture to assert, that no little indifference and a good deal of sciolism still prevail, and that urgent need exists for securing by early training a more solid foundation of correct knowledge on all Eastern subjects among all classes of the community: in other words, —that the neglect of Oriental knowledge, as a department of education, calls for immediate attention at the hands of our educators.

Let me substantiate my assertion by a few instances, beginning with the simple subject of Geography. An educated European may perhaps be pardoned for betraying ignorance of the exact position of Quettah, but is it not somewhat startling to be asked by men of rank and education in this country whether Lahore is near Benares, and whether Calcutta lies south of Bombay? Even in India itself I have met with many able civilians who have confessed to me their inability to pass an examination in the geography of India outside their own Presidency. Much the same may be said of physical geography. India is blessed with numerous magnificent rivers, yet, even among Anglo-Indians, how many of those long resident in particular districts would be able to give an accurate account of India's marvellous network of running water, or the best method of utilizing it? Then how little is generally known of the Zoology and Botany of India! Doubtless there are scientific men to whom the fauna and flora of certain districts are familiar, but few Englishmen have an adequate conception of the marvellous wealth of India's animal and plant life. Sportsmen indeed abound everywhere by hundreds, but how many care for animals except to kill or eat them? It may be very true that some forms of life are a little too exuberant. Yet what country affords such beautiful specimens of the insect world? And how is it that Indian Zoologists and Entomologists may be counted on the fingers?

Then as to the vegetable kingdom. Nowhere in the world are there such opportunities for the study of botany, and nowhere is a knowledge of botany less common. Even well-informed persons have to confess their ignorance of India's vast and varied agricultural capabilities. For example, much has yet to be learnt about India's capacity for developing the cultivation of cotton. Again, quite within living memory the remarkable discovery has been made that the tea-plant is indigenous on Indian soil. Much ignorance, too, remains to be dissipated about the culture and preparation of coffee, cinchona, ipecacuanha, and above all of tobacco. Who can tell how far the latter may one day supply the eight or nine millions of revenue which must be sought for somewhere, should the conscience of Great Britain become too sensitive to permit her Indian Government to continue its dealings in opium? Who can tell, too, how far drought and famine may be averted when more is known about irrigation, the storing of water and the conservation of woods and forests? As to geology and mineralogy, it is difficult to estimate how much has yet to be ascertained about India's mineral resources—the exploration of coal-fields, the production of salt and iron, the exploitation of gold, silver, copper, and lead.

Archæology, again, presents an unbounded field, not yet adequately investigated. We are scarcely yet alive to the duty of searching out and preserving India's valuable antiquities, and of copying important historical inscriptions, all traces of which the climate is rapidly obliterating. I will not enter on the boundless subject of ethnology, except to remark that some of the oldest amongst us can remember the time when the near relationship of Englishmen to Brāhmans and Rājputs was barely suspected. I may mention, too, that no one in India could give me any clue to the ethnical classification of the Bhīls, and that the existence of Negrito and Negroïd races on the hills is a mystery.

Perhaps I should scarcely be believed if I were to relate with richness of detail the story of an intelligent young person, supposed to be fully educated, who was present the other day at a lecture on Zanāna work, and was heard to inquire with much *naïveté* whether the Zanānas were not a tribe of Afghāns. As to Indian history, all that can be said, I fear, is that the minds of most men are a perfect blank—a complete *tabula rasa*.

In regard to the languages and dialects of India, cultivated and uncultivated, how many persons are aware that their number amounts to at least two hundred? To know even two of these well is, of course, as much as can be expected of our administrators, and I willingly admit that they are generally well versed in at least one language. But I may be pardoned for bemoaning the almost universal ignorance of the classical languages of India,—Sanskṛit, Arabic and Persian, with their respective literatures. I have often been asked by learned Europeans—Has Sanskṛit any literature? The fact is that since the abolition of Haileybury in 1858 the study of Sanskṛit has remained voluntary. It is much to be regretted that few Indian probationers address themselves to this important language, and that those who begin learning it, rapidly drop all the knowledge they have gained in this country as soon as they commence their official duties.

Still more to be regretted is the neglect of Sanskṛit by missionaries. Happily there are signs of a better appreciation of its value in the future, and I even look forward to its eventual adoption in England as an element of linguistic training. Let us not forget that Sanskṛit is as closely allied as Greek to our mother-tongue, that its symmetrical grammar is the key to all other grammars, that its system of synthesis is as useful to the mind as the study of geometry, and that its literature contains models of true poetry and some of the most remarkable treatises on philosophy, science and ethics that the world has ever produced.

Above all, let those who are preparing for an Indian career bear in mind that Sanskṛit is the only source of life, health and vigour to all the spoken languages of the Hindūs, the only repository of Hindū religious creeds, customs and observances. 'The popular prejudices of the Hindūs,' said my illustrious predecessor at Oxford, 'their daily observances, their occupations, their amusements, their domestic and social relations, their local legends, their traditions, their fables, their religious worship, all spring from and are perpetuated by the Sanskṛit language.' Yes—to know a country, its people, its needs and necessities, its mistakes and errors, all these things must be known and understood. Without such knowledge no respect can be felt for all that is good and true, no successful attempt made for the eradication of all that is evil, false and hurtful.

Indeed, I am deeply convinced that the more we learn about the ideas, feelings, drift of thought, religious and intellectual development, eccentricities, and even errors of the people of India, the less ready shall we be to judge them by our own conventional European standards—the less disposed to regard ourselves as the sole depositories of all the true knowledge, learning, virtue and refinements of civilized life—the less prone to despise as an ignorant and inferior race the men who compiled the laws of Manu, one of the most remarkable literary productions of the world—who composed systems of ethics worthy of Christianity—who imagined the Rāmāyaṇa and Mahā-bhārata, poems in some respects outrivalling the Iliad and the Odyssey—who invented for themselves the science of grammar, arithmetic, astronomy, logic, and six most subtle systems of philosophy. Above all, the less inclined shall we be to stigmatize as benighted heathen the authors of two religions, however false, which are at this moment professed by about half the human race.

And this leads me to express my sense of our remissness, whether as laymen or missionaries, in neglecting to study the sacred works on which the various religions of India rest. We cannot, of course, sympathize with all that is false in the several creeds of Hindūs, Buddhists, Jains, Pārsīs, Sikhs and Muslims. But we can consent to examine them from their own point of view, we can study their sacred books in their own languages, Sanskṛit, Pāli, Prākṛit, Zand, Gurumukhī and Arabic, rather than in imperfect translations of our own. We can pay as much deference to the interpretations of their own commentators as we expect to be accorded to our own interpretation of the difficulties of our own sacred Scriptures. We can avoid denouncing in strong language what we have never sufficiently investigated, and do not thoroughly understand.

Yes, I must speak out. It seems to me that the general ignorance of our fellow-countrymen in regard to the religions of India is really worse than a blank. A man, learned in European lore, asked me the other day whether the Hindūs were not all Buddhists. Of course ignorance is associated with indifference. I stayed in India with an eminent Indian civilian who had lived for years quite unconsciously within a few hundred yards of a celebrated shrine, endeared to the Hindūs by the religious memories of centuries. Another had never heard of a perfectly unique temple not two miles from the gate of his own compound. Ignorance, too, is often associated with an attitude of unmitigated contempt. Another distinguished civilian who observed that I was diligent in prosecuting my researches into the true nature of Hindūism, expressed surprise that I could waste my time in 'grubbing into such dirt.' The simple truth, I fear, is that we are all more or less ignorant. We are none of us as yet quite able to answer the question:—'What is Hindūism?' We have none of us as yet sufficiently studied it under all its aspects, in its own vast sacred literature stretching over a period of more than two thousand years. We under-estimate its comprehensiveness, its super-subtlety, its recuperative hydra-like vitality; and we are too much given to include the whole system under sweeping expressions such as 'heathenism' or 'idolatry,' as if every idea it contains was to be eradicated root and branch.

Again I must speak out. I deeply regret that we are in the habit of using opprobrious terms to designate the religious tenets of our Indian brethren, however erroneous we believe those tenets to be. Unfortunately it is difficult to find any substitute for the convenient expression 'heathen,' but we ought to consider that the translators of our Bible only adopted this word as an equivalent for Gentile nations, and that the term is now frequently applied to wicked, godless people. I have constantly heard it so applied by our clergy when speaking of the most degraded section of the population of our large cities,—atheists, thieves, lawless people and criminals of all kinds, such as, in former times, congregated on wild *heaths*, remote from civilized towns. We are surely untrue to our own principles when we associate all unbelievers in Christianity with such people, by the use of a common term for both. Does not our own religion teach us that in every nation he that feareth God and worketh righteousness is accepted with Him? A clergyman, long resident in India, once remarked to me that he had seen many a poor man in an Indian village, whose childlike trust in his god, and in the efficacy of his religious observances, whose simplicity of character and whose practical application of the precepts of his creed put us Christians to shame.

I deplore, too, the ignorance displayed in regard to Indian religious usages. A recent book on India by an eminent Member of Parliament describes the mark on the forehead of the Southern Rāmānujas as the trident of Śiva, whereas it really represents the footprints of Vishṇu. Errors of this kind swarm even in the works of missionaries, and are generally caused by ignorance of Sanskṛit. As to caste, its working is very imperfectly understood, and few are aware that the Hindūs regard it as an imperfect condition of life, and hold that to attain supreme happiness caste must be abandoned. Again, we are apt to indulge in a wholesale condemnation of caste and to advocate its total abolition, forgetful that as a social institution it often operates most beneficially. Doubtless caste-rules are generally a great hindrance to progress, but their very connection with religious faith and practice may often furnish a salutary check where the mere belief in Vishṇu and Śiva is powerless to exercise any restraint at all.

Then, how often do we offend caste prejudices simply from ignorance of their strength and of their connection with venerated religious usage and deep religious feeling!

I, for my part, can believe that an earnest-minded Englishman might well hesitate to eat the flesh of oxen, while resident in certain districts of India, where Hindū religious prejudices continue strongest, and where cow-killing is regarded as nothing short of impious sacrilege, remembering the words of a high Christian authority, 'if meat make my brother to offend, I will eat no flesh while the world standeth.' The Deputy-Commissioner at Rohtak was murdered the other day by a fanatical Hindū, who never spoke afterwards till the moment of his execution, except to whisper that he had a call from heaven to destroy cow-killers.

When I was at Jammu, one of the Mahārāja's Ministers told me that the punishment in Kaśmīr for killing oxen was imprisonment for life, and that he himself had such a horror of eating the flesh of oxen that, if the alternative were submitted to him of tasting beef or being beheaded, he would unhesitatingly choose decapitation.

It is said that a holy Brāhman who lived near Saugor determined to wrestle with the Deity till he should reveal to him the real cause of the general scarcity under which the land was groaning. After three days and nights of fasting and prayer, he saw a vision of some celestial being, who stood before him in a white mantle, and told him that all the calamities of the season arose from the slaughter of oxen by Englishmen and Muhammadans. Colonel Sleeman asserts that this actually occurred, and created a great sensation in the neighbourhood. At any rate, we may learn from such stories how deep-seated are the religious convictions on which the sacredness of the cow is based, and can understand how our practice of eating beef may generate bitter feelings of ill-will towards us. Let us suppose for a moment an imaginary case. Let us ask ourselves what our own feelings would be if a number of Chinese were to settle down in this country, and insist on constantly eating boiled rats with chop-sticks before our eyes. Yet our disgust would be as nothing compared with the revulsion in the mind of a pious Hindū caused by our devouring with avidity the flesh of animals which from his infancy he is taught to believe permeated with the essence of divinity.

Of course, I am not advocating a general abandonment of beef-eating throughout India. I am aware that many consider it a duty to show openly their disapproval of what they consider the absurd prejudices of a weak-minded people, and I admit that when religious customs are degrading and do violence to nature and humanity, like the rite of Satī, they ought to be put down. All I maintain is, that the time-honoured usages of particular districts, when intimately bound up with religious feelings, ought, as far as possible, to be respected. Ought we not, too, without making any concessions to what we believe utterly false in the religions of India, to be more diligent in searching for some common religious ground on which Europeans and Asiatics may take their stand together? Is it not the case that, among ourselves, people of the most opposite opinions find their religious differences softened down and their sympathies evoked by meeting face to face on the common platform of Conference and Congress Hall? Has England advanced with such gigantic strides beyond Eastern nations that no points of agreement in ideas, customs, usages, and religion can be found with an ancient people who had a polished language, an extensive literature, and a developed civilization when our forefathers were clothed in skins and could neither read nor write? Is so great a gulf now fixed between two races who once occupied the same home in Central Asia that no community of thought, no interchange of ideas, no reciprocity of feeling is any longer possible between them? I verily believe that an unfairly low estimate of the moral, social and religious condition of the people of India, and of their intellectual capacity, is really the principal obstacle to the promotion of sympathy between the two races.

The great historian Mill, whose History of India is still a standard work, has done infinite harm by his unjustifiable blackening of the Indian national character. He has declared (I quote various statements scattered through his work) that 'the superior castes in India are generally depraved, and capable of every fraud and villany; that they more than despise their inferiors, whom they kill with less scruple than we do a fowl; that the inferior castes are profligate, guilty on the slightest occasion of the greatest crimes, and degraded infinitely below the brutes; that the Hindūs in general are devoid of every moral and religious principle; cunning and deceitful, addicted to adulation, dissimulation, deception, dishonesty, falsehood and perjury; disposed to hatred, revenge, and cruelty; indulging in furious and malignant passions, fostered by the gloomy and malignant principles of their religion; perpetrating villany with cool reflection; indolent to the point of thinking death and extinction the happiest of all states; avaricious, litigious, insensible to the sufferings of others, inhospitable, cowardly; contemptuous and harsh to their women, whom they treat as slaves; eminently devoid of filial, parental, and conjugal affection.'

No wonder that young Englishmen, just imported from the ruling country, and fresh from the study of Mill's History, sometimes affect a supercilious air of superiority when first brought into contact with their Indian fellow-subjects. No wonder that Mr. Nowrozjee Furdoonjee should have delivered a lecture three or four years ago before this Association and attempted to prove that the natives of India are often treated by Europeans 'with incivility, harshness, and even contempt and personal violence—that they are frequently stigmatized as Niggers, a nation of liars, perjurers, forgers, devoid of gratitude, trust, good-nature, and every other virtue, as rude barbarians and inhuman savages.'

Of course, we know that this Indian gentleman has overstated his case, and that his description applies to a condition of things which may have partially existed thirty years ago, but which has to a great extent passed away. Still, it cannot be questioned that, conscious of our own superiority in religion, science, morality, and general culture, we are too apt to under-estimate the character and acquirements of our Indian brethren. We may regret that they are not Christians, that they have not the moral stamina of Englishmen, that their social institutions are a source of weakness and an obstacle to all fusion between European and Asiatic races, their caste-rules a bar to progress, and the low condition of their women fatal to their elevation. We may tell them plainly that we aim at raising them—men and women—socially, morally, intellectually, to our own standard. But we must bear in mind, all the while, that they are human beings like ourselves, with feelings and infirmities like our own. We must give them credit for whatever is good, true, and lovely in their own national character; we must even be ready to admit that in some points—such as patient perseverance in common duties, courtesy, temperance, filial obedience, reverent demeanour towards their elders and betters, dutiful submission to governors, teachers, spiritual pastors and masters, faithfulness in service, tenderness towards animal life, toleration of religious diversities in foreigners and each other—they may possibly be our equals, if not our superiors.

Contrast with Mr. Mill's estimate of the Hindū character the opinion of the great Abūl Fazl (well called 'the father of excellence'), Akbar's celebrated Minister, who, though a Muhammadan, wrote in his Ayīn-i-Akbarī—'The Hindūs are religious, affable, courteous to strangers, prone to inflict austerities on themselves, lovers of justice, given to retirement, able in business, grateful, admirers of truth, and of unbounded fidelity. Their character shines brightest in adversity. Their soldiers know not what it is to fly from the field of battle. When the success of the combat becomes doubtful they dismount from their horses and throw away their lives in payment of the debt of valour. They have great respect for their tutors; and make no account of their lives when they can devote them to the service of their God. They believe in the unity of the Godhead, and although they hold images in high veneration, yet they are by no means idolaters, as the ignorant suppose.'

I must admit that in another place he says that the Hindūs differ widely in different places, and that some have the disposition of angels, others of demons.

If I may be allowed to speak of my own experiences, I confess that to me the Indian character has seemed neither angelic nor demoniacal. But if the best Christian found a law in his members bringing him into captivity to the law of sin, so that when he 'would do good, evil was present with him,' how much more must this be true of the best Hindū! Surely, then, on the common ground of conflict with evil, both Christian and Hindū, though equipped for the fight with armour of very different temper, may meet and sympathize with each other. And if his own religion is to the one a power and to the other a weakness, surely the strong man armed may have some strength to spare for the encouragement and support of his more feeble brother.

I will not enter into the question of how far the social gulf which is now separating the two races is capable of being bridged over. When I was at Calcutta I found all the highest State functionaries—Lord Northbrook himself, our noble Chairman here,—the late high-minded Bishop Milman, and many others I could name, vying with each other in their efforts to conciliate the natives, and bring about more social fusion between the rulers and the ruled. I found, too, many of our devoted fellow-countrywomen doing their best to work their way lovingly and tenderly into the interior of many an Indian family. The present Viceroy, Lord Lytton, is not a whit behind his predecessors in endeavouring to counteract, by his personal example, the estrangement caused by race-antipathies. But I fear that little success will be achieved till the impenetrable barrier which now surrounds the homes of India is thrown down, till Hindūs consent to eat and drink with Europeans, and till the wives, mothers, and daughters of India are elevated to their proper position in the family circle.

Nor will I now discuss the question of the duty of redressing so-called Indian grievances, because this is acknowledged on all hands. Traversing India as I have recently done from Kaśmir to Cape Comorin, I have found all intelligent natives generally satisfied with our rule. It is useless, however, to conceal from ourselves the existence of much discontent, chiefly among the men we have educated above their stations. When I have inquired of such men: What are your grievances? What does India want which India has not got? 'We want,' they have replied, 'complete social and political equality; we want admission to the highest executive offices; we want a more economical Government; we want a more permanent and moderate settlement of the land-tax; we want less tedious and costly litigation; we want power of sending a few representatives to the House of Commons; we want a certain number of covenanted civil appointments to be competed for in this country.' These are a few specimens of alleged wants. If any of them are *real* wants which it is possible and proper to meet, the Government seems to me to be inclined to go even beyond its duty in endeavouring to meet them. Our Indian Government, too, is now doing its best (just as the Emperor Akbar did more than 300 years ago) to organize in India systematic efforts for the acquisition and dissemination of accurate information on all the points I have mentioned in this address, and indeed on every minute particular bearing on the condition of the people committed to its rule.

The best evidence of this is afforded by the statistical account of Bengal, in twenty volumes, just completed by Dr. W. W. Hunter, Director-General of Statistics, and published in London by Messrs. Trübner and Co.

Yet in the preface to this great national work—a monument of exemplary industry as well as of literary ability—Dr. Hunter owns that it represents the first organized advance towards a better knowledge of India. 'When I commenced,' he says, 'the survey, no regular census had been taken of India, and the enumeration of 1872 disclosed that the official estimates had been wrong as regards Lower Bengal alone by more than twenty-five million of souls. No book existed to which either the public or the administrative body could refer for the most essential facts concerning the rural population. Districts lying within half-a-day's journey of the capital were spoken of in the Calcutta Review as "unexplored."'

What I plead for, then, is a similar systematic organization and concentration of effort in this country for instilling a better knowledge of India into the rising generation. Unless we bestir ourselves, England will rapidly lose its position as the proper centre and focus of Eastern learning in Europe. Germany, France, and Russia are doing their best to take our place. Even Holland and Italy are rivalling us. All these countries have established chairs of most of the Indian languages, especially of Sanskṛit, Arabic, and Persian. Even now we often have to go to Germany for our Indian Professors, Librarians, Secretaries, and Cataloguers of manuscripts[1].

What are our requirements, then, with a view to more systematic organization for the promotion of Indian studies? In my opinion principally four, namely:—1. Formal University recognition by the establishment of an Indian School for obtaining degrees. 2. The appointment of Professors and Teachers of Indian subjects at Colleges and Schools. 3. The encouragement of Indian students by the foundation of Indian scholarships and fellowships. 4. Local centralization by the founding of Indian Institutes, containing libraries, museums, and lecture-rooms, at great educational centres—for example, here in London (according to the plan long advocated by my friend, Dr. Forbes Watson), and especially at Oxford. But why, it may be asked, especially at Oxford rather than at Cambridge, Edinburgh, Glasgow, or Dublin? I reply for two

[1] I am told that there is not in England a single person who knows Tibetan, although teachers of this language are to be found in Germany, France, and Russia, and although it is spoken by numbers of our own subjects and by millions inhabiting neighbouring countries.

reasons:—1st. It can be proved by statistics that a large proportion of our members of Parliament—the real rulers of India—are Oxford men. I believe the majority over Cambridge is at present represented by 136 over 100, and there are now eight Oxford first-class men in the Cabinet, including the Secretary of State for India himself. 2ndly. Our Oxford system, which lays great stress on languages, history, law, and political economy, affords the best training for every kind of Indian career.

At last, therefore, I come to the goal to which my remarks have been converging—the need of founding at Oxford an institution which shall be a centre of union, intercourse, inquiry and instruction for all engaged in Indian studies. I have already promises of £5,000 towards the erection of a building, but I require £5,000 more for the building alone. The Institute will, I hope, be equipped in the most effective possible manner—both materially and personally. It will have Lecture-rooms, Museum, Library, and Reading-room, all aiding and illustrating each other, and closely connected with it an ample staff of University Professors and teachers, many of whom will have resided in India and have an intimate knowledge of the country. It will, I trust, adapt itself to the needs of young Indians, who often go astray in this vast metropolis from the want of proper supervision; and who, as soon as our Oxford Indian School and Indian Institute are established, will probably frequent our University more than they have hitherto done. Oriental Fellowships, Indian Travelling Fellowships, Scholarships for Indians pursuing their studies at Oxford, Scholarships for Englishmen pursuing Indian studies, will, I trust, in time be connected with the Institute. It will, I hope, give prizes for essays on Indian subjects, and will invite able natives to deliver lectures in its lecture-rooms, where meetings and conferences on various topics relating to the welfare of our Indian fellow-subjects will occasionally be held. In brief, *its one aim* will be to concentrate and diffuse accurate information on every subject connected with the condition of our Indian Empire; *its one work* will be to draw England and India closer together, by promoting mutual knowledge, by furthering interchange of ideas, by encouraging reciprocity of feeling, by fostering goodwill and sympathy between the two countries.

This great aim—this great work, cannot and must not rest with the University of Oxford alone. Every society, every individual interested in the well-being of our Eastern Empire, will, I trust, lend a helping hand. The National Indian Association, with whose operations both in England and India I have cherished the warmest sympathy ever since the late lamented Miss Carpenter and myself met together for the promotion of similar aims in various parts of India, will, I am sure, co-operate with the Oxford Indian Institute, and both will direct their best endeavours towards the same high objects.

And need I add how much I believe the maintenance of goodwill and sympathy between England and India depends on the attitude and bearing of those who are highest in authority? It is said that what distinguished the great Emperor Akbar from all previous rulers was his personal attention to all the minutiæ of government, and his deference to the opinions of his subjects, however conflicting or opposed to his own. It would be impertinent in me to speak in praise of our noble Chairman on this occasion, but it seems to me that the success of Lord Northbrook's administration was not more due to his conversancy with every detail of State affairs than to his tact in preserving harmony between the discordant elements of which the Queen's Indian Empire must always consist, and his unvarying kindness and courtesy of manner towards every individual, whether Englishman, Hindū, or

Muhammadan, with whom, as the Queen's representative, he was brought into contact.

The problem before us, then, has been—How can more cordial and sympathetic feeling be promoted between the people of England and the people of India? The solution of this problem may have been demonstrated by words, but the desired end will not be effected till the people of both countries join heart and hand in united efforts for the conciliation of each other's goodwill, and for the verification of the sublime doctrine—for the establishment of the eternal truth—that 'God has made all nations of men of one blood.'

ORIENTAL WORKS

BY

MONIER WILLIAMS, D.C.L.,

BODEN PROFESSOR OF SANSKṚIT IN THE UNIVERSITY OF OXFORD.

---

1. AN ENGLISH-SANSKṚIT DICTIONARY, in one vol. 4to. Published under the patronage of the Court of Directors of the East India Company. W. H. Allen & Co., Waterloo Place, London. 1851. Price £3 3s.

2. A SANSKṚIT-ENGLISH DICTIONARY, in one vol. 4to. Published for the University of Oxford by Macmillan & Co., Bedford Street, Covent Garden, London; also W. H. Allen & Co., London. 1872. Price £4 14s. 6d.

   'This is a most laboriously and carefully constructed and excellent work, which no student of Sanskṛit can do without.'—W. D. Whitney, Professor of Sanskṛit and Comparative Philology in Yale College (from the *Harvard College Courant*).

3. A PRACTICAL GRAMMAR OF THE SANSKṚIT LANGUAGE, arranged with reference to the Classical Languages of Europe, for the use of English Students. Fourth Edition. Published for the University of Oxford by Macmillan & Co.; also W. H. Allen & Co., London. 1864. Price 15s.

   'I am accustomed to recommend Williams's Grammar to any one who takes up the study (of Sanskṛit) by himself, without a teacher, because it is more intelligible and easily managed.'—W. H. D. Whitney (from the *Harvard College Courant*).

4. A SANSKṚIT MANUAL, containing the Accidence of Grammar, and Progressive Exercises for Composition. Second Edition. W. H. Allen & Co., London. 1868. Price 7s. 6d.

5. SAKUNTALĀ; a Sanskṛit Drama. The Devanāgarī Recension of the Text, with Critical Notes and Literal Translations. W. H. Allen & Co., London. 1853. Price 21s.

6. SAKUNTALĀ. A Second and improved Edition of the above, with Index. Published for the University of Oxford by Macmillan and Co. 1876. Price 21s.

7. A FREE TRANSLATION IN ENGLISH PROSE AND VERSE OF THE SANSKṚIT DRAMA ŚAKUNTALĀ. Fourth Edition. W. H. Allen & Co., London. 1872. Price 8s.

8. ANOTHER EDITION OF THE ABOVE, illuminated and illustrated. Stephen Austin, Hertford. 1855. Price £2 2s.

Works by Professor Monier Williams (continued).

9. VIKRAMORVASĪ; a Sanskṛit Drama, published as a Class-Book for the East India College. W. H. Allen & Co., London. 1849. Price 5*s*.

10. STORY OF NALA; a Sanskṛit Poem, with full Vocabulary, and Dean Milman's Translation. Published at the Oxford University Press. 1860. Price 15*s*.

11. THE STUDY OF SANSKṚIT IN RELATION TO MISSIONARY WORK IN INDIA. Williams & Norgate, London. 1861. Price 2*s*.

12. INDIAN EPIC POETRY. Williams & Norgate, London and Edinburgh. 1863. Price 5*s*.

13. A PRACTICAL HINDŪSTĀNĪ GRAMMAR. Second Edition. Longmans & Co., London. 1865. Price 5*s*.

14. AN EASY INTRODUCTION TO THE STUDY OF HINDŪSTĀNĪ. Longmans & Co., London. 1859. Price 2*s*. 6*d*.

15. HINDŪSTĀNĪ PRIMER. Longmans & Co., London. 1859. Price 1*s*. 8*d*.

16. BĀGH O BAHĀR; the Hindūstānī Text, with Notes and Introductory Essay on the Application of the Roman Alphabet to the Languages of India. Longmans & Co., London. 1859. Price 6*s*. 6*d*.

17. ORIGINAL PAPERS illustrating the History of the Application of the Roman Alphabet to the Languages of India. Longmans & Co., London. 1859. Price 12*s*.

18. INDIAN WISDOM; or Examples of the Religious, Philosophical and Ethical Doctrines of the Hindus. Third Edition, W. H. Allen & Co., London. 1877. Price 15*s*.

19. HINDŪISM. Published by the Society for Promoting Christian Knowledge. Sixth Thousand. 1878. Price 2*s*. 6*d*.

20. MODERN INDIA AND THE INDIANS; being a Series of Notes, Impressions, and Essays. Trübner & Co., London. 1878. Price 7*s*. 6*d*.